Juridicum—Bochumer Schriften zur Friedenssicherung und zum Humanitären Völkerrecht I Bochum Studies on the International Law of Peace and Armed Conflict

Volume 70

Series Editors

Pierre Thielbörger, Institut Friedensicherung Humanitären Völkerrecht, Ruhr-Universität Bochum, Bochum, Germany

Hans-Joachim Heintze, Institut Friedensicherung Humanitären Völkerrecht, Ruhr-Universität Bochum, Bochum, Germany

In der Schriftenreihe des Bochumer Instituts für Friedensicherungsrecht und Humanitäres Völkerrecht werden regelmäßig Publikationen veröffentlicht, die sich mit aktuellen Fragen von Friedenssicherung und humanitärem Völkerrecht beschäftigen. Die Reihe erscheint seit 1988 unter dem Titel **Bochumer Schriften zur Friedenssicherung und zum Humanitären Völkerrecht**. Sie wurde 2017 nach einer Unterbrechung von zehn Jahren zunächst neu aufgelegt und wird seit 2025 bei Springer weitergeführt.

Die Bände behandeln vielfältige Themen der Friedens- und Konfliktforschung, etwa das Gewaltverbot und Selbstverteidigung, kollektive Sicherheit und das Recht der Vereinten Nationen, Friedenseinsätze, sowie die Menschenrechte, das Völkerstrafrecht, das Umweltrecht und – in all seinen Facetten – das humanitäre Völkerrecht und die humanitäre Hilfe.

This book series regularly publishes monographs and edited collections on current issues concerning the maintenance of international peace and security as well as international humanitarian law. The series has been published since 1988 under the title **Bochumer Schriften zur Friedenssicherung und zum Humanitären Völkerrecht**. It was reissued in 2017 after an interruption of ten years and has been continued by Springer since 2025.

The volumes cover a wide range of topics in peace and conflict studies, such as the use of force and self-defense, collective security and the law of the United Nations, peace missions, as well as human rights, international criminal law, environmental law and—in all its aspects—international humanitarian law as well as humanitarian action.

Vivien Wefringhaus

Circular Economy and International Law

Springer

Vivien Wefringhaus
Ruhr-Universität Bochum
Bochum, Germany

ISSN 3091-4477 ISSN 3091-4485 (electronic)
Juridicum—Bochumer Schriften zur Friedenssicherung und zum Humanitären Völkerrecht I Bochum Studies on the International Law of Peace and Armed Conflict
ISBN 978-3-658-49935-8 ISBN 978-3-658-49936-5 (eBook)
https://doi.org/10.1007/978-3-658-49936-5

This Springer imprint is published by the registered company Springer Fachmedien Wiesbaden GmbH, part of Springer Nature.
The registered company address is: Abraham-Lincoln-Str. 46, 65189 Wiesbaden, Germany

I dedicate my dissertation to my family and closest friends. Especially to my parents and grandparents who supported me throughout the entire process and have always been by my side. To my husband Tim for consistently encouraging me and helping me through this challenging phase. And to my best friend Sonja for her moral support.

Acknowledgements I would like to thank my supervisor Prof. Dr. Pierre Thielbörger M.PP. (Harvard) for offering me the opportunity to write this thesis and paving my way into the scientific research in the field of international law. I would also like to thank my second supervisor Prof. Dr. Markus Kaltenborn for providing me the first access to international law during my studies in law.

I wish to thank the Institute for International Law of Peace and Armed Conflict and all my colleagues for warmly welcoming me at the institute. Special thanks go to my colleagues Max and JP for their helpful feedback including professional and especially personal support and to my fellow scholar Jasmin for proofreading and commenting on my thesis.

I would also like to thank the Heinrich-Böll-Stiftung not only for the financial but also ideal support as well as for providing a platform for training and exchange.

Lastly, I would like to express my gratitude to all who have been part of my law journey, especially to my friends Caro, Larissa and Svenja.

Competing Interests The author has no competing interests to declare that are relevant to the content of this manuscript.

Abstract

Our earth's supply of natural resources is depleting while mountains of waste are piling up. Killing two birds with one stone, scientists recommend a transformation from the current linear economic system towards a circular economy. Nevertheless, explicit regulation to implement such an economic model is still missing at the international, regional or even national level. With due regard to the global scope of the increasing depletion of resources and littering the question arises whether relevant rules on these issues can be extracted from existing international law. Since the international community failed to set a clear framework for a resource-saving and efficient economy which takes the urgent threats into account, it is to discover in how far existing international law demands a transition towards a circular economy.

This PhD project will examine if an integrated analysis of different fields of international law leads to an implicit obligation for states to adapt their economies. By assessing the related principles and provisions under international environmental law as well as under human rights law, it aims to reveal if they imply a mandatory economic shift. The analysis will differentiate between relevant provisions concerning the issue of resource depletion on the one hand, and the current law governing waste management on the other hand. The objective is to determine the connection between these international law rules and the concept of circular economy. This thesis involves the scrutiny of principles and concepts like sustainable development and prevention in this context and takes human rights regarding resource depletion and waste management into consideration.

In a second step, the environmental and social demands will be balanced with the states' sovereignty in order to determine if an implicit obligation to transform the economy can be detected.

Keywords: Circular Economy · Resource Depletion · Waste Management · Sustainability · Human Rights · Sovereignty

Contents

Abbreviations

Art.	Article
CBD	Convention on Biological Diversity
Cf.	Confer
ECHR	European Convention on the Protection of Human Rights and Fundamental Freedoms
Ed.	Editor(s)
E.g.	Exemplum gratia (for example)
Et al.	Et alii (and others)
EU	European Union
E-waste	Electronic waste
I.a.	Inter alia (among other things)
ICCPR	International Covenant on Civil and Political Rights
ICESCR	International Covenant on Economic, Social and Cultural Rights
ICGJ	International Courts of General Jurisdiction
ICJ	International Court of Justice
ICJ Rep	International Court of Justice Reports
ILA	International Law Association
ILC	International Law Commission
ILM	International Legal Materials
ITLOS	International Tribunal of the Law of the Sea
MARPOL	International Convention for the Protection of Pollution from Ships
No.	Number
P.	Page
Para.	Paragraph
SDGs	Sustainable Development Goals
TWAIL	Third World Approaches to International Law

UN	United Nations
UNCLOS	United Nations Convention on the Law of the Sea
UN Doc	United Nations Documents
UNEP	United Nations Environment Programme
V.	Versus
VCLT	Vienna Convention on the Law of Treaties
Vol.	Volume
WEEE	Waste Electrical and Electronic Equipment Directive
WTO	World Trade Organization

1 Introduction

1.1 Outline of the Problem

The world is facing some of the most existential environmental issues in history. Besides the increasing global warming due to climate change, humanity is threatened by the depletion of natural resources.[1] At the same time, large areas of land and even parts of the ocean are suffocating in tons of waste.[2] The lack of or poor management of waste leads to a series of negative consequences for the environment and people living close to garbage dumps.[3] The reasons for this scenario are fairly obvious: A growing world population and economic systems based on growth create a high demand for natural resources.[4] Experts even predict that the demand for resources will double by 2050.[5] Especially the economies in most developed countries generate prosperity through a high consumption of natural resources which turn into waste—in most cases even after a relatively short period of use.[6] On top of that, these manufacturing and handling processes contribute significantly to greenhouse gas emissions which are the main cause of climate change.[7] These consequences result from our current economy system which

[1] Geng, Sarkis, and Bleischwitz (2019), 153.

[2] Geng, Sarkis, and Bleischwitz (2019), 153, "8 million tonnes of plastic per year".

[3] Wilson (2015), 20.

[4] Ekins et al. (2016), 2.

[5] Bringezu (2017).

[6] Andrews (2015), 307.

[7] Ritchie and Roser (2020).

V. Wefringhaus, *Circular Economy and International Law*, Juridicum—Bochumer Schriften zur Friedenssicherung und zum Humanitären Völkerrecht I Bochum Studies on the International Law of Peace and Armed Conflict 70,
https://doi.org/10.1007/978-3-658-49936-5_1

is based on a “take-make-use-dispose-model”[8]. Because of the aforementioned issues, this so-called linear economy is considered unsustainable.[9]

Accordingly, more and more scientists and scholars argue for an economic shift towards an alternative: a circular economy.[10] Implementing a circular economic system entails the careful handling of natural resources through the establishment of their cyclical use.[11] The core of a circular economy is producing durable and valuable products out of raw materials that can be separated into secondary materials at the end of their lifetime.[12] In order to minimize waste, these materials return to the production cycle and will thus be used again. Based on these pillars, such a system can be a solution for the impending depletion of natural resources as well as for the ever-increasing problem of waste. This alternative system does not only comprise better recycling quotes, but it provides a holistic approach to sustainable resource management,[13] which will be explained later in detail. In addition, the more efficient use of resources in the production contributes to cutting the greenhouse gas emissions in a considerable way. This is illustrated by the following example: A notably smaller amount—only 5% of the energy—is necessary for reprocessing metals like aluminum rather than extracting them.[14] A uniform definition for circular economy, however, does not exist.[15] It will thus be the first task to find an appropriate working definition.

Introducing a circular economy appears to be a simple solution to deal with all of the aforementioned problems. However, this concept can hardly be found in practice. One rare exception is the reference to circular economy in the latest Five Year Plan of the Chinese government.[16] Apart from some initiatives like the Ellen MacArthur Foundation[17] or national recycling laws,[18] no state or region

---

[8] Andrews (2015), 305.

[9] Schulze (2020), 180.

[10] Geng, Sarkis, and Bleischwitz (2019), 153, 155; Schulze (2020), 193, 196; Murray, Skene, and Haynes (2017), 377.

[11] Murray, Skene, and Haynes (2017), 377.

[12] Ekins et al. (2016), 167.

[13] Korhonen, Honkasalo, and Seppälä (2018), 37.

[14] See https://www.logan.qld.gov.au/downloads/file/56/aluminium-recycling accessed 13 January 2022.

[15] Schröder, Anggraeni, and Weber (2019), 80.

[16] Schröder, Lemille, and Desmond (2020), 2.

[17] See https://ellenmacarthurfoundation.org accessed 25 March 2024.

[18] See e.g. the German Waste Management Act (KrWG), https://www.umweltbundesamt.de/en/topics/waste-resources/waste-management/waste-regulations accessed 25 March 2024; Murray, Skene, and Haynes (2017), 371.

has started a genuine shift towards a circular economy. The states' emphasis on economic growth as well as lacking waste management systems in less developed countries[19] are parts of a whole range of obstacles in transforming their current economies.[20] Vis-à-vis the pressing environmental and social problems and the outstanding advantages of such a system change, the role of international law in this field becomes relevant. Eventually, this project might serve as a basis for future political action on this topic and can help to approach the goal of an accelerated implementation of circular economy.

1.2 Research Question

This thesis will focus on the question in how far international law demands a transition to a circular economy. For answering this question, the relevant fields of international law, namely international environmental law and human rights law, are to be scrutinized. As the shift towards a circular economy offers an integrated solution on the pressing issues of resource depletion and waste generation, the relevant principles and provisions under international law will be examined in regards of their implications on these two issues.

Every product's life cycle begins with the use of resources. Therefore, this project will start with an analysis of international law provisions relating to the use of natural resources. The effective management of resources, in turn, requires that products will not only be made of new resources but contain secondary materials. Designing and producing reusable and recyclable products represent a key component of a circular economy.[21] This entails the question whether international law regarding the use of resources demands the obligatory change of production directives. Secondly, the thesis will pursue the interpretation of rules relevant to waste and its consequences in order to find a basis for a potential obligation. Since the concept of circular economy aims to achieve an efficient use of resources and the minimization of waste *through* an adapted production, the decisive step finally consists in connecting the different stages in the product's life cycle. While the solution lies in unifying the whole process and its stakeholders to a functioning cycle, legal findings can only be derived from the current regulation by analyzing the relevant rules of the different phases.

---

[19] The criticized terminology surrounding less developing countries will be illuminated in Chap. 4.

[20] Schulze (2020), 193.

[21] Ekins et al. (2016), 167.

On the other side, the states' sovereignty must be taken into account. Economic considerations are generally regarded as a part of the states' internal affairs.[22] That is why the obligation of transforming their economies calls for the necessity of considering the role of sovereignty. Understanding the concept of sovereignty constitutes the framework of the question if a mandatory economic shift can be derived from international law. Findings on the relevant law concerning the issues of resource depletion and waste generation (international environmental law and human rights) have to be weighed with the prerequisites of sovereignty in a third step. Since less developed countries face different obstacles regarding an economic shift,[23] their differentiated situation has to be taken into consideration. In contrast to more developed countries, many of them did not establish appropriate waste disposal systems or suffer from lacking financial possibilities to introduce recycling concepts[24]—only naming some of their problems. Consequently, a differentiated consideration becomes necessary. Approaching the topic of circular economy from different angles and balancing the results will serve to answer the research question comprehensively.

1.3 Methodological Overview

After having identified the course of the examination including the main areas of research, the underlying methodological approach will be introduced. Whereas the concrete steps and methods will be explained in adequate depth throughout the respective chapter and section, an overview of the methodological framework will be given at this stage.

This project is based on a doctrinal analysis of the respective principles and rules in the fields of international environmental law and human rights law. As the classic method used in legal research, it involves the evaluation of legal sources, documents and jurisprudence.[25] Doctrinal analysis aims for explaining a "segment of the law as part of a larger system"[26] and thereby synthesizes concepts, principles and norms to solve a legal issue. Regarding the research

[22] Military and Paramilitary Activities in and against Nicaragua (Nicaragua v. United States of America), Merits, ICJ Reports 1986, p. 14: § 205.

[23] Schulze (2020), 193.

[24] Schulze (2020), 193.

[25] Hutchinson and Duncan (2012), 84.

[26] Hutchinson and Duncan (2012), 84.

question, it involves examining the relevant principles and concepts under international environmental law in the first place, followed by analyzing the respective human rights in order to find out in how far states are obliged to transform their economies into circular ones. The approach of doctrinal analysis starts with assembling the facts and identifying legal issues and continues by examining these issues together with the relevant law to reach a conclusion.[27] Therefore, every chapter will primarily set out the necessary facts and consequences, followed by combining them with the applicable law. Since the issues of resource depletion, waste management and ultimately circular economy are not conclusively regulated by international treaties, it must first be set out, which principles, concepts, norms, and rights may be applied to those issues. Within that scope, not only written agreements, but also other legal sources like international documents and declarations will be examined, completed by the analysis of international and regional case law. This source-based research is accompanied by a review of the actual literature in the respective fields of law. Touching upon old and new debates, this project will take a critical perspective on ongoing discussions and draw justified conclusions—wherever necessary—without getting lost in theoretical discussions leading beyond the scope of the research question.

In the following, the methodological approach will be outlined, structured along the three fields of international law, that form part of this thesis: international environmental law, human rights law and sovereignty.

Both the depletion of resources and the consequences of the actual waste management systems will be illuminated first from an environmental law perspective. In order to evaluate if this field of law provides a foundation for answering the overall research question, both hard law and soft law will be scrutinized. Concerning resource management, there does not exist an explicit hard law framework at the international level, which entirely covers this issue, as will be demonstrated in the following chapter. Therefore, the analysis directly starts with examining the soft law principles and concepts under international environmental law. The term "principles" is used equivalently to the General Principles, laid down in Art. 38 (1) (c) of the Statute of the International Court of Justice (ICJ)[28], which are referred to as "expressions of other unperfected sources of international law"[29]. "Unperfected" means that there is no sufficient state practice for a custom, but there still exist manifestations (in documents or jurisprudence) of a certain legal

[27] Hutchinson and Duncan (2012), 106.

[28] Statute of the International Court of Justice (adopted on 26 June 1945, entered into force on 24 October 1945) UN Treaty Series vol. 993, 33.

[29] Bassiouni (1990), 768, 769.

behavior.[30] Without being adopted in a formal legislative procedure, their character and legal status are parts of an ongoing debate.[31] Especially international environmental law contains a range of these generally accepted principles and it will be the task to examine their legal relevance. Since written law and customary law do not provide answers for every environmental issue, these principles are said to represent an important legal source.[32] On these grounds, they deserve closer attention and will play a prominent role in the analysis. In contrast, concepts build a category of legal models that do not achieve the status of general principles but still entail legal relevance. Both classifications will be referred to in detail and will be analyzed in terms of their legal significance with regard to the research question.

Due to lacking generally accepted interpretation rules regarding those principles and concepts, this project structures their analysis as follows:

First, it will be revealed on which grounds these principles or concepts might be useful to be considered. Second, their general content and meaning, including possible definitions and delimitations to other similar concepts, will be set out in order to classify them within the environmental law framework. As a third step, this thesis examines their scope and embedment in legal documents in search of their legal significance. This analysis will not be conducted in a general manner, but the principles and concepts will be applied to the issues relevant to this thesis. Their connections to resource depletion, waste management and ultimately to circular economy will be revealed to derive concrete legal implications on the research question. In a next step, these principles and concepts will be combined since they cover different aspects of the same issue—as will be seen in the next chapter. Consequently, it will be examined if they are mutually reinforcing each other and what results can be derived from their combined consideration.

This methodology, building the first part of Chap. 2, is also applied to Chap. 3 about waste management. Thus, principles and concepts under international environmental law applicable to waste will be scrutinized. In contrast to Chap. 2, there exists a hard law framework concerning waste which will be examined as well. After clarifying the consequences of current waste management, this framework will be illuminated concerning its implications on waste minimization and prevention, since they represent the main objectives of a circular economy. With the help of international agreements such as the Basel Convention on the Control of

[30] Bassiouni (1990), 768, 769.

[31] Kohen and Schramm (2013), 1.

[32] Bassiouni (1990), 768, 769.

Transboundary Movements of Hazardous Wastes and their Disposal (Basel Convention)[33], waste as the central term will be defined and, moreover, the current waste framework will be examined in light of the overall research question.

Human rights law marks the second field of law to be scrutinized regarding its implications on resource and waste management. This regime will be analyzed according to the interpretation rules of the Vienna Convention of the Law of Treaties (VCLT)[34] with the aid of the actual literature and case law, including resolutions, declarations and other legal documents, especially the General Comments. Whereas the methodology of the human rights interpretation will be described in detail within the respective chapter, a broad overview is to be given at this point. First, the relation between human rights and resources (Chap. 2) and waste management (Chap. 3) will be outlined in order to set out the relevance of human rights interpretation in this context. Second, the scope of rights will be defined by revealing, which rights may have implications on these issues and circular economy. After defining their content and having clarified their relation to a circular economy, their ability to create an obligation regarding an economic transformation will be evaluated. Besides the general interpretation rules under Art. 31 VCLT, also the specific characteristics of this regime will be considered by involving special interpretation rules that will be developed in the respective section.

In a next and crucial step, the results of the international environmental law analysis and the examination of human rights will be considered together. By taking into account the literature and interpreting Art. 31 (3) (c) VCLT, it will be illuminated whether a joint interpretation of both regimes is possible and if so, which implications this would involve. Furthermore, the findings of both chapters will be set in relation with each other, recalling their commonalities at a practical and legal level. Regional legislation will be included as a potential model, and it will be analyzed whether these developments can also be traced at the international level.

The last chapter examines the role of sovereignty regarding a potential obligation to transform the economy. First, it will be set out why a consideration of this broad concept is necessary in this context. Analyzing sovereignty will not be conducted in a holistic manner, but this concept will be illuminated with regard to its effect on implicit obligations. To understand sovereignty, it is indispensable

[33] Basel Convention on the Transboundary Movements of Hazardous Waste and their Disposal (adopted on 22 March 1989, entered into force on 5 May 1992) UN Treaty Series vol. 1673, 57.

[34] Vienna Convention on the Law of Treaties (adopted on 23 May 1969, entered into force on 27 January 1980) UN Treaty Series vol. 1155, 331.

to recall its theoretical foundations. Nonetheless, these basic questions will be touched upon with all due brevity in order to directly apply it to the research question. It is therefore necessary to classify economic decisions and discuss the central question of a limitation of sovereignty, concretized to this topic. In evaluating relevant case law, developments like globalization and the role of human rights will be considered to conclude in how far this concept deals with a potential obligation to transform the economy. Core task of this chapter is the weighing process, in which the results of Chap. 2 and 3 will be balanced with the concept of sovereignty to find out the character of a potential obligation. How this balancing process is to be structured, will be explained in depth in Chap. 4. As a last step, the role of less developed countries and the character of a potential obligation will be taken into account by illuminating their different situations from an environmental law and a human rights perspective.

1.4 Definition and Background of Circular Economy

The concept of circular economy is relatively new in the scientific debate,[35] especially concerning its legal implications. Due to its ongoing developing process, no uniform definition of circular economy exists—a fortiori none in international law. In order to determine, whether an obligation for states to transform their economies exists, this term and its scope are to be clarified. As a basis for the further analysis, the prerequisites and limitations of the concept need to be set out as well. The analysis of what exactly circular economy is serves to develop a working definition, which in turn builds the framework for this thesis. In light of the range of existing definitions, the aim of this section consists in establishing a groundwork for this project, which encompasses all necessary aspects of a realistic and feasible circular economy.

1.4.1 Origin and Development

In order to develop a working definition, it is essential to understand the concept's origin and background. Although its exact origin is debated,[36] the genesis of circular economy can be traced by the most important stages of its development. One of the early originators of the idea was the first president of the Royal

[35] Murray, Skene, and Haynes (2017), 370.

[36] Lazarevic and Valve (2017), 61.

Society of Chemistry who considered a factory without waste and only products as an outcome as ideal in 1848.[37] The increased recycling and repairing due to rationing during World War II, which was common only for less wealthy people before, quickly turned to the opposite after war.[38] In the 1960s it even became more profitable to purchase new things instead of repairing used ones.[39] In the 1970s the Swiss architect and economist *Walter Stahel* brought up the idea of a closed loop system, in which waste is used as a resource.[40] This "Cradle-to-Cradle" system constituted the counterpart of the linear "Cradle-to-Grave" system that describes the linear economy and dominates until today.[41] The emergence of this different conception was related to the growing awareness of the issue of waste generation as a deficiency of the linear system in the 1970s and 1980s.[42] At the same time the concept of sustainability was initiated, particularly through the Brundtland report from 1987 that deemed the economic systems of developed states as the reason for increased consumption.[43] The interrelation of both concepts and the assumption that circular economy can integrate "economic activity and environmental wellbeing in a sustainable way"[44] led to an increasing discussion about circular economy.[45] Their common roots show that sustainability influences the understanding of circular economy and that the need for a more sustainable way of consumption is a key driver for the increased significance of circular economy. That is underlined by the augmenting calls for a "holistic approach [...] towards issues of consumption"[46] and an economic shift.[47] At this stage, the focus lied on the 3 R's, namely reducing, reusing and recycling,[48]

---

[37] Murray, Skene, and Haynes (2017), 372.

[38] Andrews (2015), 307.

[39] Andrews (2015), 307.

[40] Awan, Kanwal, and Bhutta (2020), 29.

[41] Andrews (2015), 309.

[42] Schröder, Lemille, and Desmond (2020), 1.

[43] Murray, Skene, and Haynes (2017), 369; Gro Harlem Brundtland, "Report of the World Commission on Environment and Development: Our Common Future," UN Doc. A/42/427 § (1987), 142, available on https://www.netzwerk-n.org/wp-content/uploads/2017/04/0_Brundtland_Report-1987-Our_Common_Future.pdf.

[44] Murray, Skene, and Haynes (2017), 369.

[45] Cf. Awan, Kanwal, and Bhutta (2020), 20; eg. Schröder, Lemille, and Desmond (2020), 2; Korhonen, Honkasalo, and Seppälä (2018), 37.

[46] Murray, Skene, and Haynes (2017), 369.

[47] Murray, Skene, and Haynes (2017), 370.

[48] Schröder, Lemille, and Desmond (2020), 1.

while waste minimization played a minor role.[49] From the 1990s on the value of resources and reusing waste became more central to the concept.[50] In addition, circular economy was influenced by related conceptions like industrial ecology, described as "the study of material and energy flows resulting from human activities, providing the basis for developing approaches to close cycles in such a way that the ecological impact of these activities is minimized"[51]. These impacts broadened the scope of circular economy: Initially focused on a healthy relationship between economy and environment[52], it incorporated aspects like energy flows and took into account wider consequences of human activities on the environment. With the establishment of the Ellen MacArthur Foundation in 2013, the debate surrounding circular economy gained new momentum—be it the design or possible paths of implementation.[53] The EllenMacArthur Foundation commits itself to the development and the promotion of circular economy by providing research on this concept including a possible implementation and the support of different stakeholders through its engagement with businesses, organizations and governments.[54] It is noteworthy that the concept of circular economy was largely formed by businesses, initiatives and policy-makers, while especially its formation process lacked accompaniment of scientific research.[55] Although it enjoys growing attention in the scientific community in the current time, the development was driven by practitioners. Its continuous enlargement thus led to a whole range of different meanings and definitions. In order to find a suitable definition, it is necessary to determine what circular economy exactly entails. Clarifying its current scope works best by comparing it to the current linear economic system and setting out differences.

---

[49] Schulze (2020), 181.

[50] Schröder, Lemille, and Desmond (2020), 1.

[51] Lazarevic and Valve (2017), 61.

[52] Awan, Kanwal, and Bhutta (2020), 23.

[53] Lazarevic and Valve (2017), 61.

[54] See for more information about the EllenMacArthurFoundation https://ellenmacarthurfoundation.org/about-us/what-we-do accessed 25 March 2024.

[55] Korhonen, Honkasalo, and Seppälä (2018), 37.

1.4.2 Differences to the Current Linear Economy

Circular economy is described as an alternative model to linear economy regarding production and consumption.[56] When looking at the way in which states are currently managing their economies, linear economic models predominate. Natural resources and raw materials are exploited, used in production processes and—thereafter—disposed.[57] Summarized as a "take-make-use-dispose"[58] model, even exacerbated through planned obsolescence in many cases,[59] the linear economy is considered unsustainable.[60] Based on the idea of sustainable consumption, a circular economy aims for "closing the life cycle of resources, products, services, waste and materials"[61]. In contrast to the current system, it "mirrors natural life cycles"[62] and focuses on extending the value of natural materials.[63] By establishing a cyclical use of resources, a circular economy does not only reduce the need for new raw materials drastically, but also contributes to save energy and diminish emissions.[64] It is therefore capable of encountering the issue of depleting resources as well as supporting climate protection through a more efficient way of using energy.[65] Additionally, it contributes to minimizing waste generation and thus reduces its negative consequences like e.g. marine plastic pollution[66] or releasing toxins. In light of that, a circular economy can reduce negative environmental impacts through its restorative and regenerative character.[67]

Establishing a circular economy does not merely mean to reinforce recycling laws.[68] In fact, it is a completely different method to achieve a sustainable way of using resources.[69] This involves the requirement for new technologies,

[56] Da Rosa, Morais and Schmidt Ramos (2018), 35.

[57] Schulze (2020), 180.

[58] Andrews (2015), 305.

[59] Andrews (2015), 307.

[60] Da Rosa, Morais and Schmidt Ramos (2018), 37.

[61] Da Rosa, Morais and Schmidt Ramos (2018), 35.

[62] Andrews (2015), 305.

[63] Ekins et al. (2016), 128.

[64] Andrews (2015), 310.

[65] Awan, Kanwal, and Bhutta (2020), 7.

[66] Schröder, Lemille, and Desmond (2020), 2.

[67] Ekins et al. (2016), 128; Korhonen, Honkasalo, and Seppälä (2018), 37.

[68] Backes (2017), 14.

[69] Backes (2017), 13.

production processes and product designs.[70] For this reason, a transformation towards a circular economy cannot only be effected in slight adaptions of waste recycling, but demands for a holistic approach. It fundamentally changes the way of dealing with resources by concentrating on their scarcity and efficiency rather than on maximizing consumption.[71] With a new approach of product design and production processes it offers the opportunity for new business models.[72] In Europe an annual benefit of €1.8 trillion by 2030 is even estimated, if a shift to a circular economy would succeed.[73] Therefore, a transformation to this alternative cyclical model represents a "systematic change"[74] by not only remedying environmental, but also economic and financial concerns.[75] The differences between both systems will be elucidated by setting out the main requirements of a circular economy.

1.4.3 Prerequisites of a Circular Economy

Most important for developing a working definition is to determine the prerequisites of circular economy. Within the range of diverse associations and meanings of the concept, this section aims to clarify whether there is a consensus about the main requirements of a circular economy and what it consists of. The common basis of a circular economy appears to lie in the closed-loop cyclical system.[76] This involves not only creating loops of material use, but also slowing down resource and energy flows.[77] Central steps to achieve a closed cycle are the three R's: reduce, reuse and recycle.

The first pillar consists in reducing material and the use of primary resources through more efficient production processes.[78] This depends on an adapted product design, e.g. lightweight products, but also on more durability.[79] Longevity of products leads to the fact that less products need to be rebought and less

[70] Backes (2017), 14.

[71] Da Rosa, Morais and Schmidt Ramos (2018), 38.

[72] Ghisellini, Cialani, and Ulgiati (2016), 12.

[73] Ballardini, Kaisto, and Similä (2021), 1.

[74] Backes (2017), 14.

[75] Schröder, Lemille, and Desmond (2020), 2.

[76] Murray, Skene, and Haynes (2017), 372.

[77] Mies and Gold (2021), 1.

[78] Ekins et al. (2016), 156.

[79] Schulze (2020), 180.

resources need to be used for new products. The design phase thus is the crucial part for change. Another option for saving material is avoiding packaging wherever possible.[80] Materials for packaging are used to be thrown away after a short time. Many products, are they robust food items or the majority of non-food articles, are sellable with less or even no packaging. Through substituting material, e.g. with bamboo, or through new technologies, material reduction is possible as well.[81]

Reducing the exploitation of raw materials goes along with the reusability of products. Reusability refers to "any operation by which products or components [...] are used again for the same purpose for which they were conceived"[82]. Reusing products is accompanied by remanufacturing which means "taking a used product and restoring it to like-new or even better condition"[83]. This involves reparation or cleaning and contributes to a lower consumption of energy as well as of primary materials.[84] Possible models are sharing goods instead of owning them or second-hand trading.[85] Leasing or service models have the advantage that manufacturers hold the control over the products for maintaining or repairing[86] them but also the responsibility which can avoid planned obsolescence. The idea of reusing materials applies as well for packaging.[87] Crucial for assuring reusability is again the design phase,[88] in which a simple reparation or cleaning need to be considered.[89] Green supply chains are also important to reduce corruption or unethical practices.[90]

If reuse is not an option, recycling is called to the scene. It is defined as reprocessing "scrap materials into raw materials, which can then be used again to make a new product"[91]. Although the inputs necessary to recycle products are greater than with reusing products, it affords less energy and resources than disposal.[92]

---

[80] Ekins et al. (2016), 158.

[81] Ekins et al. (2016), 158.

[82] Ghisellini, Cialani, and Ulgiati (2016), 15.

[83] Ekins et al. (2016), 159.

[84] Ekins et al. (2016), 160.

[85] Backes (2017), 15; Ekins et al. (2016), 161.

[86] Andrews (2015), 310.

[87] Ekins et al. (2016), 163.

[88] Ghisellini, Cialani, and Ulgiati (2016), 16.

[89] Ekins et al. (2016), 161.

[90] Andrews (2015), 310.

[91] Ekins et al. (2016), 164.

[92] Ekins et al. (2016), 164.

In contrast to traditional recycling, a circular economy also involves the recycling of high value materials and is therefore more comprehensive than current recycling which focuses on low value raw materials.[93] Again, the strings run together in the design process, in which manufacturers must anticipate later recycling and enable the separation of components.[94] The use of sustainable materials like biomaterials facilitates the recycling process and complements a sustainable circular economy.[95] Eventually, the input of primary resources will decrease while secondary resources will gain importance and in the end replace the disposal of waste.[96] The different models and respective steps of the three main elements of circular economy illustrate the need for a closer cooperation between the different stakeholders and lead to the next category of requirements: organizational and institutional prerequisites.

The fact that a circular economy consists in creating a closed-loop system from the use of resources, over design and production processes until the management of products at the end of their lifetime requires a close cooperation of stakeholders involved in the different phases.[97] Companies engaged in product design are dependent of the availability of (secondary) resources, generated by recycling or refurbishing businesses.[98] The work of the latter depends on a design which allows the reparation and recycling of products.[99] Therefore, they need to collaborate in order to enable the circularity of resources. Besides the necessary cooperation and organization of processes the technical infrastructure for respective recycling and designing processes is to be established.[100] Part of this is an industrial symbiosis which is based on closed-loop supply chains.[101] These huge changes need to be supported not only by public infrastructure planners[102], but also by policies on the regional and national level.[103] Without appropriate legislative and political measures as well as financial support, a transformation to

[93] Korhonen et al. (2018), 545.

[94] Elia, Gnoni, and Tornese (2017), 2742.

[95] Geng, Sarkis, and Bleischwitz (2019), 154.

[96] Schulze (2020), 180.

[97] Elia, Gnoni, and Tornese (2017), 2742.

[98] Andrews (2015), 310.

[99] Andrews (2015), 312.

[100] Ekins et al. (2016), 169.

[101] Mies and Gold (2021), 1.

[102] Ekins et al. (2016), 169.

[103] Geng, Sarkis, and Bleischwitz (2019), 154.

a circular economy will not be possible.[104] In that regard, the whole range of stakeholders from enterprises, over policy-makers to consumers must take part in these transformational processes. The aim of decoupling economic growth from resource depletion will only be reached, when all these groups cooperate. In conclusion, the main prerequisites of a circular economy can be summarized firstly, in requirements regarding the production, namely reducing materials and energy, reusing products and components and recycling them, which together lead to an adapted product design and secondly, in organizational requirements such as the cooperation, policy frameworks, infrastructure and financial support. Concentrating on environmental and economic aspects, questions arise regarding the inclusion of the social perspective as the third pillar of sustainability. This leads over to the next part about current deficiencies, limits and obstacles relating to the concept of circular economy.

1.4.4 Limits and Obstacles

Since circular economy is a developing and evolving concept, a closer look reveals weaknesses. With due regard to its aim of combining environmental and economic demands, criticism of circular economy often relates to the ignorance of social aspects and consequences.[105] Although a functioning economy and the reduction of environmental impacts indirectly benefits humanity, categories like social equality, intergenerational equity, and gender, racial or religious equality can rarely be found in the discussion about the principles of circular economy.[106] For a holistic approach, the concept must also involve these questions and offer convincing answers.

Current exploitation processes do not only affect the environment, but also involve poor labor conditions.[107] A sustainable circular economy must address all three pillars of sustainability—the economic, environmental, and social dimension. It must particularly include social aspects which entail important factors like workers' safety and human rights, especially of people involved in the extraction and waste management businesses.[108] While the interrelation between circular

---

[104] See https://www.un.org/sites/un2.un.org/files/circular_economy_14_march.pdf accessed 4 April 2024, 2.

[105] Murray, Skene, and Haynes (2017), 374.

[106] Murray, Skene, and Haynes (2017), 374.

[107] Mies and Gold (2021), 1.

[108] Mies and Gold (2021), 3.

economy and human rights will be examined later on, the conclusion that human well-being and safeguarding their rights belong to a comprehensive approach to circular economy is to be drawn at this point. In order to provide answers to the criticism, this project will operate on a concept of circular economy which considers aspects like workers' human rights and human well-being. Although the social dimension has been neglected in the debate surrounding circular economy so far,[109] the beginning awareness for this dimension illustrates the dynamic character of this concept and its capability to adapt to new requirements.

Another weakness relates to unintended consequences which may result due to different reasons. More durable products lead to an increased use of material in case of i.a. upgraded electronic devices.[110] Additionally, they need more energy and their recycling is more complicated than of less durable or more natural products.[111] In these cases it is important to weigh the consequences of producing longer lasting products against the advantages of products which have a more natural design. This includes energy efficiency and affordability as well.[112] The outcome depends on their category and function: While e.g. a cell phone should be designed to be durable because recycling of its components is difficult, a necessary package would benefit from a more natural design to be recycled quicklier. Green energy involves the detrimental effect that its production necessitates areas which are used as farmland. The resulting displacement of farmland may exert pressure on the local food production.[113] This applies e.g. for biofuels that are the reason for the loss of acres of tropical forest.[114] A careful organization and distribution of land areas thus go along with a sustainable economic transformation. Additionally, new technologies like options for a greener chemistry are more expensive than conventional ones.[115] This is accompanied by the limits of material recycling: Recycling requires energy, and the complete avoidance of side-products is impossible.[116] Thus, there will never be a complete cycle without any waste. However, the use of renewable energy, especially from

---

[109] Schröder, Lemille, and Desmond (2020), 2.

[110] Ekins et al. (2016), 156.

[111] Murray, Skene, and Haynes (2017), 374.

[112] Lazarevic and Valve (2017), 64.

[113] Murray, Skene, and Haynes (2017), 374.

[114] Murray, Skene, and Haynes (2017), 376.

[115] Ghisellini, Cialani, and Ulgiati (2016), 12.

[116] Korhonen, Honkasalo, and Seppälä (2018), 42.

the sun, enables an improved cycle.[117] The aim of a circular economy can, therefore, not lie in the creation of a perfect cycle, but in improving the cyclical use of resources and the reduction of energy.

Central hurdle of such a transformation process is the market. Starting with logistical problems and the creation of new supply chains,[118] "new innovations [...] have to compete in the market with more conventional recycling [and may have] difficulties to break through in the market"[119]. Moreover, business models that rely on the availability of waste will lose their foundation when waste streams are minimized.[120] The "lack of knowledge and experience of the local officials and citizens on how to move from theory to on-the-ground implementation" marks one of the main issues relating to the implementation.[121] This requires the interorganizational cooperation between different stakeholders and enterprises including the establishment of new supply chains.[122] Another effect of increasing efficiency is that production costs decrease and so the prices for end-products, which in turn raises consumption.[123]

This leads over to the role of consumers. A functioning transformation needs to involve the demands of customers. May it be the lack of awareness of the consequences resulting from overexploitation or the common belief that refurbished or recycled products are inferior to new ones.[124] Transparent information about these processes that aims for their acceptance is a key measure for a successful implementation of circular economy.[125] These examples highlight the important role of states in framing the whole process. States are responsible for setting the legal and administrative framework for such a transformation.[126] Without clear regulation—both regarding duties and incentives for enterprises—a holistic economic shift will be impossible. Clear guidelines for planning as well as

[117] Korhonen, Honkasalo, and Seppälä (2018), 42.

[118] Ekins et al. (2016), 164.

[119] Korhonen, Honkasalo, and Seppälä (2018), 44.

[120] Korhonen, Honkasalo, and Seppälä (2018), 44.

[121] See https://www.un.org/sites/un2.un.org/files/circular_economy_14_march.pdf accessed 4 April 2024, 3.

[122] Andrews (2015), 310.

[123] Korhonen, Honkasalo, and Seppälä (2018), 43.

[124] Andrews (2015), 310.

[125] Mies and Gold (2021), 7.

[126] Ballardini, Kaisto, and Similä (2021), 2.

economic and environmental policies need to be established.[127] However, the concrete execution of potential rules lies with the private sector. Industry and companies decide about the design and the detailed structure of processes.[128] Therefore, a close coordination between those who create new law and those who execute it becomes necessary. This gives information about what can be demanded by states and where are the limits of a potential obligation. Bearing the relation between the different stakeholders in mind, possible obstacles relating to the implementation of circular economy can be avoided by coordinating the needs of companies in the process of legislation.

Staying with the role of states, the differences between states, especially between more and less developed states, must be taken into account. When regarding recycling systems and options for establishing new processes, the fact that a functioning waste management is lacking in many countries[129] remains disregarded. The focus in the debate surrounding circular economy often lies on more developed countries, although the need for change in less developed countries is even higher.[130] Considering their difficulties and requirements of development law later on in the analysis, the working definition also needs to incorporate the issues of less developed countries. Starting with divergent political and economic conditions, the current waste management systems and opportunities for recycling vary between states.[131] In establishing a new economic system, one must consider issues like corruption and the threat of new industries competing with traditional sectors or even displacing traditional workers.[132] Further difficulties lie in the unequally distributed access to technology and finance for new technologies in many less developed countries as well as in the mismanagement of waste.[133] Combined with a—in many parts—limited awareness of resource depletion and economy strategies based on "resource extraction-led models"[134], these issues do not only hinder an ambitious transformation in less developed countries, but in almost every state. Especially less developed countries could benefit from the new opportunities of establishing a circular economy

[127] See https://www.un.org/sites/un2.un.org/files/circular_economy_14_march.pdf accessed 4 April 2024, 3.

[128] Ballardini, Kaisto, and Similä (2021), 2.

[129] Schulze (2020), 181.

[130] Schröder, Lemille, and Desmond (2020), 3.

[131] Ekins et al. (2016), 165.

[132] Preston et al. (2019), 3.

[133] Preston et al. (2019), 13.

[134] Preston et al. (2019), 13.

and an integration in a transformation process that would succeed by involving regional companies and industries.[135]

One of the central questions relates to the debatable aim of nearly every state's economy: economic growth. The proverbial elephant in the room when it comes to discussion about future economic models ignites debates between persons that hold economic growth as the ultimate objective and those who are in favor of a new direction of what an economy must aim for. Without entering into the often morally connotated discussion, it is clearly required in light of depleting resources that current economies and economic growth must be decoupled from exploiting natural resources.[136] This would allow states to continuously focusing on economic growth but at the same time ensuring a more sustainable approach.[137] In that regard, it needs to be highlighted that circular economy is an "important pathway to realise the target of the sustainable use of resources, but it is not the same thing".[138] This demonstrates that even a functioning circular economy necessitates quantitative limits for resource consumption,[139] and is no panacea for every issue related to the scarcity of resources. On the contrary, the assumption that circular economy represents a mere improved waste management does not meet the great potential of such a transformation.[140] Connected thereto, this concept needs to be implemented on a global scale to achieve a real change. Concentrating on regional approaches will limit its ability to solve the issues of depleting resources and increasing waste.[141] Nonetheless, a short overview of already existing plans as well as national and regional measures will be provided in order to complete the picture.

1.4.5 Circular Economy in Practice

Although no state has completely implemented a circular economy, there can be found many initiatives and regional or national plans towards a transformation. One of the most famous examples is the Circular Economy Action Plan as a

---

[135] Preston et al. (2019), 2, 13.

[136] Lazarevic and Valve (2017), 65.

[137] Lazarevic and Valve (2017), 65.

[138] Backes (2017), 13.

[139] Backes (2017), 13.

[140] Ghisellini, Cialani, and Ulgiati (2016), 12.

[141] Lazarevic and Valve (2017), 65.

part of the Green Deal by the European Union (EU) presented in 2020.[142] It entails over 50 measures for closing the loop of resources and focuses on different sectors like construction or demolition.[143] Earlier regulation like the Waste Framework Directive (2008/98/EC) "focuses, as its name suggests, mainly on the final stages of the life cycle of products, such as recovery, recycling, and disposal of waste"[144]. These rules only "encourage" member states to implement measures for reuse and recycling and thus are incomplete in terms of legal bindingness.[145] Furthermore, it does not comprise models of sharing goods.[146] Insofar, the EU has initiated an ambitious plan, but binding legislation is still missing. Some member states, most notably the Netherlands, have incorporated steps towards a circular economy. With the objective to make their economy 100% circular by 2050 and implementing guidelines and transition agendas, the Dutch government has launched the most ambitious plan so far.[147] This is followed by France, which launched a ban of destroying unsold non-food products, a repairability index, and started phasing out single-use plastic packaging by 2040.[148] Moving over to Asia, China began orienting itself towards circular approaches in 2009 by promoting an economic development strategy at different levels from the individual business level, over eco-industrial parks towards municipalities.[149] This Circular Economy Promotion Law was followed by several further plans incorporating this objective into the recent 5-year-strategies.[150] Japan implemented circular economy approaches since the 90s with the Law for Effective Utilization

---

[142] "How countries are striving to build their circular economy" https://sustainabilitymag.com/sustainability/how-countries-are-leading-build-a-circular-economy-eu-sustainability-regenerative accessed 25 March 2024.

[143] "How countries are striving to build their circular economy" https://sustainabilitymag.com/sustainability/how-countries-are-leading-build-a-circular-economy-eu-sustainability-regenerative accessed 25 March 2024.

[144] Ballardini, Kaisto, and Similä (2021), 2.

[145] Ballardini, Kaisto, and Similä (2021), 2.

[146] Ballardini, Kaisto, and Similä (2021), 2.

[147] "How countries are striving to build their circular economy" https://sustainabilitymag.com/sustainability/how-countries-are-leading-build-a-circular-economy-eu-sustainability-regenerative accessed 25 March 2024.

[148] "How countries are striving to build their circular economy" https://sustainabilitymag.com/sustainability/how-countries-are-leading-build-a-circular-economy-eu-sustainability-regenerative accessed 25 March 2024.

[149] Awan, Kanwal, and Bhutta (2020), 23.

[150] Preston et al. (2019), 10.

of Recyclables.[151] It started by mapping all material flows crossing the country borders, but did not establish a circular economy yet.[152] India initiated a strategy for resource efficiency and acknowledged the importance of circular economy to achieve this.[153] Taking a look at African countries, Nigeria, Rwanda and South Africa founded the African Circular Economy Alliance in 2017.[154] Joined by Côte d'Ivoire and Ghana, the alliance specified different areas like food production or textiles to foster circular activities.[155] These examples show that circular economy is playing an increasing role in the national and regional policy agendas, but without concrete measures for implementing and above all, without any global agreement on it.[156] For instance, Sweden fostered the collection of materials for recycling, but did only achieve the generation of a small amount of secondary materials.[157] Growing awareness is to be noted in the private sector, where companies and even major players as Google or Renault approach circular systems due to its cost- and resource-efficiency.[158] In countries without appropriate waste management systems especially the informal sector including waste collectors and recyclers is pushing the reuse and reparation of products forward.[159] This reveals that although states have progressive waste management and recycling systems, they are far away from having established a functioning circular economy.[160] However, these examples underscore the increasing attention and implementation of this concept on different levels.

---

[151] Ghisellini, Cialani, and Ulgiati (2016), 15.

[152] Joe Isles, "Which country is leading the circular economy shift?" https://ellenmacarthurfoundation.org/articles/which-country-is-leading-the-circular-economy-shift accessed 25 March 2024.

[153] Preston et al. (2019), 13.

[154] Preston et al. (2019), 13.

[155] See https://www.aceaafrica.org/#:~:text=The%20African%20Circular%20Economy%20Alliance%20%28ACEA%29%20is%20a,delivers%20economic%20growth%2C%20jobs%2C%20and%20positive%20environmental%20outcomes accessed 25 March 2024.

[156] Preston et al. (2019), 9.

[157] Preston et al. (2019), 9.

[158] Preston et al. (2019), 10.

[159] Shresta, "The Integration of Circular Economy into Municipal Solid Waste Managemnt of Kathmandu Metropolitan City in Nepal", 54 https://essay.utwente.nl/77393/1/2012685_Zubin_Shrestha_17-18.pdf accessed 25 March 2024.

[160] Preston et al. (2019), 9.

1.4.6 Developing a Working Definition

After clarifying the origin, prerequisites, potential limits and the current state of implementation, the cornerstones for developing a definition are set out. To say it in advance: There is no internationally accepted definition of circular economy.[161] Existing definitions differ in their focus on various aspects or dimensions due to a divergent understanding of this concept or different priorities.[162] Since the objective is not to draft a complete new "better" definition, the most appropriate definitions—in light of the previous findings—will be presented and after that complemented by missing aspects. The aim consists in drafting a working definition which summarizes all the relevant aspects mentioned above and builds the framework for the further analysis. Even though it attempts to include all important facets, the definition cannot result in an overarching foundation encompassing every single (future) interest due to the still evolving character of circular economy.[163] Common to the existing definitions is the reference to completely transforming the current way of producing and consuming.[164] A basic definition including the main prerequisites is this of *Ballardini*, referring to circular economy as a "general term covering all activities that reduce, reuse, and recycle materials in production, distribution, and consumption processes"[165]. Highlighting its differences to a linear economy and current production and consumption schemes, *Ghisellini* describes it as a method to "optimize natural resource use through efficiency increase towards a transition from open to closed cycles of materials and energy and to less wasteful industrial processes"[166]. Other authors already establish the connection to sustainable development in their definition like *Awan*, defining it as "resource reduction to meet the sustainability agenda of the existing and future generation"[167]. *Murray* extends the focus of this concept by including human well-being in its definition.[168] The definition of the

---

[161] Awan, Kanwal, and Bhutta (2020), 21.

[162] Awan, Kanwal, and Bhutta (2020), 21; Murray, Skene, and Haynes (2017), 369.

[163] Korhonen et al. (2018), 548.

[164] Ballardini, Kaisto, and Similä (2021), 1.

[165] Ballardini, Kaisto, and Similä (2021), 1.

[166] Ghisellini, Cialani, and Ulgiati (2016), 26.

[167] Awan, Kanwal, and Bhutta (2020), 20.

[168] Murray, Skene, and Haynes (2017), 369.

which are used in the production of cell phones, also more basic resources like sand, which forms the foundation of building material, need to be included in this context. When speaking of resource depletion, it does also involve more far-reaching aspects such as water shortages or depleting minerals like phosphorus, which is crucial for plant growth.[16] As biological components like renewable biomass gains importance in the production and energy sector, the resources that are relevant in a circular economy partly overlap with the resources covered by biological diversity. Nonetheless, animals and microorganisms as well as other living resources are excluded from this consideration. Although not every special problem regarding a certain type of resource can be thematized here, the entirety of all non-living resources forms part of this project.

2.1 Principles and Concepts Under International Environmental Law

Since depleting resources have huge consequences on the environment, the first step of the analysis consists in scrutinizing the environmental legal framework concerning circular economy. In the context of international environmental law, the general principles and concepts—although their classification as binding rules remains in most of the cases disputed—[17]as well as their reflections in international treaties mark a crucial step in the development of this field of law.[18] These principles and concepts were "derived from the balancing and mutual limitation of sovereign rights"[19] and thus build an appropriate starting point for the analysis. Therefore, the project benefits from analyzing the roots of this field of law to generate a better understanding of its linkage to circular economy. A special focus will lie on their scope and connections to the management of resources as well as their legal value, in order to reveal if they can build a pillar for a potential obligation. Regarding the research question, the following principles and concepts deserve a closer consideration: sustainable development, the precautionary principle as well as the preventive principle, and the common concern of humankind. Discussions about their acceptance and legal character will not be conducted in a

[16] See https://www.conserve-energy-future.com/causes-effects-solutions-depletion-natural-resources.php accessed 25 March 2024.

[17] Proelß (2022), 99.

[18] Brunnée (2003), 70.

[19] Brunnée (2003), 43.

general manner,[20] but their legal implications and importance regarding a potential obligation to transform the economy into a circular one will be examined in the respective section. The central question will be whether these principles and concepts can result in concrete obligations on their own or combined with each other, or at least build the foundation for such an obligation in connection with other rules under international law such as human rights.

2.1.1 Sustainable Development

As a crucial concept in the context of the United Nations (UN) work in the field of international development and environmental protection,[21] the concept of sustainable development will be analyzed in light of the issue of resource depletion. The impending depletion of highly needed natural resources such as minerals[22] leads to the conflict of how to manage their exploitation. Thus, the management of resources lies in the area of conflict between environmental, economic and social interests. With respect to potential social and economic conflicts as well as the severe ecological consequences, the concept of sustainable development is playing a major role.[23] Providing a tool of reconciling these three dimensions, it may therefore be capable to resolve these tensions in the field of resource depletion. Moreover, the limited supply of resources directly affects the living conditions of future generations, which raises the issue of inter- and intragenerational equity.[24] The latter form inherent components of sustainable development,[25] as will be shown below, which renders the analysis of this concept necessary in light of this intergenerational conflict. In terms of the legal value of sustainable development, the concept builds part of the evolving field of international environmental law, which will be illustrated on the basis of its actual influence. Regarding its disputed legal character, it will be revealed if a concrete obligation to transform the economy can be derived from this concept, or if rather its influences on the law

---

[20] See for a general discussion Ekardt (2020), 178.

[21] Beyerlin (2013), para. 1.

[22] UN Interagency Framework Team for Preventive Action, "Toolkit and Guidance for Preventing and Managing Land and Natural Resources Conflict", available at https://www.un.org/en/land-natural-resources-conflict/pdfs/EU-UN%20Introduction%20and%20overview.pdf accessed 4 April 2024.

[23] Velenturf and Purnell (2021), 1441.

[24] See https://en.unesco.org/themes/education-sustainable-development/what-is-esd/sd accessed 4 April 2024.

[25] Barral (2012), 380.

may be used in combination with other rules and concepts under international law to build a pillar for such an obligation.

After clarifying the term "sustainable development", the relevant principles of the Stockholm Declaration on the Human Environment (Stockholm Declaration)[26] and the Rio Declaration on Environment and Development (Rio Declaration)[27] will be interpreted regarding their implications on sustainable development. Discovering the linkages between this concept and circular economy and determining its legal notion will mark the first step in clarifying the legal basis of a potential obligation. This section aims for an analysis of sustainable development with focus on its connections to circular economy and the issue of depleting resources rather than comprehensively examining every detail of this concept. In order to elucidate their relationship, the UN Sustainable Development Goals (SDGs) are of supplementary significance. The following section will culminate in the discussion about the legal character of this concept related to circular economy and eventually answer the question if sustainable development demands a change to use secondary materials instead of new resources on its own or if it contributes to such an obligation by combining it with other rules or concepts under international law.

2.1.1.1 Definitions of Sustainability and Sustainable Development

What exactly is sustainable development and what is the difference with regard to the term 'sustainability'? Even though it builds a relevant component in a range of international legal instruments, its scope is rather vague than clear.[28] Referring to the Brundtland report's definition—which is cited in nearly every article about sustainable development—it is considered as "meet[ing] the needs [...] of the present without compromising the ability to meet those of the future".[29] The main point thus consists in the needs of present and future generations. It

[26] UN General Assembly, "Report of the United Nations Conference on the Human Environment," UN Doc. A/CONF.48/14/Rev. 1 § (1972), available at https://documents-dds-ny.un.org/doc/UNDOC/GEN/NL7/300/05/IMG/NL730005.pdf?OpenElement.

[27] UN General Assembly, "Report of the United Nations Conference on Environment and Development," UN Doc. A/CONF.151/26 § (1992), available at https://www.un.org/en/development/desa/population/migration/generalassembly/docs/globalcompact/A_CONF.151_26_Vol.I_Declaration.pdf.

[28] Beyerlin (2013), para. 1.

[29] Brundtland, Report of the World Commission on Environment and Development: Our Common Future, 38.

entails the preservation of the planet's ecosystem including its natural resources.[30] The intra- and intergenerational aspect is accompanied by its aim of balancing economic, environmental, and social needs. The equal improvement of these three pillars of economic, environmental and social development shall guarantee a prosperous and secure future.[31] This can only be achieved by minimizing the current exploitation of raw materials and pollution.[32] Both the use of renewable and non-renewable resources must be adapted to the actual supply and rebuilding capacity.[33] In terms of the social perspective, global security for everyone is an element of sustainable development.[34] *Ekardt* argues for a broader scope of this concept which includes "cross-generational and global justice"[35] and thus enlarges the three-pillar model. Additionally, *Da Rosa, Morais and Schmidt Ramos* extend the concept with cultural and political factors.[36] Since this concept is evolving continuously, there seems to be a trend to include different aspects in the definition. As *Ekardt* himself states that not every important aspect per se constitutes an element of this concept,[37] the incorporation of further aspects should not blur the boundaries of sustainable development, since its core about intra- and intergenerational equity and the generations' needs remains the same. Hence, the Brundtland Report's definition will build the basis for the further analysis.

In terms of clarity, the difference between 'sustainability' and 'sustainable development' must be set out: In contrast to sustainability, which is classified as a "long-term goal", the term sustainable development is used to describe "the processes and pathways to achieve it"[38]. This shows that sustainability represents the objective, while sustainable development represents the action. It does not set a target to be achieved but requires a process to be initiated. Therefore, sustainable development is more likely to lead to a potential obligation for states to take action than a mere goal. Although some authors believe that the term 'sustainable development' was replaced by 'sustainability',[39] most of the international law

[30] Beyerlin (2013), para. 14.

[31] Velenturf and Purnell (2021), 1441.

[32] Da Rosa, Morais and Schmidt Ramos (2018), 37.

[33] Ekardt (2020), 30.

[34] Ekardt (2020), 30.

[35] Ekardt (2020), 28.

[36] Da Rosa, Morais and Schmidt Ramos (2018), 37.

[37] Ekardt (2020), 30.

[38] See https://en.unesco.org/themes/education-sustainable-development/what-is-esd/sd accessed 4 April 2024.

[39] Da Rosa, Morais and Schmidt Ramos (2018), 37.

literature still refers to 'sustainable development' as a concept of international environmental law.[40] For this reason, the project will concentrate on sustainable development.

Before determining the content and the legal scope of this concept in a next step, it is important for understanding its development to trace back the states' first commitments to sustainable development. In the UN General Assembly's Resolution 35/56 states initially made a commitment not only to support economic development, but also towards integrating environmental soundness as well as social development.[41] They expressed their growing awareness of how development and poverty depend on a healthy environment and a sufficient supply of resources.[42] In 1987 they explicitly addressed sustainable development by seconding the Brundtland Report's definition and agreeing that "an equitable sharing of the environmental costs and benefits of economic development between and within countries and between present and future generations is a key to achieving sustainable development"[43]. This resolution amends the report by stating that the quality of growth must be changed, especially by preserving the supply of resources.[44] Referring to resources at various points, these initial documents highlight the importance of the adapted use including extraction and management of natural resources. In order to analyze the legal relevance of sustainable development and its linkages to the depletion of resources, the concept's content will be determined in the following section.

2.1.1.2 Scope of Sustainable Development

In order to figure out the exact scope of sustainable development, the underlying declarations, namely the Stockholm and Rio Declaration, will be analyzed. These declarations paved the way for the present understanding of this concept[45]

---

[40] Barral (2012), 380; Beyerlin (2013); Birnie, Boyle, and Redgwell (2009), 199; Sands et al. (2012), 207.

[41] UN General Assembly, "International Development Strategy for the Third United Nations Development Decade," UN Doc. A/RES/35/56/Add. 1 § (1980), 118 et. seq., https://documents-dds-ny.un.org/doc/RESOLUTION/GEN/NR0/390/75/IMG/NR039075.pdf?OpenElement.

[42] Beyerlin (2013), para. 3.

[43] UN General Assembly, "Report of the World Commission on Environment and Development," UN Doc. A/RES/42/187 § (1987), para. 4, http://www.un-documents.net/a42r187.htm.

[44] UN General Assembly, Report of the World Commission on Environment and Development, para. 5.

[45] Brunnée (2003), 62.

and therefore build the starting point for the analysis. Especially the Rio Declaration with twelve principles incorporating aspects of sustainable development marks an important cornerstone of this concept. Central to both declarations is their focus on the relation between economic development and environmental protection, which is laid down in the Principles 9, 10 and 11 of the Stockholm Declaration. They refer to the interdependencies between these aspects by stating that "raw materials are essential to environmental management since economic factors as well as ecological processes must be taken into account"[46]. Economic development and environmental protection are thus described as objectives that support each other.[47] *Beyerlin* even qualifies "environmental protection as an integral part of any development measure"[48]. At the same time, Principle 11 requires that "environmental policies of all States should enhance and not adversely affect the present and future development potential"[49], which seems to give priority to economic development. In contrast, Principle 3 of the Rio Declaration demands for "equitably meet[ing] the developmental and environmental needs of present and future generations"[50]. Although not explicitly providing criteria for balancing both aspects, it suggests that economic needs should be treated equally as environmental ones rather than prescribing a hierarchy.[51]

A focus of these declarations lies, in fact, on the intertemporal dimension of this concept.[52] In addition to Principle 3 of the Rio Declaration, Principle 1 and 2 of the Stockholm Declaration refer to safeguarding the environment for present and future generations.[53] Principle 2 explicitly incorporates natural resources in this context. This intertemporal perspective marks a notable shift in the field of international environmental law away from the previous concentration on transboundary pollution between neighboring states.[54] Environmental concerns are no longer restricted to transboundary harm, but are now viewed as global concerns

---

[46] UN General Assembly, Report of the United Nations Conference on the Human Environment, Principle 10.

[47] Beyerlin (2013), para. 2.

[48] Beyerlin (2013), para. 11.

[49] UN General Assembly, Report of the United Nations Conference on the Human Environment, Principle 11.

[50] UN General Assembly, Report of the United Nations Conference on Environment and Development, Principle 3.

[51] Beyerlin (2013), para. 12.

[52] Beyerlin (2013), para. 10.

[53] UN General Assembly, Report of the United Nations Conference on the Human Environment, Principle 1, 2.

[54] Brunnée (2003), 42.

which entail a collective responsibility of states.[55] This broader perspective is reflected in the current understanding of sustainable development which incorporates the inter- and intragenerational responsibility of states.[56] This aspect is, in turn, related to the idea of inter- and intragenerational equity.[57] *Barral* even describes sustainable development as the combination of inter- and intragenerational equity.[58] Intergenerational equity constitutes a principle in international law that requires states to take into account environmental concerns in every of their economic decisions to safeguard the environment for future generations.[59] By intragenerational equity one means equally distributing the "outcomes of development within one generation as much internally (within one national society) as internationally (between more and less developed states)"[60] These different but supplementary forms of equity build the core of sustainable development and they can only be pursued by their mutual integration. Therefore, preserving the environment must be integrated in economic development for the current and future generations, which is underscored by Principle 4 of the Rio Declaration.[61] The social aspect was included not before 1997, when the UN General Assembly acknowledged social development as a third pillar in sustainable development.[62] Accordingly, both the environment and humanity are reflected in this concept.[63]

But what does it entail in light of the depletion of resources? *Beyerlin* takes Agenda 21 as a rather "broad catalogue of recommendations"[64] than a clear composition of concrete rules for taking action. Nonetheless, one can find several specific references to the use of natural resources. Core provision of the Stockholm Declaration is Principle 21 that prescribes the balancing of the states' sovereign right to exploit their own resources with the duty not to cause transboundary harm.[65] By requiring a balance between the states' sovereignty and the

---

[55] Brunnée (2003), 42.

[56] Beyerlin (2013), para. 10.

[57] Brunnée (2003), 48.

[58] Barral (2012), 380.

[59] Barral (2012), 380.

[60] Barral (2012), 380.

[61] Barral (2012), 380.

[62] UN General Assembly, "Programme for the Further Implementation of Agenda 21," UN Doc. A/RES/S-19/2 § (1997), para. 3, available on https://documents-dds-ny.un.org/doc/UNDOC/GEN/N97/774/73/PDF/N9777473.pdf?OpenElement.

[63] Beyerlin (2013), para. 13.

[64] Beyerlin (2013), para. 5.

[65] UN General Assembly, Report of the United Nations Conference on the Human Environment, Principle 21.

consideration of transboundary harm, this principle will build the basis for weighing the first two substantive chapters' findings with the requirements of the states' sovereignty at the end of this project. However, this principle will also serve to clarify the scope of sustainable development in relation to the use of resources. It turns the spotlight on the question whether states are entitled to use their own resources without limitations with respect to the demands of sustainable development. Hence, it does not come as a surprise that "sustainable use of natural resources" has evolved as a special emanation of sustainable development.[66] Its content will be scrutinized in the next section.

2.1.1.3 The Sustainable Use of Natural Resources

From the concept of sustainable development there can be derived a range of subnotions like sustainable management, maximum sustainable yield, and—closely connected to the issue of depleting resources—sustainable use.[67] The idea of this special emanations results from the main aim of sustainable development, namely, to meet the needs of present and future generations, which predominantly includes the sufficient supply of natural resources. In order to safeguard these resources also for future generations, they have to be exploited in a sustainable way.[68] At the moment, there does not exist any established definition on sustainable use, however, its broad implementation in especially regional agreements, ia. the Yaoundé Declaration on the Conservation and Sustainable Management of Forests, shows that this emanation creates limitations upon the use of different resources like water, materials or other important resources.[69]Linked to biological diversity, Art. 2 of the Convention on Biological Diversity (CBD) offers a definition that connects the use of resources with the consideration of future generations: "the use of these components in a way and at a rate that does not lead to the long-term decline of biological diversity, thereby maintaining its potential to meet the needs and aspirations of present and future generations"[70]. In this context "sustainable" means that the environment must be capable to cope with the exploitation and to regenerate from the interferences.[71] In case of renewable resources it requires an extraction rate that is aligned with the time, the resources

---

[66] Beyerlin (2013), para. 11.

[67] Beyerlin (2013), para. 1.

[68] Sands et al. (2012), 207.

[69] See for more sources Sands et al. (2012), 207.

[70] The Convention on Biological Diversity (adopted on 5 June 1992, entered into force 29 December 1993) UN Treaty Series vol. 1760, 79.

[71] Brunnée (2003), 49.

need to be formed anew. Non-renewable resources have to be used up only to a point to which a sufficient supply for future generations remains.[72] It challenges the states' sovereign right to exploit their natural resources by imposing restrictions on the current rate of exploitation to preserve them for future generations.[73] These limitations do not only apply to resources within a state's territory, but also to areas beyond national jurisdiction.[74] The development of this concept has been reflected in a range of regional and international agreements about specific natural resources: One example is the International Convention for the Conservation of Atlantic Tuna.[75] However, also non-marine resources have become part of treaties, to mention the African Nature Convention, the International Tropical Timber Agreement and the CBD, all incorporating the idea of sustainable use.[76] With similar terms like "rational" or "appropriate", these international agreements have contributed to the implementation of the concept of sustainable use.[77] The idea behind this concept and its reflections in international instruments is that resources should be used for the benefit of people instead of ending up as waste.[78] This goes back to the principles of the Stockholm and Rio Declaration: Principle 5 Stockholm Declaration highlights the danger of exhaustion of non-renewable resources, while Principle 3 relates to the restoration of renewable materials. Both the Stockholm and Rio Declaration expressly refer to the exploitation of resources and constitute the limit of this right to freely use their own resources where damage or pollution beyond their own territory is likely to occur (Principle 21 Stockholm Declaration and Principle 2 Rio Declaration). They also demand a coordinated and cooperative[79] approach from the states in achieving a sustainable management of resources (Principle 13 Stockholm Declaration and Principle 18 Rio Declaration). Sustainable use is thus one integral component of bringing together environmental protection and development. The review of the examples in treaty law and the principles of the declarations have shown that the main point of this concept consists in constituting limitations of

[72] Birnie, Boyle, and Redgwell (2009), 199.

[73] Sands et al. (2012), 210.

[74] Sands et al. (2012), 213.

[75] International Convention for the Conservation of Atlantic Tunas (adopted on 14 May 1966, entered into force on 20 May 1969) UN Treaty Series No. 9587, 64.

[76] Birnie, Boyle, and Redgwell (2009), 199; Sands et al. (2012), 211.

[77] Sands et al. (2012), 212.

[78] Gabčikovo-Nagymaros Project (Hungary v Slovakia), Judgement (Separate Opinion of Vice-President Weeramantry), ICJ Rep 7 107 (International Court of Justice (ICJ) 1997).

[79] Da Rosa, Morais and Schmidt Ramos (2018), 41.

the sovereign right of exploitation. As *Brunnée* sums up the core of this concept, it "makes certain aspects of domestic resource management a matter of international concern"[80]. How far-reaching these limitations are and what exactly is required of states remains unclear. What is clear is that Principle 21 Stockholm Declaration (and Principle 2 Rio Declaration) as well as the treaty rules *did* in some way limit the free exercise of the right of exploitation.[81] The question of what states are obliged to regarding their use of resources can be answered by determining the normative content of the concept of sustainable use and of the concept of sustainable development in general. In order to not only repeat the current discussion about the legal content of these concepts, their connections to the research question and circular economy have to be set out before. This allows to combine the question about the legal character of sustainable development and its sub-notion of sustainable use with the question if these concepts require the transformation towards a circular economy and, hence, to discuss their potential normative value specifically in light of the research question.

2.1.1.4 Connection to Circular Economy

Returning to the thesis' main purpose, the discussion of sustainable development should not be pursued detached from the topic of circular economy. Although it is necessary to understand the concept of sustainable development on its own to draw conclusions if it could serve as a pillar for a potential obligation, findings on the role of sustainable development concerning an economic transformation can only be made if the relation between sustainable development and circular economy is clarified. First, the concrete links between both concepts will be revealed by comparing their objectives and content. The SDGs, adopted by the UN General Assembly in 2015, will serve as additional information reflecting the states' interests regarding the content and concrete aims of sustainable development.[82] Second, it will be scrutinized of what character the relationship between both concepts is.

By improving the efficiency of resource cycles which leads to the minimization of resource use and waste, circular economy can serve as a solution for a range of environmental problems like pollution by waste as well as it may ensure the supply of resources for generations of human beings. It thus encompasses the environmental and social aspect of sustainability and enables to economize sustainably. Therefore, its aim is closely related to the three pillars of sustainable

[80] Brunnée (2003), 48.

[81] Brown Weiss (1992), 730.

[82] Biermann, Kanie, and Kim (2017), 26–31.

development.[83] Through providing a holistic approach for a sustainable management of resources, it is capable of contributing to the objective of sustainable development, which is balancing environmental, social and economic concerns.[84]

Moreover, circular economy and sustainable development share the same roots. Both concepts are based on the awareness that the earth's supply of resources and capability to cope with the immense interferences by humanity are not infinite. Hence, they have been developed in an attempt to reconcile the current standard of living with a protection of livelihoods and existential rights. Nonetheless, critical voices argue that despite their shared roots, the concepts evolved in different directions and that their relationship weakened.[85] *Velenturf and Purnell* even speak of adverse affects of circular economy practices on sustainability by consolidating unsustainable practices e.g. in the petrochemical industry.[86] On top of that, they affirm that the concept of sustainable development has developed further, while circular economy remained without any advancement.[87] Further critique relates to the lower attention circular economy pays to inter- and intragenerational equity and to the fact that circular economy does not represent a counter design to economic growth.[88]

It is true that inter- and intragenerational equity are no key components of circular economy. However, the whole concept is aligned with decreasing resource consumption and thus stopping the depletion of resources. This directly benefits future generations and serves to a better distribution of resources within the actual generation. Inter- and intragenerational equity are, hence, more than a side effect of circular economy, but one of its main objectives. Furthermore, the analysis of the prerequisites and components of circular economy in Chap. 1[89] has demonstrated, that this concept did evolve towards including more aspects than just saving resources. It has become a comprehensive approach for an improved economy that includes environmental aspects like resource extraction and waste, as well as social elements such as intergenerational equity or human rights.[90] On these grounds, it cannot be argued that circular economy and sustainable development have developed in completely divergent directions. Anyhow, *Velenturf and*

[83] Murray, Skene, and Haynes (2017), 373.

[84] Ghisellini, Cialani, and Ulgiati (2016), 12.

[85] Lowe (1999), 25; Velenturf and Purnell (2021), 1438.

[86] Velenturf and Purnell (2021), 1438.

[87] Velenturf and Purnell (2021), 1438.

[88] Velenturf and Purnell (2021), 1441.

[89] See 1.4.3.

[90] See 1.4.3.

Purnell themselves state that circular economy is of "tremendous potential for sustainable development"[91]. Even though these concepts are not absolutely congruent, the following assessment of the SDGs will reveal concrete intersections between them:

The SDGs are concrete targets which are legally non-binding.[92] Following after the Millennium Development Goals and broadening their scope, the SDGs represented the common political aim of a sustainable future.[93] Concerning the UN General Assembly's intention to set goals instead of principles which might develop to legally binding rules later on, they have to be distinguished from other reflections of sustainable development in treaties or the concept per se.[94] Therefore, the SDGs will not be analyzed in light of their capability to support the normative character of sustainable development, but to highlight the linkages with circular economy. First of all, the goal to ensure sustainable consumption and production patterns in SDG 12 is closely related to circular economy.[95] It does not expressly refer to the term "circular economy", but literally involves sustainable management and efficient use of natural resources in Target 12.2. Target 12.4 entails the "environmentally sound management of chemicals and all wastes throughout their life cycle" and the aim to "reduce their release [...] in order to minimize their adverse impacts on human health and the environment". On that account, it covers the issue of depleting resources as well as that of waste and its consequences, which are addressed by circular economy. The reference to the life cycle underscores the similarity to the core principles of circular economy: the consideration of a product's entire life cycle and the aim of a closed-loop system. Target 12.5 even mentions reduction, recycling and reuse which build the basic prerequisites of circular economy.[96] Hence, SDG 12 sets the objective of reduction of waste and sustainable use of resources, for which circular economy represents a holistic solution. This marks the first evidence of the close relation between sustainable development and circular economy. Beyond that, circular economy also contributes to other targets of the SDGs: Through an increased efficiency of resource use, circular economy supports a reduction of exploitation of natural resources, which is demanded by SDG 6 regarding the sustainable management of the resource water, by SDG 14 relating to the sustainable use

[91] Velenturf and Purnell (2021), 1437.

[92] Ekardt (2020), 31.

[93] Biermann, Kanie, and Kim (2017), 26.

[94] Biermann, Kanie, and Kim (2017), 26.

[95] Velenturf and Purnell (2021), 1443.

[96] See 1.4.3.

of marine resources and by SDG 15 regarding the sustainable use of terrestrial ecosystems. Target 9.4 expressly aims for an increased resource-use efficiency in industries which is directly linked to the core area of circular economy: the industrial production. Staying with economic processes, SDG 8 involves sustainable economic growth that can be achieved by decoupling economic growth from environmental degradation (Target 8.4), which is again one objective of circular economy.[97] Further targets touch upon the other side of the product's life cycle, namely waste: Target 6.3 includes the elimination of dumping and hazardous chemicals and materials in water, whereas Target 14.1 refers to the reduction of marine debris and pollution. Target 3.9 covers the reduction of deaths and illnesses by pollution and contamination. These dangers caused by waste can be tackled by establishing closed-loop systems with less or without any waste at all. Additionally, SDG 7 (Affordable and Clean Energy), especially Target 7.2 involves sharing of renewable energy that builds one component of a circular economic approach. Concluding with Target 8.8, which incorporates secure working environments, and Target 1.4 aiming for an equal right to i.a. natural resources, the human-related elements of circular economy form also part of the SDGs. This comparison highlights that nearly every aspect of circular economy builds a target of the SDGs and is therefore closely related to sustainable development. The majority of the SDGs is thus relevant for the management of resources,[98] and is thus related to circular economy.[99]

It is nonetheless to be admitted that the review of these rather vague goals[100] does not lead to the conclusion that the SDGs expressly aim for establishing a circular economy. It follows from these close connections, however, that the current linear economy with the excessive use of resources and waste generation is "fundamentally incompatible with sustainable development"[101]. Circular economy is also viewed by some voices of the literature as a concept that is able to achieve sustainability.[102]The crucial point besides the content-related connections is, therefore, how the relation between sustainable development and circular economy is designed in concrete terms. Is circular economy a necessary condition or one of many tools of sustainable development? *Wilson* argues that it is "one of

---

[97] See 1.4.4.

[98] Schulze (2020), 184.

[99] Velenturf and Purnell (2021), 1443.

[100] Biermann, Kanie, and Kim (2017), 27.

[101] Velenturf and Purnell (2021), 1442.

[102] Schröder, Anggraeni, and Weber (2019), 77; Da Rosa, Morais and Schmidt Ramos (2018), 41.

various concepts proposed for sustainable development".[103] *Velenturf and Purnell* even ascribe to it that it is not capable of solving the issue of overconsumption.[104] The role circular economy plays with regard to sustainable development depends on what one understands of circular economy. If it is viewed as a mere approach for more recycling, circular economy indeed can be just one out of many tools for sustainable development. In fact, the previous assessment of its components in Chap. 1 has shown that circular economy incorporates more elements and represents a comprehensive approach for sustainable production and consumption. It did evolve from a technological fixated to a holistic concept that involves economic, as well as environmental and social elements.[105] Although it certainly cannot be the only pathway to achieve sustainability, thinking about current limitations and difficulties, it is, however, one of the most promising concepts to solve not only the issue of depleting resources but also that of waste including renewable energies and considering human rights. *Da Rosa, Morias and Schmidt Ramos* agree that achieving sustainability depends on optimizing the use of natural resources.[106] This again is addressed by circular economy. For these reasons, circular economy is more than a mere tool, but the most important approach and therefore a necessary condition for sustainable development as it delivers a possible solution for most of its objectives. With their clarified relation, it is now to scrutinize the legal implications which may follow from these closely connected concepts.

2.1.1.5 Legal Character of Sustainable Development

The question if sustainable development can build a pillar for a mandatory economic transformation depends on its normative value. Related to this is the general discussion about what sustainable development is: a principle of international law? Customary law? A concept with no legal implications at all? Or can a normative value be ascribed to it? As this part aims to answer the question about its normative character in light of its connections with circular economy, the lively discussion about the legal character of sustainable development in general will be entered to create a starting point for the concrete analysis applied to circular economy.

---

[103] Wilson (2015), 130.

[104] Velenturf and Purnell (2021), 1446.

[105] See 1.4.6.

[106] Da Rosa, Morais and Schmidt Ramos (2018), 39.

In the literature, there is a continuing debate about the normative value of sustainable development which reaches from taking it for a principle of customary law to qualifying it as a mere political objective without normative quality.[107]Between these two extremes, authors also propose a sort of middle way or reveal its implications without a concrete label.[108] In general there can be distinguished three different groups of classification: Rules, principles and political objectives. A rule is a concrete and binding regulation, while a principle "expresses a general truth, which guides our action"[109] and must be taken into consideration by officials without requiring a particular outcome.[110] With due regard to the current uncertainties about its concrete content, it cannot be classified as a rule. The debate therefore concentrates on the differentiation between a binding principle, a political value or something in between. In contrast to a political objective, a principle, which is of the same structure as such an objective as its "language [...] is more vague and general"[111], it must not be disregarded in legal argumentations and therefore does have legal implications.[112]

2.1.1.5.1 Sustainable Development as a Principle?

Starting with the strongest attribution of normativity, sustainable development is according to some voices closely connected with customary law. *Sands* even describes it directly as a principle of customary law.[113]He refers to the Separate Opinion of Judge *Weeramantry*[114] in the ICJ Gabčikovo-Nagymaros Case[115] and argues that Principle 21 Stockholm Declaration is "sufficiently well established to provide the basis for an international cause of action; that is to say, to reflect an international customary legal obligation"[116]. Concerning the classification of Principle 21 as customary law he is seconded by *Brunnée*, who takes the ICJ

[107] Beyerlin (2013), para. 15; Brunnée (2003), 57.

[108] Barral (2012), 378.

[109] Sands et al. (2012),189.

[110] Sands et al. (2012), 189.

[111] Ellis (2008), 2.

[112] Ellis (2008), 2; Sands et al. (2012), 189.

[113] "little doubt that the concept of 'sustainable development' has entered the corpus of international customary law" Sands et al. (2012), 208.

[114] Gabčikovo-Nagymaros Project (Hungary v Slovakia), Judgement (Separate Opinion of Vice-President Weeramantry), ICJ Rep 7.

[115] Gabčikovo-Nagymaros Project (Hungary v Slovakia), Judgement, Merits, ICJ Rep 7 (International Court of Justice (ICJ) 1997).

[116] Sands et al. (2012),188.

Advisory Opinion on the Legality of the Threat and Use of Nuclear Weapons[117] as an evidence. Since the ICJ in its Advisory Opinion on Nuclear Weapons states that the "general obligation of States to ensure that activities within their jurisdiction and control respect the environment of other States [...] [is] now part of the corpus of international law relating to the environment"[118] and classifies it as customary law, *Brunnée* hits the weak point of *Sands'* argumentation that it does not include the classification of the concept of sustainable development per se.[119] In its generality the categorization of sustainable development as customary law cannot be derived from his argumentation. Sustainable Development is not equivalent to the content of Principle 21, even though this principle plays an important role in determining the scope of sustainable development.[120] More in line with the argumentation by *Brunnée*, the stated case law sources do by no means suffice for representing enough state practice. Moreover, these two cases, which on top of that do not expressly ascribe the customary law status to sustainable development, cannot substitute the lacking state practice. The character of a principle of customary law thus cannot be ascribed to sustainable development.

Nonetheless, the ICJ Gabčikovo-Nagymaros Case and the Separate Opinion of Judge *Weeramantry* deserve a closer consideration, as they were the first general judicial statements concerning the concept of sustainable development. "This need to reconcile economic development with protection of the environment is aptly expressed in the concept of sustainable development."[121] In this statement of the ICJ, it expressly refers to sustainable development as a concept, leaving open the question about its normative quality.[122] The judgement itself thus does not provide any guidance of how to treat sustainable development in a legal assessment. Further details were, however, offered by Judge *Weeramantry*, who calls it the "principle of sustainable development" and considered it as a "principle with normative value which is crucial to the determination of this case"[123]. He

---

[117] Advisory Opinion on the Legality of the Threat or Use of Nuclear Weapons, ICJ Rep 1996 226 (International Court of Justice (ICJ) 1996).

[118] Advisory Opinion on the Legality of the Threat or Use of Nuclear Weapons, ICJ Rep 1996 para. 29.

[119] Brunnée (2003), 53.

[120] See 2.1.1.2.

[121] Gabčikovo-Nagymaros Project (Hungary v Slovakia), Judgement, Merits, ICJ Rep 7 at 75.

[122] Beyerlin (2013), para. 16.

[123] Gabčikovo-Nagymaros Project (Hungary v Slovakia), Judgement (Separate Opinion of Vice-President Weeramantry), ICJ Rep 7 at 85.

develops the statement of the Judgement of balancing environmental and developmental considerations that is enabled by sustainable development by setting out that beyond its importance for the actual case, sustainable development also will have to be considered in future environmental disputes and thus builds "an integral part of modern international law"[124].[125] He bases his argumentation on the agreement of both Hungary and Slovakia which accepted this principle as applicable to the dispute as well as the necessity for a principle that balances environmental and developmental concerns and ascribes to it general acceptance and sufficient establishment in international law.[126]

Criticism to this classification starts right there: While scholars like *Natarajan* state that sustainable development entails the criteria for bringing together environmental and developmental aspects, he criticizes that it "fell short of assigning a hierarchy of norms and actions for states to observe"[127] and thereby solving these conflicts. As a representative of the Third World Approaches to International Law (TWAIL) movement, *Chimni* refers to the scepticism especially of TWAIL about the practicability of sustainable development, attesting it lacking preciseness which allows manipulation by powerful states.[128] Besides the conceptual critique, *Natarajan* nonetheless calls it a "legal concept"[129]. However, these views challenge the alleged acceptance and establishment of the concept.

2.1.1.5.2 Or Just Another Political Objective?

Connected thereto is the label that implies the lowest level of normativity: sustainable development as a mere political value. This group of authors considers the concept to be an important political goal, which covers a broad field, but has no legal implications at all.[130] From this point of view, it does not trigger any legal consequences and gains meaning only in political discussions. The reason why they ascribe no normative quality to sustainable development goes back to the vagueness of this concept. *Beyerlin* explains its lacking certainty with the range of different interpretations and definitions of sustainable development that

---

[124] Gabčikovo-Nagymaros Project (Hungary v Slovakia), Judgement (Separate Opinion of Vice-President Weeramantry), ICJ Rep 7 at 86.

[125] Gabčikovo-Nagymaros Project (Hungary v Slovakia), Judgement (Separate Opinion of Vice-President Weeramantry), ICJ Rep 7 at 85.

[126] Gabčikovo-Nagymaros Project (Hungary v Slovakia), Judgement (Separate Opinion of Vice-President Weeramantry), ICJ Rep 7 at 87, 91.

[127] Natarajan (2012), 187.

[128] Chimni (2013), 265.

[129] Natarajan (2012), 187.

[130] Beyerlin (2013), para. 1; Lowe (1999), 30.

impede deducing clear behavioral rules for states regarding environmental protection.[131] *Birnie et al.* name the missing or unclear criteria for this concept as the main ground for its incapability to imply legal consequences.[132] In their opinion, these lacking standards hinder its development towards a normative concept.[133] Normative quality of a concept thus requires that its content is clear enough for states to know which behavior fulfills the prerequisites of the concept and which violates it. The question behind its legal character is thus also whether the content sustainable development is clear enough or still too vague.

Within these voices, several scholars go beyond a mere political value: *Ellis* speaks of a policy objective "that informs and influences the development and interpretation of international law"[134]. *Beyerlin* considers it to be a political idea which "although lacking normativity of their own, can be catalysts in the process of further developing international law"[135]. Statements like these describe the bridge between a political objective with no legal implications and an international law principle. Even authors that deny the classification of sustainable development as a principle of international law argue in favor of a strong influence of this concept on international law.[136] Especially in international environmental law also principles or concepts without formal legal bindingness have a notable impact on the law.[137] More important than the concrete label are thus the actual legal implications of sustainable development.[138]

2.1.1.5.3 Concrete Legal Implications of Sustainable Development

What do these legal implications of sustainable development consist in? Again, the ICJ Gabčikovo-Nagymaros Case provides helpful information on this question. The court speaks of taking into consideration "new norms and standards", referring in the same sentence to the effects for present and future generations and the environment.[139] By that it obliges the parties—not the court in its decision—to take norms like sustainable development into account when they decide

[131] Beyerlin (2010), 445.

[132] Birnie, Boyle, and Redgwell (2009), 125.

[133] Birnie, Boyle, and Redgwell (2009), 126.

[134] Ellis (2008), 1.

[135] Beyerlin (2013), para. 19.

[136] Beyerlin (2010), 443; Barral (2012), 379; Brunnée (2003), 43.

[137] Brunnée (2003), 58, 59.

[138] Viñuales (2021), 292.

[139] Gabčikovo-Nagymaros Project (Hungary v Slovakia), Judgement, Merits, ICJ Rep 7 at 75.

on their projects without prescribing a particular outcome.[140] *Sands* agrees that sustainable development is not able to determine the result, but has to be part of the negotiations.[141] *Ellis* also applies the concept to the decision-making of states: Rather than a specific outcome, she joins the opinion that a state has to take this concept into consideration.[142] She develops further that it "can provide guidance on the manner in which decisions are taken, in particular by pointing to a range of factors that must be taken into consideration"[143]. The key term these authors refer to is "take into consideration" The Commission on Sustainable Development expressly refers to this article and proposes to "take into consideration rules of environmental, social, human rights and other sustainable development law"[144] when deciding on conflicts of rules. Regarding this function, *Ellis* concludes that due to the lower attention decision-makers currently devote to the issue of balancing environmental and developmental concerns, the concept of sustainable development serves to adequately reflect these conflicts in legal decisions.[145] With due regard to its treatment in international judgements and documents an interpretive function can be ascribed to sustainable development.

2.1.1.5.4 Sustainable Development as a Normative Concept

This view leads over to a group of scholars that attribute to sustainable development an even stronger normativity. *Viñuales* considers it to be a normative concept, which is applied in legal practice like in treaties and judicial decisions.[146] In his opinion, sustainable development represents a "prescriptive or permissive preposition which entails legal effects"[147]. This point of view is partly shared by *Lowe* who holds it for an "aspirant to the status of a norm that purports to direct the conduct of states and other actors within the international legal system"[148]. He recognizes that legal norms do not have to be formed in a traditional

---

[140] Boyle (1997), 18.

[141] Sands et al. (2012), 318.

[142] Ellis (2008), 7.

[143] Ellis (2008), 14.

[144] Commission on Sustainable Development, "International Legal Instruments and Mechanisms (Chapter 39 of Agenda 21), Report of the Secretary-General Addendum," E/CN.17/1996/17/Add.1 § (1996), para. 18, available at https://www.un.org/esa/documents/ecosoc/cn17/1996/ecn171996-17a1.htm accessed 18 July 2022.

[145] Ellis (2008), 20.

[146] Viñuales (2021), 289.

[147] Viñuales (2021), 289.

[148] Lowe (1999), 31.

way, but its normative status can evolve through judicial reasoning.[149]With reservation he adds that these sort of norms do not directly lead to legal consequences, but "can be used by a tribunal to modify the application of other norms"[150] and therefore describes it as a "modifying norm".[151] *Barral* goes beyond that by claiming that sustainable development with its flexible but identifiable material content has direct legal implications and is therefore a primary norm of international law.[152] With respect to the further assessments, particularly the stated case law, this conclusion is not reflected by the current state practice.[153] The allocation as a modifying concept is in fact consistent with its treatment in the ICJ Gabčikovo-Nagymaros Case. Sustainable development has to be taken into consideration by decisionmakers to resolve conflicts between opposing norms and therefore is able to modify other rules.[154] In elaborating its argumentation, *Lowe* qualifies sustainable development as a concept that is of a different kind of normativity which unfolds its force in connection with other norms of international law.[155] In light of the aforementioned judgements and especially the explanations of *Weeramantry*, *Lowe's* classification as a modifying norm or concept circumscribes its legal implication adequately. *Birnie et al.* second this understanding by stating that it can influence the development of treaties as well as judicial reasonings and therefore impacts on the development of law.[156]

To sum up its normative content in general, sustainable development modifies existing law by serving as an interpretative rule for conflicting norms and balancing environmental and developmental concerns as well as it indirectly regulates a state's conduct by influencing treaty formation and judgements. What that means with due regard to circular economy, depends on the answer to the question whether its scope is still too broad to create a normative value and therefore on its implications on the issue of resource depletion.

---

149 Lowe (1999),31.
150 Lowe (1999), 34.
151 Lowe (1999), 33.
152 Barral (2012), 390.
153 Lowe (1999), 24.
154 Lowe (1999),33.
155 Lowe (1999), 21.
156 Birnie, Boyle, and Redgwell (2009), 127.

2.1.1.5.5 Legal implications of Sustainable Development on Circular Economy

Continuing with the concrete relevance for establishing a circular economy, its legal implications on the use of resources will be scrutinized. As sustainable development is described as a "process of change in which the exploitation of resources, the direction of investments [...] are all in harmony and enhance both current and future potential to meet human needs"[157], its capability to reconcile environmental, social and economic concerns regarding the use of resources becomes clear. Its normative value relates to bringing together conflicting rules and aim for their mutual support[158], but which norms and which concrete concerns can be solved by sustainable development has not yet been set out.

The message behind its role of interpreting conflicting norms, is that sustainable development so far depends on other rules and cannot decide a dispute on its own.[159] According to *Ellis* it has "normative, but no independent legal weight"[160]. The same applies to the establishment of treaties: Sustainable development is part of a range of international agreements such as the World Trade Organization (WTO) Agreement[161], the UN Framework Convention on Climate Change[162], or the Paris Agreement[163]. *Viñuales* argues that it is not the concept itself, but the relevant treaty norm which decides a case.[164] Furthermore, *Barstow Magraw and Hawke* consider that its legal implication is dependent from the concrete text of the treaty.[165] These conclusions are based on the judgement of the ICJ Pulp Mills Case which describes sustainable development as the measure to balance economic and environmental issues, but refers to the concrete Art. 27

[157] Ellis (2008), 4.

[158] Commission on Sustainable Development, International Legal Instruments and Mechanisms (Chapter 39 of Agenda 21), Report of the Secretary-General Addendum, para. 17.

[159] Viñuales (2021), 294.

[160] Ellis (2008), 13.

[161] Marrakesh Agreement Establishing the World Trade Organization (adopted on 15 April 1994, entered into force on 1 January 1996) UN Treaty Series vol. 154, 33, preamble.

[162] United Nations Framework Convention on Climate Change (adopted on 9 May 1992, entered into force on 21 March 1994) UN Treaty Series vol 1771, 107.

[163] Paris Agreement (adopted on 12 December 2015, entered into force on 4 November 2016) UN Treaty Series vol. 3156.

[164] Viñuales (2021), 294.

[165] Barstow Magraw and Hawke (2008), 622.

of the underlying treaty, which incorporates this concept.[166] How to precisely balance these concerns in the respective case must be determined by the concrete treaty norm.[167]

In order to get closer to the topic of resource exploitation, the legal implications of the sub-notion of sustainable use will be assessed in the following section. *Ellis* opines that identifying the elements of sustainable development serves as a basis for determining in how far sustainable development contributes to international law.[168] Sustainable development can be seen as an umbrella concept, involving different concepts like inter- and intragenerational equity or sub-notions like the aforementioned sustainable use.[169] It might therefore take the analysis one step further to the implication on circular economy by concentrating on the legal implications of this sub-notion of sustainable use. Here again, the ICJ Pulp Mills Case provides the first linkage to resources as it refers to the connection between the equitable use of a shared resource and the balancing of economic and environmental aspects, incorporated in sustainable development.[170] *Sands* derives from the various reflections in international agreements the responsibility of states to ensure the sustainable use of resources.[171] In contrast, *Lowe* disagrees about a general rule of sustainable use of natural resources and demands to take into account the respective situation.[172] As with the concept of sustainable development, the normative character of sustainable use must be determined related to a specific object or resource.[173] This sub-notion forms also part of international legal instruments such as the CBD.[174] In combination with this treaty, the object to which sustainable use refers is the flora and fauna that is necessary to safeguard biological diversity.[175] When it comes to specific obligations, the respective treaty norms play an important role in determining the normative content of this

166 Pulp Mills on the River Uruguay (Argentina v Uruguay), Judgement, ICJ Rep 113 (2006) para. 177 (International Court of Justice (ICJ) 2006).

167 Viñuales (2021), 291.

168 Ellis (2008), 16.

169 Sands (1995), 379; Lowe (1999), 26.

170 Pulp Mills on the River Uruguay (Argentina v Uruguay), Judgement, ICJ Rep 113 (2006) para. 177.

171 Sands et al. (2012), 206.

172 Lowe (1999), 29.

173 Beyerlin (2010), 445.

174 In various articles, including the preamble; Birnie, Boyle, and Redgwell (2009), 199.

175 Beyerlin (2013), para. 21.

sub-notion.[176] In the case of the CBD, the reference of sustainable use to the biological diversity is clear. But related to natural resources in general, *Birnie et al.* find it "difficult to treat these regimes, or the limited indications of customary rules derived from case law, as adding up to the systematic endorsement of an obligation of conservation and sustainable use of all natural resources in international law"[177]. They argue that different to common areas, where international cooperation has developed further, there does not exist sufficient state practice for similar obligations within a state's territory.[178] However, its ability to influence treaties and judgements shows that its impact does not only result from written treaty rules, but also from the concept itself. This is supported by the view of *Viñuales* who ascribes to it the ability to not only interpret, but also "to update a treaty that [...] given its date of conclusion, could not possibly imply any such consideration"[179]

That is the reason why sustainable use of natural resources is also considered as an "independent normative standard of international law"[180] but with the limitation that concrete action requires the agreement of states.[181] *Beyerlin* even alleges that due to its integration in various international law instruments it gained the status of customary law.[182] He develops further that the sustainable use of natural resources demands states to ensure a sustainable exploitation as well as an equal distribution between states.[183]Measured against the reference in treaties and case law that is restricted to a concrete application regarding a specific resource, it cannot be assumed that it has gained the status of customary law as an independent principle. To create a concrete obligation, sustainable use requires the connection to a specific rule. Transmitted to the concrete obligation to transform the economy into a circular one, sustainable use must be put in combination with a specific norm of international law in order to build a legal basis for this obligation. Since it is a general concept whose implications go beyond its written reflections in treaties, it can therefore be combined with other norms than those of the treaties which expressly incorporate sustainable use. Hence, its application to a concrete topic—here the use of resources—clarifies the content

176 Sands et al. (2012), 215.

177 Birnie, Boyle, and Redgwell (2009), 200.

178 Birnie, Boyle, and Redgwell (2009), 200.

179 Viñuales (2021), 297.

180 Birnie, Boyle, and Redgwell (2009), 200.

181 Birnie, Boyle, and Redgwell (2009), 200.

182 Beyerlin (2013), para. 21.

183 Beyerlin (2013), para. 20.

of sustainable development in a satisfactory manner. Consequently, safeguarding resources for future generations constitutes a clear behavior for states to orient themselves thereto and thereby frames the normative content of this concept.

With the special emanation of sustainable use, the concept of sustainable development thus offers legal implications related to the use of natural resources. Although a concrete obligation cannot be derived from this concept alone, its normative value goes beyond a mere political objective. As a modifying norm, it is capable to influence other rules and principles of international law, which entails the power to further develop legal provisions. It is therefore crucial for the further analysis as a combination with the following principles and concepts such as the precautionary principle or the common concern of humankind as well as with human rights provisions may build a pillar for an obligation to establish a circular economy.

2.1.2 Precautionary and Preventive Principle

Action in advance represents a necessary condition in order to encounter the issue of resource depletion. In international environmental law, there exist two principles which cover different fields of preemptive action: the precautionary principle and the preventive principle.[184] For the question if one or both of these principles can serve as a pillar for the obligation of a mandatory economic transformation, their content and application with regard to the issue of depleting resources need to be clarified. Therefore, their scope and character will be revealed in a first step. Secondly, their linkages to resource management will be set out to determine potential implications on circular economy. After analyzing them on their own, these principles will be examined in combination with the previous findings about sustainable development since this concept serves as a modifying norm.

In order to get a better impression of both principles, their general content will be set out briefly, before entering in the main analysis: Starting with the precautionary principle, Principle 15 of the Rio Declaration determines—according to the majority of scholars[185]—its content well in stating that a "lack of scientific certainty shall not be used as a reason for postponing cost-effective measures to prevent environmental degradation"[186]. It basically means that states

[184] Schröder (2014), para. 4.

[185] Brunnée (2003), 49; Sands et al. (2012), 218; Birnie, Boyle, and Redgwell (2009), 203.

[186] UN General Assembly, Report of the United Nations Conference on Environment and Development, Principle 15.

shall apply measures to avert potential damage to the environment and human health even when the consequences are not fully investigated. In other words, scientific uncertainty should not be used as a reason to continue with hazardous activities or refrain from protective measures.[187] Key component besides the serious and irreversible damage is the aspect of scientific uncertainty.[188] In contrast, the preventive principle is based on evidence of harm.[189] Similarly, it requires states to avoid activities that cause significant damage to the environment, but only applies when the creation of serious harm is evident.[190] Focusing on the exact prerequisites of both principles in the next sections, the main difference already became clear and lies in the likelihood of the damage.[191] The principle of prevention applies when the threatening harm is certain, e.g. when environmental damage has already occurred and so the risks of a hazardous activity are known.[192] On the contrary, the precautionary principle requires a lower level of certainty and does not necessitate scientific certainty.[193] *Cooney* describes the difference in a simplistic way by stating that: "Prevention [...] is about preventing known risks, precaution is about preventing unknown risks"[194]. Consequently, these principles also differ in terms of the sort of necessary action. Regarding the issue of depleting resources, their differences and especially the degree of certainty must be determined in order to specify the influence of these principles on a potential obligation to transform the economy. Therefore, the principles will be scrutinized separately in a first step to figure out possible interdependencies in a second step.

2.1.2.1 Precautionary Principle

For a detailed analysis, the origin as well as the exact scope of the precautionary principle will be determined, followed by its legal nature and consequences. Going back to national law concepts, especially the German "Vorsorgeprinzip", the precautionary principle evolved from the idea that environmental harm could be avoided by taking protective measures in advance.[195] At the international level,

[187] Schröder (2014), para. 2.
[188] Handl (2012), 5.
[189] Schröder (2014), para. 4.
[190] Schröder (2014), para. 4.
[191] De Sadeleer (2002), 74.
[192] De Sadeleer (2002), 75.
[193] Schröder (2014), para. 4.
[194] Cooney (2004), 8.
[195] Schröder (2014), para. 6.

it emerged in the 1970 s and builds now part of a variety of national, regional and international agreements and agendas.[196] Its main component of scientific uncertainty developed in the face of the complex cause-and-effect relationships of many activities, for which complete evidence could not be reached.[197] With regard to these uncertainties, "the principle provides guidance on the management of difficult environmental decisions [...] in the context of the impact of human civilization or new technology on the environment and human, animal and plant health"[198] according to *Schröder*.[199] As the consequences of activities on environmental and human health are directly associated with releasing toxins and the pollution by waste, the precautionary principle will play an important role in the following chapter about waste. However, *Sands* assumes that the precautionary principle has been applied to protect different areas of the environment.[200] *Schröder* even describes it as a "guiding principle of modern international law [...] relating to protection of the environment and conservation of natural resources"[201]. This direct application of the precautionary principle to conserving natural resources serves as a first hint that the principle does not only play a role with pollution. The principle's concrete field of application will therefore be determined.

2.1.2.1.1 Scope of the Precautionary Principle

Whether depleting resources undoubtedly are addressed by the precautionary principle must be figured out by determining its prerequisites and applying them to the issue of resource depletion. Since Principle 15 of the Rio Declaration forms the consensus of the understanding of this principle,[202] it will serve as the basis for the further analysis. Firstly, it requires "threats of serious or irreversible damage"[203]. According to this wording, not every kind of environmental harm suffices for the application of the precautionary principle.[204] Related to resources, it must be distinguished between non-renewable and renewable resources. Once,

---

[196] Cooney (2004), 11.

[197] Cooney (2004), 5.

[198] Schröder (2014), para. 8.

[199] See also Cooney (2004), 1.

[200] Sands et al. (2012), 219.

[201] Schröder (2014), para. 1.

[202] Brunnée (2003), 49; Sands et al. (2012), 218; Birnie, Boyle, and Redgwell (2009), 203.

[203] UN General Assembly, Report of the United Nations Conference on Environment and Development, Principle 15.

[204] Brunnée (2003), 49; Sands et al. (2012), 218; Birnie, Boyle, and Redgwell (2009), 203.

a non-renewable resource has been used up, it cannot be recovered, as its name suggests. The depletion of those resources is thus irreversible. Furthermore, the overexploitation of renewable resources—although not being irreversible—can have a serious impact as the following example will show:

The massive use of wood leading to deforestation affects the habitats of many species and whole ecosystems, letting alone consequences like desertification or erosion which in turn also impact on human settlements and their livelihoods.[205] The drastic consequences on global warming through the loss of forests describe the global nature of this example for the overexploitation of natural resources.

But is the depletion of resources considered as an environmental damage? This can be traced based on the current application of the precautionary principle in treaty law. A range of national, but also international environmental treaties include the precautionary principle implicitly or explicitly.[206] *Freestone* directly highlights its connection to natural resources by stating that the precautionary principle "infiltrated virtually every international environmental and natural resource treaty regime and is increasingly being adopted by national legal systems"[207]. He refers explicitly to the UN Agreement about the Conservation and Management of Straddling Fish Stocks and Highly Migratory Fish Stocks[208], which in Art. 6 connects the precautionary principle with the management and exploitation of fish stocks. This application of the precautionary principle shows that environmental damage can also be seen in mismanagement of natural resources. Although this agreement is only related to living resources, this marks the first evidence of a connection between this principle and the exploitation of natural resources. Due to the similar location of the issue of depleting resources, its transferability to this issue is not too far-fetched.

The next and most important aspect is the lack of full scientific uncertainty. There must be lacking certainty on whether the aforementioned irreversible or serious environmental damage actually will occur. This involves a lack of data which can be traced back to missing investigation or which lies in the nature

---

[205] See https://www.nationalgeographic.com/environment/article/deforestation accessed 25 March 2024.

[206] Sands et al. (2012), 220.

[207] Freestone (1999), 135.

[208] The UN Agreement for the Implementation of the Provisions of the UN Convention on the Law of the Sea of 10 December 1982 relating to the Conservation and Management of Straddling Fish Stocks and Highly Migratory Fish Stocks (adopted on 4 August 1995, entered into force on 11 December 2001) UN Treaty Series vol. 2167, 3.

or complexity of the issue itself.[209] In terms of the irreversibility of the possible damage, it cannot be waited for scientific evidence.[210] Applied to depleting resources, data is often missing while predictions about the actual date when a resource is used up or about the concrete consequences remain vague or unreliable.[211] Resource management thus entails a range of uncertain factors. Nonetheless, a differentiation between these factors must be undertaken. Not every aspect of depleting resources is uncertain: Concerning the consequences on ecosystems, the exact rate of depletion, and especially related to living resources, there are more factors of uncertainty like the interdependence between human actions and the environment. What is certain, in turn, is that a huge range of natural resources will be used up in time. For example, copper and zinc are estimated to be declined soon.[212] The boundary, however, cannot be drawn between living and non-living resources, as to both factors of uncertainty apply. Also, renewable and non-renewable resources encompass certain as well as uncertain aspects. Since the main difference between the precautionary and the preventive principle lies in the degree of certainty of a potential outcome, their "boundary […] in conservation/NRM [= natural resource management] is a blurred one"[213]. Therefore, it can be noted that although a clear distinction cannot be made, the precautionary principle is at least applicable to the uncertain factors of depleting resources.

Principle 15 limits the required action of states to their capabilities and thus makes concrete measures dependent from the states' financial and organizational possibilities.[214] This limitation to the states' capabilities is assumed to weaken the principle.[215] However, before evaluating different approaches to the precautionary principle, its consequences need to be set out. In other words: What are the states required to do according to this principle? *Sands* provides a general approach that requires states to "act carefully and with foresight when taking decisions that concern activities that may have an adverse impact on the environment"[216]. Searching for more specific measures, the interpretations quickly get

---

[209] Cooney (2004), 26.

[210] Sands et al. (2012), 220.

[211] Cooney (2004), 26.

[212] See https://www.conserve-energy-future.com/causes-effects-solutions-depletion-natural-resources.php accessed 25 March 2024.

[213] Cooney (2004), 27.

[214] Handl (2012), 5.

[215] Schröder (2014), para. 9; Cooney (2004), 7.

[216] Sands et al. (2012), 222.

blurred. Scholars agree that there is a wide range of possible actions and measures states are required to take.[217] Similar to the discussion about sustainable development, *Schröder* states that a specific measure is dependent from a concrete formulation in treaty law.[218] *Cooney* seconds this by remarking that without such a specific formulation, the principle does not lead to a concrete decision.[219] Dependence on concrete formulations and the respective context seem to hinder a self-sustaining meaning of the precautionary principle. In order to determine its more or less concrete legal implications, the question about its legal character must be answered.

2.1.2.1.2 Legal Character

Different to the discussion surrounding the legal nature of sustainable development, the sources and opinions tend more to a recognition of the precautionary principle as a principle of customary law. *Brunnée* describes it as the "most likely candidate for customary law status", not concealing current doubts.[220] This is—according to some authors—justified by its incorporation in several international environmental agreements, judicial decisions and national legislation which reflect a broad state practice.[221] One example is the Advisory Opinion by the Seabed Chamber of the International Tribunal of the Law of the Sea (ITLOS) from 2011, stating that there is a "trend towards making this approach part of customary international law"[222].[223] Critical voices, however, refer to its still vague content and hesitance of international courts to accept it as customary law.[224] Some scholars thus consider that there is only sufficient evidence for state practice

[217] Birnie, Boyle, and Redgwell (2009), 203; Freestone (1999), 136; Schröder (2014), para. 9.

[218] Schröder (2014), para. 11.

[219] Cooney (2004), 5.

[220] Brunnée (2003), 57.

[221] Freestone (1999), 137; Brunnée (2003), 50.

[222] Advisory Opinion on the Responsibilities and Obligations of States Sponsoring Persons and Entities with Respect to Activities in the Area, ITLOS Reports 2011, 10 para. 135 (International Tribunal of the Law of the Sea (ITLOS) 2011).

[223] Handl (2012), 5.

[224] Schröder (2014), para. 20; Sands et al. (2012), 223, 228; cf. Gabčikovo-Nagymaros Project (Hungary v Slovakia), Judgement, Merits, ICJ Rep 7 para. 113.

in the EU, so that the precautionary principle has gained merely regional customary law status.[225] Although a regional recognition of the precautionary principle as customary law supports the trend of a wider acceptance of this principle, a universal recognition as customary law cannot be derived therefrom.

Further insights on the principle's acceptance are, however, possible through the lenses of a sectoral approach. When looking at its influence on a specific field of law such as biodiversity, evidence for a global application can be found.[226] *Cooney* hence assumes that it gained a status of customary international law in some sectors.[227] Evidence for such recognition related to resources can be found in its incorporation in treaty law concerning biodiversity and species conservation.[228] I.a. in the preamble of the CBD, the precautionary principle is applied to loss of biodiversity.[229] In addition, in the ICJ Pulp Mills case, this principle is "relevant in the interpretation and application of the provisions"[230] concerning the shared resource of a river. Although this recognition in agreements and judicial reasonings is considered as a strong argument for its acceptance, *Schröder* rightly points to the fact that the jurisprudence as well as the legislation concerning the precautionary principle is still inconsistent.[231] Furthermore, the relevance in the interpretation and an incorporation merely in the preamble instead of concrete rules do not argue for a status as a binding rule of (sectoral) customary law. Parallels can be drawn with the application of sustainable development again. The precautionary principle seems to play a role regarding the interpretation of other provisions. This is supported by *Cooney*, ascribing the strong promotion of environmental protection and even human rights to this principle.[232] Rather than a customary law principle, it is used for interpreting rules and providing guidance in environmental decisions. Judge *Weeramantry* attests that the precautionary principle "is gaining increasing support as part of the international law

[225] Schröder (2014), 17; cf. United Kingdom of Great Britain and Northern Ireland v. Commission of the European Communities, Judgment, 1998/-02265 European Court Reports (European Court of Justice 1998).

[226] Sands et al. (2012), 228.

[227] Cooney (2004), 12.

[228] Cooney (2004), 12.

[229] "where there is a threat of significant reduction or loss of biological diversity, lack of full scientific certainty should not be used as a reason for postponing measures to avoid or minimize such a threat" Preamble CBD.

[230] Pulp Mills on the River Uruguay (Argentina v Uruguay), Judgement, ICJ Rep 113 (2006) para. 164.

[231] Schröder (2014), para. 18.

[232] Cooney (2004), 12.

of the environment"[233]. With its incorporation in treaty law and growing acceptance in judgements, its recognition is more pronounced than this of sustainable development. Regarding the increasing voices that hold it for customary law, the development to a binding principle is visible.

2.1.2.1.3 Concrete Implications of the Precautionary Principle

Like every general principle under environmental law, figuring out concrete measures remains difficult. *Cooney* and *Brunnée* argue that the precautionary principle restricts human actions and thus has impacts on the rights and obligations of states.[234] As introduced above, the formulation and context as well as its position in an agreement—may it be part of the preamble or the operative text—play a major role in determining concrete obligations.[235] Therefore, it is deemed as being merely relevant in the decision-making process rather than determining the outcome of a decision.[236] At the same time, it does have an influence when using it for balancing different measures or aspects.[237] Its flexible approach does not only allow several measures to implement it but, furthermore, "provides a new lens with which to view existing obligations"[238]. This offers the possibility to take a diverse look at current obligation like human rights and will also play a role in the chapter about waste when analyzing current treaty law. Its actual influence, however, lies in guiding decisions and enabling precautionary action despite a lack of scientific evidence.

To improve the effectiveness of that principle, scholars developed a further approach that addresses a weak point of the precautionary principle. *Cooney* summarizes the need to improve this principle by the following statement: "Where the principle is given its fullest effect, however, it may lead to prohibition of activities which pose any environmental threat, and require proponents of any proposed activity to demonstrate that it is safe."[239] As suggested in the last part of this statement, it is discussed whether the burden of proof should lie with the person opposing the activity, as it is established with traditional views, or if a

[233] Nuclear Tests (New Zealand v France), Request for an Examination of the Situation in Accordance with Paragraph 63 of the Court's Judgment of 20 December 1974, Dissenting Opinion of Judge Weeramantry, ICJ Reports 1995, 288 342 (International Court of Justice (ICJ) 1995).

[234] Cooney (2004), 1; Brunnée (2003), 50.

[235] Birnie, Boyle, and Redgwell (2009), 203.

[236] Cooney (2004), 25.

[237] Cooney (2004), 6.

[238] Freestone (1999), 141.

[239] Cooney (2004), 6.

shift of the burden to the actual polluter would be a better alternative.[240] Applied to the issue of resource depletion, this would require the companies to prove that the exploitation will not lead to environmental harm, or rather the states to legislate respective rules. This approach goes back to the Wingspread Statement, demanding that "the proponent of an activity, rather than the public, should bear the burden of proof"[241]. Such a shift of the burden of proof would allow to hold the relevant stakeholders liable and enable a better assessment of risks but also of alternatives.[242] Although this approach has not gained uniform acceptance yet, it shows the development and potential of the precautionary principle regarding alternative measures to protect the environment such as the concept of circular economy in resource management.

Regarding its unspecific consequences, its possible interrelation with other principles and provisions will be illuminated later. Before analyzing these connections of the precautionary principle, the other principle concerning action in advance must be scrutinized to figure out if that principle connected to the certain aspects of resource depletion leads to more specific measures.

2.1.2.2 Preventive Principle

A holistic picture of the principles that require action in advance demands the analysis of the preventive principle. Since the development of the precautionary principle is connected to the principle of preventive action,[243] its capability to generate specific obligations needs to be set out. The main difference to the precautionary principle lies, as already stated above, in the certainty of environmental damage. For a better understanding, its exact scope and its legal consequences will be examined.

2.1.2.2.1 Scope of the Preventive Principle

The preventive principle aims for the minimization of foreseeable harm and demands for action in advance.[244] Although there is no consensus about its exact wording, the Draft Articles on Prevention of Transboundary Harm from Hazardous Activities by the International Law Commission (ILC) serve as basis

---

[240] Sands et al. (2012), 222.

[241] Raffensperger and Tickner (1999).

[242] Cooney (2004), 8.

[243] Proelß (2022), 104.

[244] Rayfuse (2016), 22; Duvic-Paoli (2018), 8.

for further insights on this principle.[245] The preventive principle can be seen as the counterpart to the curative approach which entails reparation and compensation.[246]In contrast to the law of state responsibility, which applies retrospectively, preventive action rather requires to avoid environmental harm in advance.[247] In order to complete the categorization of the preventive principle, the difference to the likewise important polluter pays principle is to be set out briefly: Again, the distinction lies in the time of application. The polluter pays principle establishes a liability mechanism, whereas the preventive principle can be applied before damage has actually occurred.[248] Since the objective of a circular economy consists in averting the threatening depletion of resources instead of managing its consequences, both the analysis of state responsibility and the polluter pays principle will not lead to fruitful findings on an obligation concerning the establishment of a circular economy. Therefore, scrutinizing the preventive principle is considered to be more promising in building a pillar for such an obligation.

What are then the prerequisites of the preventive principle? First of all, it is applicable to certain risks, which means that there is scientific evidence for threatening environmental harm.[249] As discussed within the precautionary approach, it therefore applies to the certain aspects of depleting resources. Generally, a certain fact is that resources *are* depleting. For many resources even a clear time frame of their overexploitation exists.[250] In terms of its complex consequences on the ecosystems and the interrelation between these and human activity, there remain uncertainties, which are covered by the precautionary principle. The proven fact of overexploitation thus can be subsumed under the preventive principle. Controversy, however, arises regarding its spatial application. Preventive action is required by a state concerning environmental harm that is rooted in its territory or under its jurisdiction or control.[251] With due regard to the location where

---

[245] International Law Commission, "Draft Articles on Prevention of Transboundary Harm from Hazardous Activities, with Commentaries," *Yearbook of the International Law Commission*, no. vol. II, Part Two (2001): 148.

[246] International Law Commission, "Draft Articles on Prevention of Transboundary Harm from Hazardous Activities, with Commentaries," 148.

[247] Duvic-Paoli (2018), 6.

[248] Muigua (2022), 8.

[249] See 2.1.2.

[250] See https://www.conserve-energy-future.com/causes-effects-solutions-depletion-natural-resources.php accessed 25 March 2024.

[251] International Law Commission, "Draft Articles on Prevention of Transboundary Harm from Hazardous Activities, with Commentaries," 150.

environmental damage occurs, the traditional approach restricts its scope to transboundary harm.[252] The ILC Draft Principles pick up on this view and limit its spatial scope by excluding "activities which cause harm only in the territory of the State within which the activity is undertaken"[253]. This restriction would drastically limit the principle's extent to activities of states which happen within their own territory and affect different states. Applied to the issue of resource depletion, scenarios which would be covered by this principle are hardly imaginable. The overexploitation within a state's territory would need to cause direct environmental consequences to another state. This again would have to be underscored by scientific evidence. To conclude that: The preventive principle could not be applied to resource depletion in the most cases. Detached from the application to resource management, more and more scholars argue for turning away from the restriction to transboundary harm.[254]They refer to the development of this principle towards territorial unlimitedness which explicitly involves preventing environmental harm within a state's own territory.[255] The scholars' main argument relates to "putting the emphasis on the objective of environmental protection for its own sake (outside sovereignty considerations)"[256] that allows a duty of prevention "irrespective of the location of harm"[257]. In favor of this argument, it cannot only be referred to the development of the preventive principle itself—since the adoption of the ILC Draft Principles of 2001 several years have passed in which the principle evolved—but also to the development of international environmental law and particularly its principles in general. As stated above, this field of law made a progress from rules and principles only thematizing the issues between neighboring states and transboundary effects towards a general protection of the environment, irrespective of national boundaries. This overall development supports the scholars' view that the transboundary criterion has become outdated. Hence, the preventive principle is also applicable to issues like depleting resources within areas under national jurisdiction as well as to the global nature of this issue.

---

[252] Duvic-Paoli (2018), 111.

[253] International Law Commission, "Draft Articles on Prevention of Transboundary Harm from Hazardous Activities, with Commentaries," 151.

[254] Rayfuse (2016), 22; Muigua (2022), 28; Proelß (2022), 112; Duvic-Paoli (2018), 8; Sands et al. (2012), 201.

[255] Muigua (2022), 28.

[256] Duvic-Paoli (2018), 113.

[257] Duvic-Paoli (2018), 113.

2.1.2.2.2 Legal Consequences

After clarifying its scope, it is to be scrutinized whether the preventive principle leads to concrete measures, paving the way for a mandatory economic transformation. Similar to the precautionary principle, it relies upon the anticipation of damage.[258] What that anticipation exactly consists of will be examined by looking at the legal consequences and implications. In order to control or limit activities causing environmental harm, it is necessary to investigate potential risks and plan these activities in advance.[259] Again, the ILC Draft Principles represent a starting point for determining the required measures. Regarding precise measures, it needs to be highlighted, that the ILC Draft Principles were drafted in the context of hazardous activities and are focused on transboundary harm rather than on a generally non-hazardous action as exploitation which will result in environmental damage only by overusing resources. Thus, they merely provide an interpretive aid and are not of a binding character. In Art. 3 it demands from states to "take all appropriate measures to prevent significant transboundary harm or at any event to minimize the risk thereof"[260] which prioritizes the prevention before the minimization. The commentary concretizes this as an obligation for states to legislate rules incorporating international standards.[261] Both prevention and minimization are obligations of due diligence according to the commentary.[262] Such an obligation of due diligence does not include a guarantee that environmental harm is totally prevented, but rather requires the states to use its best efforts to prevent or minimize the risk.[263] The character of a due diligence obligation consists in demanding proactive action,[264] including "effective national legislation and administrative controls"[265]. This standard of due diligence is applied in the ICJ Pulp Mills Case to a similar obligation of preservation and prevention of the

---

[258] De Sadeleer (2002), 61.

[259] Muigua (2022), 28.

[260] International Law Commission, "Draft Articles on Prevention of Transboundary Harm from Hazardous Activities, with Commentaries," 153.

[261] International Law Commission, "Draft Articles on Prevention of Transboundary Harm from Hazardous Activities, with Commentaries," 153.

[262] International Law Commission, "Draft Articles on Prevention of Transboundary Harm from Hazardous Activities, with Commentaries," 154.

[263] International Law Commission, "Draft Articles on Prevention of Transboundary Harm from Hazardous Activities, with Commentaries," 154.

[264] Duvic-Paoli (2018), 12.

[265] Muigua (2022), 28.

aquatic environment and encompasses besides the adoption of rules, their vigilance and enforcement.[266] Hence, it can be noted that the preventive principle entails a duty to ensure, in other words an obligation of conduct, rather than a result-based prohibition like the standard in state responsibility.[267] In contrast to a prohibition, the preventive principle relies on positive measures to anticipate risks and protect the environment.[268] This approach builds a promising pillar by enabling to derive a positive obligation of conduct from this principle. As stated earlier, the application of the preventive principle to the issue of resource depletion is not uncontested and relates only to the certain aspects of depleting resources. Nonetheless, its capability to demand positive anticipatory action makes it become a good candidate for a pillar for a mandatory economic shift. Its implications on such an obligation though depend on its legal bindingness and its preciseness, which will be scrutinized hereafter.

The duty to prevent harm was considered to having become a general principle of international law by the Iron Rhine Case.[269] The ICJ Pulp Mills Case even referred to it as a customary law rule.[270] Scholars like *De Sadeleer* agree with the application of the preventive principle as a customary law principle and justify this with its implementation in many international agreements.[271] It influences on treaty law by placing the focus on the preventive effect of these provisions.[272] Its character as customary law seems to be less contested than that of the previous principles and concepts. Nonetheless, it is not clear which formulation of the preventive principle is considered as customary law. In other words, it is not specified which measures are required under the preventive principle to fulfil a state's due diligence obligation.[273] Therefore, further concretizations of this principle are to be scrutinized.

[266] Pulp Mills on the River Uruguay (Argentina v Uruguay), Judgement, ICJ Rep 113 (2006) at 197.

[267] Proelß (2022), 106.

[268] Duvic-Paoli (2018), 9.

[269] Arbitration regarding the Iron Rhine Railway (Belgium v Netherlands), Award, ICGJ 373 paras. 59, 222 (Permanent Court of Arbitration (PCA) 2005).

[270] Pulp Mills on the River Uruguay (Argentina v Uruguay), Judgement, ICJ Rep 113 (2006) para.s 101, 197.

[271] De Sadeleer (2002), 66.

[272] De Sadeleer (2002), 73.

[273] De Sadeleer (2002), 63.

In general, the preventive principle entails the formulation and implementation of rules that prevent environmental harm including enforcement mechanisms.[274] In how far these obligations are concretized will be figured out by first setting out its implementation in treaty law and declarations. Since due diligence does not constitute a certain action itself but rather a standard of conduct, it is to be integrated in the assessment whether this obligation of conduct is violated.[275] This standard is dependent from the circumstances of the individual case and the character of the activity.[276] The preventive principle is part of a range of environmental treaties concerning i.a. the conservation of species, the pollution of the sea, and hazardous waste and substances.[277] As the latter vote for a closer look at this principle in the chapter about waste, the incorporation in the CBD[278] shows its connections to resource conservation. Even more related to the conservation of natural resources, it is part of the Guidelines and Principles on Shared Natural Resources by the UN Environment Programme (UNEP)[279]. Bearing in mind its application to *shared* natural resources and potential harm *on* the resources as well as its merely interpretive function, the guidelines can help to determine more specific measures of the preventive principle concerning resource management. These guidelines aim for balancing the sovereign right of exploitation with the protection of the other state's rights regarding the resources.[280] This is enshrined in Principle 3, particularly in the duty of avoiding adverse environmental effects through the utilization of the resource under No. 3. Principle 1 explicitly requires the prevention of "adverse environmental effects which may result from the utilization of such resources"[281] and thereby forms a direct link between prevention and the use of resources.

---

[274] International Law Commission, "Draft Articles on Prevention of Transboundary Harm from Hazardous Activities, with Commentaries," 154.

[275] Proelß (2022), 113.

[276] Rayfuse (2016), 22.

[277] Sands et al. (2012), 202.

[278] See Art. 14 CBD.

[279] UN Environment Programme, "Governing Council Approval of the Report of the Intergovernmental Working Group of Experts on Natural Resources Shared by Two or More States," *International Legal Materials*, no. vol. 17 No. 5 (September 1978): 1091–99.

[280] Duvic-Paoli (2018), 112.

[281] UN Environment Programme, "Governing Council Approval of the Report of the Intergovernmental Working Group of Experts on Natural Resources Shared by Two or More States," 1098.

Since the character of duties is often determined by formulations in treaties, they can also illuminate what is required under due diligence.[282] Examples from international instruments are the monitoring of environmental damage, administrative controls, the implementation of clean production methods and environmental impact assessments.[283] Especially concerning new production methods and the latter assessments, the duty to use the best available technology has evolved.[284] The best available technology is defined by the Integrated Pollution Prevention and Control (IPPC) Directive in its Art. 2 (11) as "the most effective and advanced stage in the development of activities and their methods of operation which indicate the practical suitability of particular techniques for providing in principle the basis for emission limit values designed to prevent and, where that is not practicable, generally to reduce emissions and the impact on the environment as a whole"[285]. Even though this definition is originated in the EU context, it provides the basis for how to understand the term 'best available technology'. Therefore, it represents an accepted concretization of the due diligence standard. The requirement to adapt production patterns by using the best available technology marks a shift from acting retrospectively to directly tackle the source of potential pollution or damage.[286] Making use of the best available technology and addressing the roots of issues also forms the core of the principle of rectification at source, which can be treated as a sub-notion of the preventive principle.[287] This principle specifies the need to "tackle the source of pollution by requiring the polluters to make use of best available technologies"[288] and is recognized e.g. in the Helsinki Convention on the Protection of Transboundary Watercourses[289]. This specification of the preventive principle thus paves the way for establishing new production processes which are considered to be the best available technology. In terms of resource management and product design, circular economy—as set out extensively in Chap. 1—can be considered as a holistic and promising alternative concept. Though still including limitations and

---

[282] De Sadeleer (2002), 66.

[283] De Sadeleer (2002), 63.

[284] De Sadeleer (2002), 72.

[285] European Council, "Integrated Pollution Prevention and Control (IPPC) Directive," 96/61/EC § (1996).

[286] De Sadeleer (2002), 77.

[287] De Sadeleer (2002), 75.

[288] De Sadeleer (2002), 75.

[289] Convention on the Protection and Use of Transboundary Watercourses and International Lakes (adopted on 17 March 1992, entered into force on 6 October 1996), UN Treaty Series vol. 1936, 269.

difficulties, it is argued that this concept represents the most future-orientated and pragmatic approach to improve resource management and production processes. Hence, the duty to use the best available technology is strongly related with implementing a circular economy.

The wider preventive principle can thus lead to more specific consequences than the precautionary principle with the limit that there needs to be a scientific certainty of consequences of resource depletion. Although it must be noted that there is no explicit customary law which requires states to use the best available technology in resource management and therefore directly demanding for the establishment of a circular economy, there can be derived such a consequence by interpreting this principle. Considering its character as a principle, these linkages cannot lead to a binding rule of economic transformation alone. With its specifications and its consolidated acceptance, however, the preventive principle serves as a promising pillar for deriving such an obligation under international law. Combining it with the previous principles and concepts in the following and with human rights later, thus, will reveal whether further implications on a mandatory economic transformation are possible.

2.1.2.3 Combination of Principles and Sustainable Development

Since especially in the context of depleting resources, the preventive and the precautionary principle both apply to different aspects, an integrated consideration of those including the modifying concept of sustainable development can lead to further insights. A clear distinction between these principles is, due to their gradual transition, not entirely possible.[290] Additionally, they are said to influence on other norms and provisions and their exact scope can only be determined through their formulations in treaties. More than the preventive principle, the precautionary principle is dependent on additional parameters, defining its consequences.[291] Particularly, in the context of natural resource management, they often overlap with sustainable development and its sub-notion of sustainable use.

Birnie et al. explicitly ascribe to the precautionary principle the intention to regulate the uncertain aspects of a sustainable use of resources.[292] *Duvic-Paoli* highlights the parallels between the prevention and precautionary principle and their incorporation in the concept of sustainable development.[293] She even argues

---

[290] Proelß (2022), 111.

[291] Freestone (1999), 155, 156.

[292] Birnie, Boyle, and Redgwell (2009), 136.

[293] Duvic-Paoli (2018), 3.

that sustainable development can be implemented through the procedural and substantive measures under the preventive principle.[294] Sometimes scholars speak of mixed terms like "concept of precautionary resource utilization and management"[295], underscoring their connectedness. But where does their relation lie more in detail?

Between the precautionary principle and the concept of sustainable development, there exist several connections: *Cooney* describes the precautionary principle as a "fundamental tool for sustainable development"[296]. *Brunnée* develops this by stating that it "complements the intertemporal concepts of sustainable development"[297]. Since sustainable development and especially the sustainable use of resources aim for safeguarding the supply of resources for future generations, the precautionary principle ensures this by applying anticipatory measures to avoid such harm. Precautionary action is, therefore, a necessary measure to encounter the uncertain aspects of resource depletion which are addressed by the sustainable use of resources at the same time.[298] Both objectives are thus interrelated.[299] The precautionary principle and the concept of sustainable development are both based on the presumption that safeguarding natural resources prevails over the freedom of exploitation.[300] *Freestone* even conceives the precautionary principle as a key component to achieve sustainable development.[301] This is supported by the Bergen Ministerial Declaration, which states that for achieving sustainable development, "policies must be based on the precautionary principle"[302]. Hence, it is uncontested that the precautionary principle forms an integral component of sustainable development by providing anticipatory measures in order to protect the supply of resources for future generations.[303] As revealed above, sustainable development is a modifying norm and can thus help to derive more concrete measures from the wide precautionary principle. This can be already found in the New Delhi of Principles of International Law Relating

294 Duvic-Paoli (2018), 4.

295 Cooney (2004), 19.

296 Cooney (2004), 1.

297 Brunnée (2003), 49.

298 Voigt (2009), 48.

299 Sands et al. (2012), 219.

300 Freestone (1999), 162.

301 Freestone (1999), 135.

302 UN General Assembly, "Report of the Economic Commission for Europe on the Bergen Conference," A/CONF.151/PC/10 § (1990), 19 para. 7.

303 Brunnée (2010), 626; Cooney (2004), 2.

to Sustainable Development by the International Law Association (ILA): They encompass in Principle 1.2 the management of natural resources according to a sustainable use of them and waste minimization.[304] Principle 4.1 summarizes the connection between the precautionary principle and sustainable development by stating that it is "central to sustainable development in that it commits States [...] to avoid human activity which may cause significant harm to human health, natural resources or ecosystems, including in the light of scientific uncertainty"[305]. In Principle 4.2 more concrete measures under the precautionary principle in connection with sustainable development are set out including "planning based on clear criteria and well-defined goals; consideration in an environmental impact assessment"[306]. Together with sustainable development, the precautionary principle can lead to comparable measures as the preventive principle. These principles can be seen as first evidence of this reinforcing power of sustainable development in the context of resource management. The Sofia Guiding Statement 2, having interpretive function to the New Delhi Declaration, even votes in favor of interpreting rules and principles of international law generally in light of sustainable development.[307]

Moreover, the concept of sustainable development demonstrates a close relationship with the preventive principle.[308] Regarding its roots of preventing transboundary harm, the preventive principle is often equated with Principle 21 Stockholm Declaration,[309] which in turn illuminates its connection with sustainable development.Principle 21 thus represents the interface between exploiting resources in a sustainable manner and averting environmental damage. The prevention of environmental harm and the sustainable use of a state's natural resources appear to be two sides of the same coin. Eventually, both the preventive principle and the concept of sustainable development share the same objective and are associated with the same formulation of a customary law principle. Nonetheless, the preventive principle has evolved to a principle with a wider scope,

---

304 Schrijver (2002), 302.

305 Schrijver (2002), 303, 304.

306 Schrijver (2002), 303, 304.

307 International Law Association, "Sofia Guiding Statements on the Judicial Elaboration of the 2002 New Delhi Declaration of Principles of International Law Relating to Sustainable Development," Resolution No. 7/2012 § (2012).

308 De Sadeleer (2002), 66.

309 Duvic-Paoli (2018), 1.

including its detachment from the requirement of transboundary harm.[310] Furthermore, Principle 21 concentrates on natural resource management, whereas the preventive principle can be applied to different sources of environmental harm.[311] While Principle 21 is clearly rooted in balancing sovereign rights with environmental damage, the prevention of such damage itself forms the objective of the principle of prevention.[312] Hence, these two principles are to be distinguished with respect to their scope and objective. Their close connection, however, leads to the conclusion that the preventive principle and the concept of sustainable development in general serve the same purpose of safeguarding natural resources. Despite their remaining vagueness and current limitations, they reinforce each other and through their mutual support, they gain increasing importance.

In conclusion, the Guidelines for Applying the Precautionary Principle to Biodiversity Conservation and Natural Resource Management, which serve as an inspirational source rather than as a legal argument, describe the relationship between these principles and concepts well: In Guideline 2 they vote for an integration of the precautionary principle with other principles and rights that are "relevant to conservation and NRM, including prevention, […] inter-generational and intra-generational equity, the right to development, the right to a healthy environment and human rights to food, water, health and shelter."[313] Therefore, they highlight the mutual reinforcement of both the preventive and precautionary principle together with the concept of sustainable development. These principles and the sustainable development are not only applicable to the issue of resource depletion but are—in combination—capable to lead to concrete measures regarding the conservation of resources which have particular legal effect. Although their separate treatment does not suffice for deriving an obligation for an economic transformation, together they form a strong argument for an alternative resource management. As mentioned in the guidelines, these principles are not only relevant to each other, but also to other principles and human rights. Before leading over to their connection with human rights, the last concept under international environmental law will be analyzed regarding implications on resource management and potentially on an obligation to establish a circular economy.

---

[310] See 2.1.2.2.

[311] De Sadeleer (2002), 64.

[312] Sands et al. (2012), 201.

[313] Precautionary Principle Project, "Guidelines for Applying the Precautionary Principle to Biodiversity Conservation and Natural Resource Management,", 4, available on http://www.onlyoneplanet.com/marinePPguidelines2005.pdf accessed on 16 August 2022.

2.1.3 Common Concern of Humankind

A fairly new perspective to classify environmental protection and thus the conservation of natural resources on which life depends is to consider it for its own sake. From an ethical point of view, the idea of protecting the environment detached from human benefit signifies a shift away from an anthropocentric approach towards an ecocentric thinking.[314] This global human responsibility for the environment is reflected in the concept of common concern of humankind. As a concept providing a comprehensive approach for global environmental concerns, it is considered necessary to include it into the analysis as well. First, its scope and content will be determined in light of the question whether resource depletion constitutes a common concern of humankind. Second, its legal implications will be analyzed in order to reveal its potential for establishing a circular economy. In a last step, this concept will be interpreted together with the aforementioned principles and the concept of sustainable development to detect if further findings follow from their combination.

2.1.3.1 Scope and Content of the Common Concern of Humankind

What exactly is the concept of common concern of humankind and does the depletion of natural resources—which on top of that takes place within a state's jurisdiction—fall under the scope of this concept? In order to answer these questions, primarily, the general content of this concept will be determined, followed by subsuming resource depletion thereunder. Connected thereto, the question of national jurisdiction will be illuminated by comparing this concept to a similar principle, namely the common heritage of mankind. Using the words of *Brunnée*, the common concern of humankind "identifies certain issues as of concern to all members of the international community"[315] and especially relates to shared environmental issues of all states with their transboundary nature.[316] The concept, therefore, builds a framework for international cooperation in the field of cross-border problems.[317] It applies to global environmental issues which require action of the international community as a whole[318] and thereby extends the scope of environmental law from balancing sovereign rights towards a global

[314] Jonas (2017), 27, 29.

[315] Brunnée (2003), 45.

[316] Brunnée and Nollkaemper (1996), 309; Bowling, Pierson and Ratté (2021), 2.

[317] Bowling, Pierson and Ratté (2021), 2.

[318] Bartenstein, Durner, and Epiney (2022), 71.

approach of solving these issues.[319] For a better understanding of this concept's current application, its development will be outlined briefly: The term 'common concern of humankind' is reflected in international treaty and case law since the 1990's, but similar formulations relating to global issues were used all over the 20th century, i.a. in the Brundtland Report.[320] Today, a range of international law agreements incorporated the term 'common concern of humankind' or variations thereof, e.g. the CBD or the Paris Agreement in their preambular texts. These reflections have in common that they demand for international action to address common issues and thereby overcome national boundaries.[321]

In order to get a closer and more detailed look at this term, the following part will focus on the wording: The component "humankind", which can be considered as the most recent terminology,[322] refers to a large group of individuals who are confronted with a shared problem.[323] "Concern" is considered as an issue or negative consequences that—according to *Zaker*—involves a normative demand for addressing this problem.[324] The term "common" leads to the global and transboundary nature of this issue and clarifies that the threatening problem cannot be encountered except through global action.[325] Coming back to the examples from the CBD and Paris Agreement, not the climate or biological diversity themselves are common concerns, but rather the negative consequences like the loss of biodiversity and global warming with its adverse effects.[326]Therefore, not an area or its resources per se represent the common concern, but potential risks and their threat are subject of this concept.[327]

Is the depletion of natural resources then a common concern? For answering this question, its current application in international environmental law is to be scrutinized. As already stated above, climate change and the loss of biological diversity are considered as common concerns in the respective treaties. What they have in common is their global character and the requirement for global action to

319 Brunnée and Nollkaemper (1996), 309.

320 Bowling, Pierson and Ratté (2021), 4; Brundtland, Report of the World Commission on Environment and Development: Our Common Future, 7.

321 Brunnée (2003), 45; Shelton (2009), 83.

322 Wolfrum (2009), para.1.

323 Shelton (2009), 83.

324 Ahmad (2021), 33.

325 Ahmad (2021), 34.

326 Shelton (2009), 85; Brunnée (2010), 565.

327 Brunnée (2010), 564.

encounter these issues.[328] Climate change is seen as a common concern due to its drastic consequences for present and future generations because—according to the UN General Assembly Resolution 43/53—"climate is an essential condition which sustains life on earth"[329] Since natural resources constitute a similar necessary condition for different fields of human life and well-being, the role of resources can be also seen as highly important. Besides these fields, the destruction of the ozone layer is considered as an elaborated subject of the concept of common concern.[330] These application fields show that specific environmental processes are of interest of the international community and thus are seen as common concerns.[331] As *Birnie et al.* state, the scope of the common concern of humankind is not limited to these explicitly regulated issues.[332] *Brunnée and Nollkaemper* even consider the CBD a "model for the application of the concept of common concern to natural resources located within the jurisdiction of states"[333] The fact that the CBD already subsumes a part of natural resources, namely the living resources, under the concept of common concern, suggests that the depletion of resources in general can be summarized under this concept. Similar to the loss of biodiversity, the scarcity of (also non-living) natural resources affects the environment and humanity negatively and constitutes an issue of global scope.[334] *Brunnée* therefore holds that besides the global resources like the atmosphere, also physical materials within the states' territories demand for international cooperation.[335] *Birnie et al.* even go one step further by arguing that a state's environment can constitute a "matter of international concern independently of any transboundary effects"[336].

Can resource exploitation within a state's territory thus be assumed as a subject of common concern? In order to figure this out, it is necessary to illuminate the linkage of this concept to natural resources more in detail. The World Charter for Nature, itself not a binding instrument, provides a link between the overall goal of the UN of achieving international cooperation in solving global problems

328 Birnie, Boyle, and Redgwell (2009), 128.

329 UN General Assembly, "Protection of Global Climate for Present and Future Generations of Mankind," A/RES/43/53 § (1988), 133.

330 Biermann (1996), 426, 438.

331 Brunnée (2010), 564.

332 Birnie, Boyle, and Redgwell (2009), 128.

333 Brunnée and Nollkaemper (1996), 309.

334 See 2.1.

335 Brunnée (2003), 45.

336 Birnie, Boyle, and Redgwell (2009), 128.

and safeguarding natural resources, referring to both in its preamble.[337] This reflection of natural resources in an UN General Assembly document underscores the international awareness of the importance of natural resources on the one hand, and its global character on the other. Furthermore, the ILA in its Sofia Guiding Statement 3 explicitly calls the sustainable use of all natural resources a common concern[338] and thus highlights their strong interrelation. Although these documents are not of a binding nature, they demonstrate that the international community has already agreed on the global significance of depleting resources.

By examining whether natural resources fall within the scope of the concept of common concern, it needs to be opposed to another well-known concept, namely that of common heritage of mankind. In contrast to the concept of common concern of humankind, the common heritage concept or principle entails a spatial-oriented focus. The common heritage of mankind is applicable to geographical areas and is closely linked to the global commons like the seabed, the high seas and Antarctica.[339] In other words, it builds the framework for the protection of shared areas.[340] Naming one example in treaty law, Art. 136 of the United Nations Convention on the Law of the Sea (UNCLOS)[341] explicitly describes the Area (the seabed) and its resources as the common heritage of mankind. One of its major impacts is the establishment of international administration of global commons, e.g. the International Seabed Authority.[342] Both concepts entail parallels like the awareness for a global responsibility. However, the concept of common concern of humankind is not limited to shared areas but is equally applicable to issues beyond and within national jurisdiction.[343] When considering the scarcity of natural resources, the majority of them lies within the states' territories. Certainly, both concepts partly overlap due to the fact that the global commons provide necessary resources like minerals or natural gas as well. However, as a result of their low exploitation so far, they are less at risk of resource scarcity. Therefore, the issue of depleting resources concentrates on resources within national boundaries. With its focus on global commons, the

337 UN General Assembly, "World Charter for Nature," A/RES/37/7 § (1982), 17.

338 International Law Association, Sofia Guiding Statements on the Judicial Elaboration of the 2002 New Delhi Declaration of Principles of International Law Relating to Sustainable Development.

339 Brunnée (2010), 564.

340 Bowling, Pierson and Ratté (2021), 2.

341 United Nations Convention on the Law of the Sea (adopted on 10 December 1982, entered into force on 16 November 1994) UN Treaty Series vol. 1833, 3.

342 Cf. Art. 156 UNCLOS et seq.

343 Shelton (2009), 83.

common heritage concept restricts itself to shared natural resources.[344] Although a more sustainable exploitation of those shared resources is demanded by the common heritage concept,[345] it does not touch the core of the issue. That is why the analysis of the concept of common concern may be more fruitful applied to the issue of depleting resources than that of the concept of common heritage. The regulation on exploiting shared resources based on the common heritage concept though reflects the awareness of the threatening scarcity and the necessary careful management of resources in general.[346] The conclusion, that the depletion of natural resources and the concept of common concern are interrelated, can be drawn at this point. What is more important, however, is which legal implications result from the concept of common concern of humankind concerning depleting resources. That is to be figured out by analyzing its legal character in the following.

2.1.3.2 Legal Character

Such as the legal nature of the foregoing principles and concepts, concrete legal implications of the common concern of humankind are contested.[347] From a candidate for customary international law to an imprecise target, the concept of common concern evokes diverging views. In order to determine whether general or even concrete legal duties can be derived from this concept, these different opinions will be evaluated. Starting with the strongest legal implication, the concept's classification as customary law will be illuminated. *Biermann* refers to its wide international acceptance in treaty law, limiting its statement at the same time by pointing to the fact that specific consequences have yet to be examined.[348] Its aforementioned reflections in the CBD as well as in the Paris Agreement represent examples for this growing acceptance. Additionally, earlier reflections of similar concepts, e.g. that of natural heritage in the Convention Concerning the Protection of the World Cultural and Natural Heritage[349], highlight the acknowledgment of an international responsibility for the global nature. On these grounds, *Brunnée*

[344] Bowling, Pierson and Ratté (2021), 2.

[345] Wolfrum (2009), para.22.

[346] Shelton (2009), 84.

[347] Biermann (1996), 426.

[348] Biermann (1996), 431.

[349] UN Educational, Scientific and Cultural Organization (UNESCO), Convention Concerning the Protection of the World Cultural and Natural Heritage, adopted by the General Conference at its seventeenth session, Paris, 16 November 1972.

seconds the assumption of a global recognition of this concept.[350] Yet, the vagueness of the concept of common concern impedes the classification as a binding rule of customary law. Compared with the common heritage concept, which is considered as a part of customary law by *Wolfrum*, the content of the common concern concept is assumed to be not so far developed.[351] Its missing occurrence in international jurisprudence,[352] moreover, speaks against its customary law status.

Nonetheless, a normative effect is also ascribed to the concept of common concern.[353] A first impression of what that effect can consist of is shown by the consequences of the concept in the CBD: The classification of biodiversity as a common concern of humankind entails a balancing process of sovereignty with biodiversity, which in turn leads to obligations to adhere to international standards for the conservation of biodiversity.[354] Accordingly, states must meet these standards in order to bear their responsibility. This example could lead to the assumption that the general target of a common concern is necessarily dependent on a concretization by international, regional or national treaty law, which is supported by *Proelß*.[355] At first glance, *Brunnée* seems to follow this argumentation by stating that the concept itself does not impose concrete rules of conduct.[356] She adds, however, that the common concern of humankind poses a limit to a state's sovereignty "even where other states' sovereign rights are not affected"[357]. This limit is derived from the classification of "certain types of degradation of areas or resources beyond the limits of national jurisdictions, and even of resources physically located within the territory of individual states, as of a concern to all"[358]. Thereby, these resources are not intended to be internationalized, but rather these concerns are globalized.[359] Under the concept of common concern the affected resources are not considered to be under global property, but its depletion or degradation does not longer remain a national concern. What does this globalization of environmental concerns such as this of depleting resources

[350] Brunnée (2010), 565.

[351] Brunnée (2010), 565.

[352] Bowling, Pierson and Ratté (2021), 7.

[353] Ahmad (2021), 35.

[354] Bowling, Pierson and Ratté (2021), 9.

[355] Proelß (2022), 100.

[356] Brunnée (2003), 45.

[357] Brunnée (2003), 45.

[358] Brunnée (2010), 566.

[359] Brunnée and Nollkaemper (1996), 309.

mean? A global responsibility raises the issue to greater importance and evokes action of all stakeholders involved.[360] While a detailed balancing of this concept and the previous ones against sovereignty will form a part of the fourth chapter, it can be concluded at this point that the concept recognizes the sovereign rights of states[361] regarding their resources, but builds the basis for joint protective action for the concern that involves benefits for the international community.[362] *Brunnée* even ascribes to the concept the capability to restrict states' sovereign rights regarding their resources beyond the scope of Principle 21 Stockholm Declaration.[363] Again, this development can be understood on the basis of the Rio Declaration that broadened the spatial scope of international environmental law[364] and finds itself in the general development of this field of law towards a more global approach. *Birnie et al.* speak of a globalization of this field of international law as well, referring to the development of international environmental law after the Rio Declaration away from simply governing neighboring states' relations.[365] They also argue in favor of a limitation of the states' free decision of how to exploit their own resources due to their significance on a global level.[366] In terms of global issues like climate change and the scarcity of resources, spatial boundaries are considered inappropriate.[367]

Concerning legal effects, the derivation of global responsibility from the concept of common concern can be connected to the well-known field of state responsibility.[368] Including the depletion of resources under the law of state responsibility would allow to hold states accountable for potential actions that aggravate this problem. As an issue which affects the whole international community, scholars contemplate about linking common concerns and obligations owed erga omnes.[369] On that note, *Biermann* follows from the statement in the ICJ Barcelona Traction Case that recognizes erga omnes obligations for subjects,

[360] Ahmad, (2021), 29.
[361] Ahmad (2021), 30.
[362] Brunnée (2010), 564.
[363] Brunnée (2003), 55.
[364] Birnie, Boyle, and Redgwell (2009), 129.
[365] Brunnée (2003), 55.
[366] Birnie, Boyle, and Redgwell (2009), 130.
[367] Birnie, Boyle, and Redgwell (2009), 130.
[368] Brunnée (2003), 55.
[369] Shelton (2009), 86; Birnie, Boyle, and Redgwell (2009), 130.

in which the international community has a legal interest regarding their protection,[370] that these obligations apply to common concerns.[371] The linkage between the concept of common concern and erga omnes obligations in the law of state responsibility will not help to determine what this obligation consists in. Furthermore, the law of state responsibility, as stated earlier, does not comprise a promising approach to derive a positive obligation for an economic transformation therefrom due to its retrospective application. Nonetheless, the combination of the concept of common concern with erga omnes obligations will serve to set its importance vis-à-vis the states' sovereignty. By revealing that the careful handling of resources is an obligation owed erga omnes, the issue gains increasing significance which influences its status compared to the state's sovereignty. Erga omnes obligations offer a range of parallels to the concept of common concern: According to Art. 48 of the Draft Articles on State Responsibility, the international community is entitled to invoke the responsibility of a state if such an obligation is breached.[372] These obligations elevate activities within national jurisdiction to a global responsibility and thereby supersede the sovereign domain of a state.[373] Due to this common ground, *Biermann* concludes that fundamental norms like common concerns of humankind—which include environmental concerns like climate change and depleting resources—also fall within the scope of erga omnes obligations.[374] For the sake of completeness, it has to be added that the ICJ is rather reserved in making use of erga omnes obligations outside the human-rights context.[375] Therefore, a general recognition that erga omnes obligations are covering common concerns like depleting resources is not supported by the current jurisprudence. A connection between those is, however, also not to be dismissed.

More important than its relation to state responsibility are, certainly, the concrete legal implications of the concept of common concern. Ideas for specific measures can be found in the World Charter of Nature, again. Although not representing a binding instrument in the field of common concern, it explicitly refers to this concept by mentioning the "right and duty of the international community

[370] Case Concerning the Barcelona Traction, Light and Power Company, Limited (Belgium v Spain), Second Phase, Judgment, ICJ Rep 1970, 3 para. 33 (International Court of Justice (ICJ) 1970).

[371] Biermann (1996), 451.

[372] International Law Commission, "Report of the International Law Commission on the Work of Its Fifty-Third Session," A/56/10 § (2001), 126.

[373] Birnie, Boyle, and Redgwell (2009), 131.

[374] Biermann (1996), 451.

[375] Birnie, Boyle, and Redgwell (2009), 131.

to act in matters of common concern" and listing certain measures regarding the use of resources.[376] In its No. 22 it recognizes the "sovereignty of States over their natural resources", whereas No. 10 demands that "Natural resources shall not be wasted, but used with a restraint [...] in accordance with the following rules". In No. 10 (c) it requires that "Resources, including water, which are not consumed as they are used shall be reused or recycled". No. 10 (d) refers to non-renewable resources and prescribes that they "shall be exploited with restraint, taking into account their abundance, the rational possibilities of converting them for consumption, and the compatibility of their exploitation with the functioning of natural systems"[377]. The World Charter for Nature thus incorporates concrete measures regarding the use of resources that correspond to the measures under a circular economy. It is needless to say, that this charter cannot directly interpret the concept of common concern and can only serve as non-binding interpretational aid. However, it builds a first framework of how the concept can be specifically used in practice. Additionally, it shows that the vague concept of common concern can also lead to concrete measures rather than remaining an empty shell.

Another approach for concretizing this concept is to derive the duty of cooperation therefrom, or at least find a connection between them. The global responsibility for these common concerns is viewed as involving a duty between states to work together in order to encounter the common problems.[378] Due to the fact that a global issue cannot be solved by one state alone, the need for international cooperation arises.[379] *Biermann* speaks of cooperation as a requirement of the concept of common concern and suggests financial transfer as a measure of cooperation.[380] Outside the debate on the concept of common concern, the duty to cooperate is considered as an independent principle in international law.[381] Regarding environmental protection, it is laid down in Principle 7 of the Rio Declaration, representing an explicit reflection of that duty.[382] Several environmental treaties nowadays incorporate duties of cooperation—such as Art. 6, 7 and

[376] UN General Assembly, World Charter for Nature, 18.
[377] UN General Assembly, World Charter for Nature, 18.
[378] Birnie, Boyle, and Redgwell (2009), 129.
[379] Bowling, Pierson and Ratté (2021), 2.
[380] Biermann (1996), 454.
[381] Shelton (2009), 86.
[382] Muigua (2022), 30.

8 Paris Agreement—underscoring its establishment in international environmental law.[383] Sharing the same burden requires to take joint efforts,[384] which builds the objective of the concept of common concern. Regarding common concerns, cooperation can consist of financial support or technology transfer, as laid down e.g. in the Art. 10 of the Amendment of the Montreal Protocol on Substances that Deplete the Ozone Layer[385]. The important aspect of cooperation is between whom it is necessary. Of course, every state has to take measures to combat environmental problems. Nonetheless, not all states are equally responsible or able to apply these measures. Therefore, cooperation is particularly necessary between more and less developed countries.[386] *Biermann* even develops a rule of international environmental solidarity therefrom.[387] This cooperation is commonly known as the concept of common but differentiated responsibilities. Within the following section about balancing sovereignty with the previous findings, the special role of less developed countries and accordingly the concept of common but differentiated responsibility will play a crucial role and will be considered more in detail in this part. For now, it is important to see the connection between common concerns and the duty to cooperate, including common but differentiated responsibilities. They are also described as the "other side of the common concern coin"[388]. Their interrelation will be of significance in the balancing process. In search of concrete legal implications of the concept of common concern, this linkage shows that also organizational measures like cooperation in terms of financial or technological support can be derived from this concept.

More precise obligations, on the contrary, cannot be directly subsumed under the concept of common concern of humankind. Its legal core of establishing an international responsibility towards common environmental issues like resource depletion builds, however, an important contribution to the question, in how far the issue of depleting resources is addressed by international law. Its elevation to a common concern and thus the necessity to collectively encounter this issue alone marks a significant step towards a general acceptance of mandatory protective measures. What is then to be analyzed is the implication of this concept in combination with the aforementioned principles and concepts.

---

383 Biermann (1996), 462.

384 Wolfrum (2009), para.9.

385 Montreal Protocol on Substances that Deplete the Ozone Layer (adopted on 16 September 1987, entered into force on 1 January 1989), UN Treaty Series, vol. 1522, 3.

386 Birnie, Boyle, and Redgwell (2009), 130; Biermann (1996), 461.

387 Biermann (1996), 465.

388 Bowling, Pierson and Ratté (2021), 12.

2.1.3.3 Combination of the Principles and Concepts under International Environmental Law

In order to determine whether more concrete measures can be derived from the concept of common concern, the analysis will now focus on a combination with the foregoing principles and concepts under international environmental law. The global nature of an issue like resource depletion evokes a common responsibility, which involves that sovereign rights must be exercised in a manner which is not only specified by treaty law but also by other legal instruments.[389] As a result, the legal consequences and standards of the concept of common concern were not only derived from hard law agreements, but also from soft law instruments. This perspective coincides with constitutionalist approaches that vote—to put it briefly—for international law as a uniform legal system. Without entering into the fundamental and theoretical debate between constitutionalism and fragmentarism, the common ground of constitutionalist strands lies in the classification of different sources of international law like treaties or customary law as an overall system, from which principles can emerge which, in turn, influence treaty and customary law.[390] Such an idea of international law as a framework system opens up the possibility to not only concretize a concept of common concern with treaty rules, but examine its consequences with the aid of other soft law principles and declarations, such as i.a. the Rio and Stockholm Declaration and the concept of sustainable development as well as the precautionary and preventive principle. Whether this combined interpretation of principles and concepts is compatible with international legal processes will be determined by examining a concrete treaty and its influences of principles. Before, however, the connections between the aforementioned principles and concepts and the concept of common concern need to be set out.

Birnie et al. state that the connection between the concepts of sustainable development and common concern as well as the preventive and precautionary principle is rooted in the Rio Declaration.[391] The core element of this declaration consists in balancing economic and environmental aspects and—applied to resources—goes in the same direction as Principle 21 of the Stockholm Declaration, which weighs the sovereign right of exploitation with avoiding environmental harm. The fact that these declarations involve the components of sustainable development (balancing economic and environmental aspects) as well as of the preventive principle (avoiding environmental harm), already

---

[389] Birnie, Boyle, and Redgwell (2009), 130.

[390] Peters (2014), 1.

[391] Birnie, Boyle, and Redgwell (2009), 129.

demonstrates the close relationship between both. *Shelton* even categorizes this balancing process, which is the central component of sustainable development, as a common concern of humanity, adding the respect for human rights.[392] Regarding the balancing progress, the Ad Hoc Working Group of Legal and Technical Experts seconds this by stating that the concept of "common concern called for a balance between the sovereign rights of nations to exploit their natural resources and the interests of the international community in global environmental protection"[393]. The ILA also characterizes the sustainable use of all natural resources as a matter of common concern in its Sofia Guiding Statement 3.[394] On these grounds, not only the concept of sustainable development is directly labeled as a common concern, but also its sub-notion of sustainable use. *Bowling et al.* also draw linkages between the concept of common concern and reconciling economic development with environmental protection.[395] In the Principle 1.3 of the New Delhi Declaration, the ILA states that the "protection, preservation and enhancement of the natural environment, particularly the proper management of climate system, biological diversity and fauna and flora of the Earth, are the common concern of humankind"[396]. Especially the protection and preservation provide a link to the preventive and precautionary principle. In this light, *Birnie et al.* describe the precautionary principle as "particularly evident in matter of global concern"[397], thereby underscoring their relation. Parallels are the "seriousness and possible irreversibility of the risks involved"[398] that apply for the depletion of resources, and which are directly considered by the precautionary principle. Returning to the balancing of sovereign rights and the environment, *Brunnée and Nollkaemper* even attribute to the precautionary principle that "it narrows the margins of sovereign discretion in relation to common concerns"[399].

The combination of those principles and concepts, particularly with regard to the use of resources, leads to a more comprehensive treatment of the issue of

392 Shelton (2009), 86.

393 UN Environment Programme, "Report of the Ad Hoc Working Group of Legal and Technical Experts on Biological Diversity on the Work of Its Second Session," UNEP/Bio.Div/WG.2/2/5 § (1991), 4.

394 International Law Association, Sofia Guiding Statements on the Judicial Elaboration of the 2002 New Delhi Declaration of Principles of International Law Relating to Sustainable Development.

395 Bowling, Pierson and Ratté (2021), 7.

396 Schrijver (2002), 302.

397 Birnie, Boyle, and Redgwell (2009), 130.

398 Birnie, Boyle, and Redgwell (2009), 137.

399 Brunnée and Nollkaemper (1996), 310.

resource depletion. From the balancing of economic and environmental aspects rooted in the Stockholm Declaration until the sustainable use of resources and protective action in advance, these principles and concepts cover all relevant aspects of the issue of resource depletion. Weighing the sovereign rights of exploitation with the interests of a global community in environmental protection marks the aim of the concept of common concern and reflects at the same time the core content of sustainable development. Avoiding environmental harm in advance, which is a central requirement of encountering issues of common concern, builds the basis for the preventive and—depending on the probability—also the precautionary principle. These strong linkages between the concept of common concern on the one side and the principles of prevention and precaution as well as the concept of sustainable development on the other side suggest that they form concretizations of the common concern concept. Accordingly, the concept of common concern can be classified as an overall concept, framing the aforementioned international environmental law principles and concepts and elevating them to a higher level of significance. They, in turn, serve to specify the concept of common concern, and derive concrete measures therefrom. The modifying function of sustainable development enables to interpret the concept of common concern and strengthen its implications on the sustainable management of resources. The different measures under the preventive principle like the use of the best available technologies, which points in the direction of a circular economy, can also be seen as a concretization of how to meet the vague requirements of the concept of common concern. Together with the necessity to take action despite a lack of full scientific certainty from the precautionary principle, a combination underscores the urgency of encountering the issues of common concern. Especially regarding the management of resources, these principles and concepts pave the way for finding specific measures that pursue one goal, which is the common concern of hindering the depletion of natural resources. The concept of common concern of humankind as a more comprehensive concept entails the capability to build a framework for these principles and concepts regarding resource depletion. Although it cannot intensify their legal bindingness, it raises their concrete legal consequences to a higher degree of relevance and integrates them as necessary components for the whole issue of resource depletion. Their strong relation enables a mutual reinforcement and thus argues in favor of constitutionalist approaches.

This argument can be proven by taking a closer look at the development of treaty obligations, which follow from a joint influence of these principles and concepts. With due regard to its similar scope compared to depleting resources, the CBD serves as an example again: Beginning with the preamble, the central issue, namely the loss of biodiversity, is explicitly described as a common concern. Following from this recognition, Art. 1 CBD constitutes the objective of the conservation of biological diversity. In Art. 3 CBD the reference to the sovereign right of exploitation and the obligation to ensure that activities do not cause damage to the environment unify both components of sustainable development and the preventive principle. These two articles, together with the preambular text, already highlight the direct influence these principles and concepts have on treaty law. The overarching character of the concept of common concern is demonstrated by its placement in the preamble as an overall objective, which embraces the following concrete obligations. Furthermore, Art. 6 (a) CBD incorporates national strategies, plans, or programs for the conservation and sustainable use of biological diversity. Thereby, the sub-notion of sustainable use found entry into the text. From a more general duty of weighing the sovereign right of exploitation with environmental concerns, the CBD mirrors the concretization of the concept of sustainable development to the more specialized notion of sustainable use in its articles. In the latter part of the convention, the duties refer to the concept of common concern by spelling out obligations of cooperation. Art. 16 CBD demands the transfer of technology, Art. 17 CBD requires the exchange of information, whereas Art. 18 CBD entails the duty of technical and scientific cooperation. These obligations are attributable to the general duty of cooperation, also involved by the concept of common concern.[400] In this regard, the influences of all these principles and concepts can be traced in one agreement. Together, they build the basis for a hard law instrument and set concrete treaty obligations applicable to a similar or partly overlapping topic like that of depleting resources.

Again, it must be kept in mind that the CBD is exclusively applicable to living resources related to biodiversity and does not cover all natural resources.[401] Additionally, these concrete and binding obligations are set out in treaty law and do not directly flow from the concepts and principles discussed. This example, however, demonstrates their high capability to influence treaty law and their even stronger impact being thought together and reinforcing each other. It represents, moreover, a further proof that these principles and concepts are not only independent and detached from each other, but rather come together and influence each other, leading to strong hard law obligations. These interdependencies as well as their fruitful combined interpretation argue in favor of constitutionalist approaches. Furthermore, the visible relations in the agreements like the CBD

---

[400] See 2.1.2.2.

[401] See differentiation in 2.

and the demonstrated acceptance of framing concepts like the common concern of humankind strengthens this perspective of a uniform legal system.

2.1.3.4 Conclusion on International Environmental Law

In that sense, a general conclusion of the principles and concepts under international environmental law examined in this section, is possible: The previous parts about the different principles and concepts and especially the latter part about their combination highlights their legal significance and strong influence in international law. However, to derive an obligation of an economic transformation therefrom, a strong impact on hard law, completed by a range of soft law instruments, does not suffice. Although these principles and concepts are widely accepted, the state practice and their fragmented treatment in international jurisprudence currently speaks against a recognition as customary international law. Their contribution for the research question thus cannot consist in building the sole basis for such a mandatory economic transformation. Generally, principles under international law are seen as components, guiding the interpretation of other rules and integrating different aspects in political and legal decisions.[402] They can provide guidance in balancing national and international interests,[403] which is important especially in the context of resource management. One of the most promising features is the capability to build a framework for the interpretation of rules,[404] keeping in mind the framing character of the concept of common concern and the modifying nature of sustainable development. Notable is the statement of the UNEP, attesting to them the capability of promoting the development of international environmental law and laying the foundation for new rules in treaty or customary law.[405] Their capability under international law can thus not solve the issue of resource depletion alone, but serves as a basis for the further development of this field of law. It allows, furthermore, to structure and rearrange other duties in the treaty context.[406] These implications make them interesting for a joint analysis together with another important field of international law, directly affected by the issue of depleting resources: human rights

[402] UN Environment Programme, *UNEP Training Manual on International Environmental Law*, 2006, 23, available on https://wedocs.unep.org/20.500.11822/20599 last accessed 6 September 2022; Rayfuse (2016), 13.

[403] Brunnée and Nollkaemper (1996), 309.

[404] Rayfuse (2016), 13.

[405] UN Environment Programme, *UNEP Training Manual on International Environmental Law*, 24.

[406] Brunnée (2003), 55.

law. In the following, their connections and interdependencies will be scrutinized in order to determine their consequences on the research of a mandatory transformation towards a circular economy.

2.2 Human Rights

Besides the consequences of resource depletion on the environment, the overuse of natural capacities has huge impacts on humanity as well. For an extensive analysis of the framework governing this issue the effects on human beings must be included. After clarifying the scope and methodology of the human rights interpretation, the relevant rights will be analyzed in light of their connection to the issue of resource depletion. In a second step, the influence of the principles and concepts under international environmental law on these rights will be detected in order to reveal whether an obligation concerning an adapted use of resources or even regarding an economic transformation can be derived therefrom.

2.2.1 Relevance and Course of the Human Rights' Examination

2.2.1.1 Relation between Resources and Human Rights

Before starting the analysis of human rights related to the issue of resource depletion, the connection between them must be set out. Generally, it is to be noted that human rights treaties do not involve explicitly how natural resources need to be managed in order to meet the standards of the human rights regime.[407] Nonetheless, scholars like *Gilbert* argue in favor of treating the management of resource as a human rights issue.[408] It will be shown in the following in how far natural resources and human rights are interconnected and whether resources have to be regarded from a human rights perspective. First, the general consequences of a scarcity of resources on human beings will be illuminated in order to clarify the significance of human rights for this issue. In how far resource depletion is connected to concrete rights on a legal level will be part of the ensuing scrutiny about specific human rights.

Their first common point of reference consists in the general influence of the environment on human beings. Although an in-depth analysis of the interrelation

[407] Gilbert (2018), 63.

[408] Gilbert (2018), 63.

between the environment and human rights will be part of the section about the right to a healthy environment, the general connections are to be outlined at this point. Humanity is directly and indirectly affected by a degrading environment.[409] Taking a look at the huge impacts of natural disasters or processes with severe consequences such as desertification on human life provides vivid examples of their mutual dependence. Besides these concerns, the environment including all natural resources constitutes the livelihood of humans.[410] Natural resources are used to build houses, to feed the population, and—generally—to fulfil the basic needs of human beings.[411] Therefore, it becomes clear that humanity depends on the availability of resources. Concerning the questioned obligation to safeguard natural resources, these connections need to be transmitted to a legal level.

On this occasion, a brief digression must be inserted to build the bridge between the terms "basic needs" and "human rights". The question arises if the fulfillment of needs is part or even central component of the human rights regime. Without entering in the ethically shaped discussion, whether a state should be responsible for satisfying human needs,[412] it is important to understand their meaning: Broadly speaking, needs and rights are no equivalent terms and have to be distinguished.[413] While needs are "things that a person must have in order to have a satisfactory life"[414], a right is defined as an "opportunity to act and to be treated in particular ways that the law promises to protect for the benefit of society"[415]. Human rights, therefore, do not incorporate every human need, but cover only that spectrum of needs, which is incorporated in the law. Hence, basic needs do form part of human rights only to the extent that these rules prescribe. In how far the need for natural resources is incorporated in the human rights system must be determined by analyzing the content of the respective rights.

Why are human rights then relevant for the question on an obligation to transform the economy in order to safeguard natural resources? It is undisputed

[409] The Office of the High Commissioner for Human Rights, "Human Rights, Poverty Reduction and Sustainable Development: Health, Food and Water—A Background Paper" (Johannesburg: World Summiot on Sustainable Development, September 26, 2002), 2.

[410] Shelton (2011), 265.

[411] Leib (2011), 76.

[412] See for a detailed analysis of this topic Streeten (1980), 108.

[413] Streeten (1980), 107.

[414] Cambridge Dictionary see https://dictionary.cambridge.org/de/worterbuch/englisch/need.

[415] Cambridge Dictionary see https://dictionary.cambridge.org/de/worterbuch/englisch/right.

that humanity will reach a point when resources will not be sufficiently available anymore.[416] Due to the dependence of human beings on the availability of resources, a lacking conservation of resources would then directly impact on human rights[417]. These rights play a crucial role in determining whether there is an obligation to safeguard natural resources under international law and thus build the subsequent pillar for answering the research question.

2.2.1.2 Defining the Scope of the Analysis

Management of natural resources forms a large field and is related to a whole range of human rights. In order to determine the scope of this analysis, it is necessary to identify the exact concern within this field. This chapter is based on the question, in how far the depletion of resources demands for an economic shift. That brings the topic of a threatening scarcity of resources into focus. Which aspects and—subsequently—which human rights are relevant to this?

First of all, human rights move into focus when considering their potential violations in the exploitation process. Resource use starts with the process of extraction, which provides the platform for different human rights violations: Exploiting natural resources goes along with negative consequences for the workers and for nearby residents. Especially the exploitation of fossil fuels affects the environment of indigenous people.[418] Therefore, human rights like the right to safe and healthy working conditions in Art. 7 (b) of the International Covenant on Economic, Social and Cultural Rights (ICESCR)[419], aiming for the prevention of hazards in the working environment,[420] could be suitable when discussing about the use of resources. Similarly, the right to security in Art. 9 of the International

[416] See https://www.theworldcounts.com/stories/depletion-of-natural-resources accessed 26 December 2022.

[417] Office of the High Commissioner of Human Rights and UN Environment Programme, "Human Rights and the Environment—Rio + 20: Joint Report OCHR and UNEP" (Rio de Janeiro, June 19, 2012), 20.

[418] UN General Assembly, "Implications for human rights of the environmentally sound management and disposal of hazardous substances and wastes", Report of the Special Rapporteur Marcos Orellana (2021), A/76/207: para.48, available at https://documents-dds-ny.un.org/doc/UNDOC/GEN/N21/201/78/PDF/N2120178.pdf?OpenElement accessed 13 January 2022.

[419] International Covenant on Economic, Social and Cultural Rights (adopted on 16 December 1966, entered into force on 3 January 1976) UN Treaty Series vol. 993, 3.

[420] Committee on Economic, Social and Cultural Rights, "General Comment No. 23: The Right To Just and Favourable Conditions of Work," E/C.12/GC/23 § (2016), para. 25.

Covenant on Civil and Political Rights (ICCPR)[421] involves the threats happening in the extraction process,[422] not only for workers, but also for everyone who is suffering from environmental degradation resulting from mining sites.[423] On top of that, it can be applied to the contamination of indigenous peoples' farmlands caused by exploitation sites.[424] Although the process of exploitation can result in a range of consequences that directly violate human rights, its analysis does not serve to answer the posed research question. These rights are surely closely connected to resources, but do not lead to any further conclusions on the topic of resource *depletion*. Solutions for these violations would consist in higher safety standards for extraction sites and processes, not in the more efficient use of natural resources. Certainly, if a perfect cycle of resource use would be possible, a circular economy could render the exploitation of resources unnecessary. Leaving this out of consideration, these rights aiming for more safety of the people involved in these processes cannot demand for the complete elimination of a whole industry sector. They require safe working places, which could be achieved through many less drastic measures. Hence, the exploitation process and pertinent rights will not be part of this analysis.

The second field related to the management of resources is the question of their distribution, particularly regarding indigenous people. Discussed in connection with indigenous people is their right to land and the respective natural resources therefrom.[425] Although the distribution of resources and the question of who benefits from their exploitation marks an important part in the legal consideration of resource management, this aspect cannot provide further findings on how to prevent their depletion. The role of indigenous people in the management of resources thus builds a separate field of investigation regarding participation and benefit-sharing.[426] It addresses the issue how to distribute resources in the

[421] International Covenant on Civil and Political Rights (adopted on 16 December 1966, entered into force on 23 March 1976) UN Treaty Series vol. 999, 171.

[422] UN General Assembly, "Report of the Special Rapporteur on the Implications for Human Rights of the Environmentally Sound Management and Disposal of Hazardous Substances and Wastes, Marcos Orellana," A/76/207 § (2021), para. 15.

[423] UN General Assembly, Report of the Special Rapporteur on the implications for human rights of the environmentally sound management and disposal of hazardous substances and wastes, Marcos Orellana, para. 16.

[424] UN General Assembly, Report of the Special Rapporteur on the implications for human rights of the environmentally sound management and disposal of hazardous substances and wastes, Marcos Orellana, para. 48.

[425] Sands et al. (2012), 782.

[426] For more information on this topic see Gilbert (2018).

present, not the question how to deal with a threatening scarcity with regard to future generations. This thesis focuses on the consequences of a scarcity of natural resources on the entire humanity and the opportunity of a cyclical use. Therefore, the special rights of indigenous people regarding their access to natural resources will be excluded from this analysis as well. Nonetheless, their particular vulnerability to the consequences of depleting resources will not be disregarded.

Furthermore, it needs to be decided if both procedural and substantive rights will form part of the analysis. Since procedural rights like the right to information, participation or access to justice shall ensure that "decision-making takes place with informed input from those potentially affected"[427], they concentrate on providing necessary information and opportunities to assert one's right. Substantive rights rather affect a decision directly by incorporating the content-related basis for a potential lawsuit.[428] Even though the procedural questions about how to litigate for a better resource management constitute an important scientific field, the research question, in how far states are obliged to transform their economies, relates to the substantive part of rights. This project involves the discussion, *if* rights contain such an obligation rather than *how* it could be enforced. Therefore, the focus will lie upon substantive rights.

Another differentiation to be kept in mind defining the examination's scope relates to the character or generation of human rights. When looking for an obligation to transform an economic system, economic, social, and cultural rights move into focus. Since resources build the foundation of a satisfactory life in all its different spheres such as housing and food, the rights concerning adequate living conditions play a dominant role. Furthermore, their concentration on positive obligations like the duty to fulfil makes them more promising in order to derive a positive obligation to transform the economy therefrom. The negative obligation to respect a right does not involve any need for resources[429] as it only comprises a state's duty to not interfere with this right. Omissions do not require the use of any resources. For that reason, a focus will lie on the duty to *fulfil* the following rights, since this duty encompasses a positive state action. Incorporating the adequate standard of living and well-being, they are also closely related to environmental issues, which mainly influence these living conditions.[430] Therefore, they can serve as a potential bridge between human rights and the environment.

[427] Shelton (2011), 265.

[428] Shelton (2011), 265.

[429] Streeten (1980), 107.

[430] Sands et al. (2012), 780.

Nonetheless, the civil and political rights shall not be completely disregarded, as they are "equally capable of creating practical and enforceable obligations in relation to environmental and related matters"[431]. Especially the right to life (Art. 6 ICCPR) deserves a closer consideration, which will be shown in the following. In consequence, this part concentrates on the rights under the ICESCR as well as the ICCPR. Although not every state represents a party of these covenants, they are nearly universally adopted, and the main rights—also reflected in the Universal Declaration of Human Rights—have reached the status of customary law by now.[432] With due regard to the research question considering a global obligation, regional human rights law will only be addressed supplementary. Hence, this thesis will illuminate the relevant rights under the ICCPR and ICESCR.

For the sake of completeness and in order to understand the relevance of human rights for answering the research question about an obligation to transform the economy, the differences between the states' duties under both covenants will be set out briefly: Different from Art. 2 (1) ICCPR, which incorporates an immediate duty to respect and ensure the rights granted, a progressive realization of the ICESCR rights is demanded.[433] Less immediate than the rights under the ICCPR, Art. 2 (1) ICESCR requires that a state "undertakes to take steps", which includes both obligations of conduct and obligations of—a rather indeterminate—result.[434] Lastly, the efforts prescribed under the ICESCR are limited by the state's maximum available resources, recognizing the diverse financial situations of every state,[435] but also weakening the demanded duties. These differences, directly affecting the obligations under these covenants, need to be kept in mind when analyzing the respective rights.

What will then fall under the scope of this chapter are the rights that directly apply to the consequences of resource depletion. As already mentioned in the beginning, the rights that address the basic human needs depend on the availability of natural resources. If the connection of these rights with the availability of resources is strong enough needs to be figured out in a detailed interpretation. The following rights deserve a closer consideration: As the most basic right, the right to life in Art. 6 ICCPR will mark the starting point for the analysis. Furthermore, the right to the highest attainable standard of health in Art. 12 ICESCR as well as the right to adequate food and housing in Art. 11 ICESCR will be

---

431 Sands et al. (2012), 787.

432 Hannum (1998), 145.

433 Saul, Kinley and Mowbray (2014), 134.

434 Saul, Kinley and Mowbray (2014), 137.

435 Saul, Kinley and Mowbray (2014), 143, 144.

analyzed with due regard to their relation to natural resources. After considering the written rights in the ICCPR and ICESCR, the right to water and the right to a healthy environment are to be examined. These rights constitute the scope of the following analysis.

2.2.1.3 Methodology of the Human Rights' Interpretation

After clarifying which rights form part of the examination, it needs to be set out how they will be interpreted. As it is generally conducted with treaties, the VCLT will build the basis for the interpretation of the aforementioned rights. Although the ICCPR and ICESCR were adopted before the VCLT entered into force, the customary law character of the convention's interpretation rules is accepted.[436] Both covenants constitute treaties under the definition of the VCLT.[437] The analysis follows the interpretation structure in Art. 31 (1) to (3) VCLT. It orients itself to the three main interpretive methods, namely the ordinary meaning, context, and object and purpose in Art. 31 (1) VCLT. Without an explicit hierarchy, Art. 31 (1) VCLT incorporates these methods in one rule.[438] Art. 31 (2) defines the extent of the context, referring to the preamble, annexes, as well as agreements between all the parties in connection with the conclusion of the treaty (a), and instruments made by one or more parties in connection with the conclusion of the treaty and accepted by the other parties (b). Furthermore, Art. 31 (3) widens the scope of interpretive methods by adding subsequent agreements between the parties (a), subsequent practice in the application of the treaty (b), and "any relevant rules of international law applicable in the relations between the parties" (c). The latter rules of international law deserve a special focus regarding the question if international environmental law principles and concepts influence the interpretation of human rights.

Concerning human rights, special characteristics to their interpretation have evolved: These are rooted in the non-reciprocal character of human rights and tendencies of attributing a constitutional nature to them.[439] Derived from the teleological principle of object and purpose, the principle of effectiveness plays a crucial role.[440] This principle demands for interpreting human rights extensively

[436] Fitzmaurice (2013), 739.
[437] Fitzmaurice (2013), 739.
[438] Fitzmaurice (2013), 746.
[439] Fitzmaurice (2013), 759.
[440] Fitzmaurice (2013), 746.

to ensure that every rule has a "definite force and effect"[441] (*effet utile*).[442] It aims for rendering the protection effectively. Besides that, the evolutive interpretation forms a special interpretation method, based on the object and purpose and bridging Art. 31 (3) (c) and Art. 31 (1).[443] The evolutive interpretation respects legal and societal developments and changes, and highlights that treaties and their interpretation are not static. Therefore, the European Convention on the Protection of Human Rights and Fundamental Freedoms (ECHR)[444] describes human rights treaties as a "living instrument [...] which must be interpreted in the light of present day conditions"[445]. These interpretation methods are common in the decision of human rights courts.[446]Although the respective jurisdiction of these tribunals and—linked to that—the limited application of their judgments need to be kept in mind, their interpretive approaches and relevant case law will also be considered. Questions on the ordinary meaning and purpose can be answered best by interpreting every right separately, whereas the discussion about the relevance of international environmental law shall be conducted in a general manner, considering the respective rights together. Therefore, the analysis will be divided into a right-by-right analysis, revealing the rights' connections to resource depletion by examining their ordinary meaning, context, and object and purpose, and a second part, in which the rights are analyzed together, determining the influence of international environmental law.

2.2.2 Analysis of Rights

2.2.2.1 Right to Life

Most fundamental of all human rights is the right to life. Not only due to its protection of the most basic foundation of every human being, but also because

[441] Fitzmaurice (2013), 752.

[442] Fitzmaurice (2013), 764.

[443] Fitzmaurice (2013), 752.

[444] European Convention for the Protection of Human Rights and Fundamental Freedoms (adopted on 4 November 1950, entered into force on 3 September 1953) UN Treaty Series vol. 213, 221.

[445] Case of Tyrer v. The United Kingdom, Jugment, No. 5856/72 (European Court of Human Rights April 25, 1978).

[446] Fitzmaurice (2013), 739, 752.

of its influences on every other human right,[447] the right to life marks the starting point of this analysis. As its reflection in Art. 6 (1) ICCPR sets out, "every human being has the *inherent* right to life", which "shall be protected by the law". The wording itself does not contain any explicit connection to the meaning of resources for this right. "Life" is a comprehensive but at the same time specific term, which broadly speaking means to be alive.[448] What exactly falls under the right to be alive can only be figured out by consulting the further methods of interpretation. The element "inherent" provides a unique characteristic to this right, which prohibits on the one hand any form of derogation[449] and a narrow interpretation on the other hand.[450] Interpreting its object and purpose and bearing in mind the principle of effectiveness, seconds this prohibition of a narrow and restrictive interpretation. This includes that the interpretation cannot stop at the negative obligation not to interfere with a person's right to life but must allow to take positive obligations into consideration as well.[451] The life of human beings is reliant to a functioning livelihood with adequate living conditions. If these basic conditions are destructed or unavailable, a state must become active and is responsible to take measures to change this circumstance. The right to life thus cannot be rendered effective by an inactive or passive state. Transmitted to the issue of depleting resources, it has already been discussed that human life depends on the availability of resources in most areas. That marks a direct connection between the right to life and natural resources.[452] It is clear, however, that only life-threatening situations can be subsumed under Art. 6 ICCPR[453] rather than any type of lacking resources. A positive duty of states to safeguard resources

[447] Human Rights Committee, "General Comment No. 36: Article 6 of the International Covenant on Civil and Political Rights, the Right to Life," CCPR/C/GC/36 § (2018), para. 2.

[448] See also Human Rights Committee, *Portillo Cáceres et al. v. Paraguay* (CCPR/C/126/D/2751/2016), para. 7.3.

[449] Human Rights Committee, General Comment No. 36: Article 6 of the International Covenant on Civil and Political Rights, the Right to Life, para. 2.

[450] Human Rights Committee, "General Comment No. 6: The Right to Life" (1982), para. 5; Schabas and Nowak (2019), 122.

[451] For example, *Teitiota v. New Zealand* (CCPR/C/127/D/2728/2016), para. 9.4; *Toussaint v. Canada*, para. 11.3; Human Rights Committee, General Comment No. 6: The Right to Life, para. 5.

[452] Gilbert (2018), 93.

[453] *Toussaint v. Canada* (CCPR/C/123/D/2348/2014), para. 11.3; *Portillo Cáceres et al. v. Paraguay*, para. 7.5; Human Rights Committee, General Comment No. 36: Article 6 of the International Covenant on Civil and Political Rights, the Right to Life, para. 7.

in order to avoid a future lack can thus only be assumed if such a lack leads to life-threatening situations in the future.

According to the Human Rights Committee, states must therefore "take appropriate measures to address the general conditions in society that may give rise to direct threats to life"[454], explicitly including a degrading environment and unsustainable development. Likewise, *Atapattu* states that human life is not possible without these basic living conditions and characterizes environmental protection as such a necessary condition.[455]. This connection between environmental protection and the right to life also forms integral part of the Human Rights Committee's decision about the Torres Straits Islanders[456], discussing a violation of the right of life through failing to provide adaptation and mitigation measures to address the consequences of climate change.[457] The Committee holds that the state party is obliged i.a. to provide compensation, to secure the communities' safe existence on the islands and to take steps to prevent similar violations in the future.[458] Therefore, it derives a state's duty to prevent environmental degradation in the future in order to ensure the right to life. Even though, this does not represent a binding decision and does not involve the use of resources, it highlights the close connection between the right to life and the basic conditions of living provided by the environment. Similarly, the case of Portillo Cáceres et al. v. Paraguay emphasizes the negative effects of a degrading environment on human well-being and the right to life.[459] This leads over to the relevance of the environment, and more specifically of natural resources, in the human rights regime. Since the discussion about a separate right to a healthy environment has developed, the analysis of this right including its relation to the right to life will be conducted separately. For other than life-threating consequences more specific rights under the ICESCR must be examined. Regarding these rights, their mutual interdependence with the right to life must be kept in mind, as the right to life builds the foundation of

---

[454] Human Rights Committee, General Comment No. 36: Article 6 of the International Covenant on Civil and Political Rights, the Right to Life, para. 26.

[455] Atapattu (2002), 99.

[456] Human Rights Committee, Views adopted by the Committee under article 5 (4) of the Optional Protocol, concerning communication No. 3624/2019, No. CCPR/C/135/D/3624/2019 (September 22, 2022).

[457] Human Rights Committee, Views adopted by the Committee under article 5 (4) of the Optional Protocol, concerning communication No. 3624/2019 para. 8.3.

[458] Human Rights Committee, Views adopted by the Committee under article 5 (4) of the Optional Protocol, concerning communication No. 3624/2019 para. 11.

[459] *Portillo Cáceres et al. v. Paraguay*, para. 7.4 and notes 45 and 46.

all other human rights and is itself influenced by other rights.[460] For a better understanding, in how far resources are embedded in the human rights system, the following sections will involve more specific rights.

2.2.2.2 Right to the Highest Attainable Standard of Health

Closely linked to the right to life is the right to the highest attainable standard of health in Art. 12 ICESCR. Since it is considered a crucial requirement for addressing human well-being,[461] the right to health deserves an examination regarding its implications on resource use. At first glance, the relation between health and natural resources remains unclear, as the wording does not mention any dependence of human health on the availability of resources. However, Art. 12 (2) (b) explicitly mentions the improvement of i.a. environmental hygiene as a necessary step to achieve by state action. This highlights that the environment plays an important role concerning human health. *Leib*, therefore, assumes a healthy environment to be a necessary "prerequisite for human health and well-being"[462]. Although a state cannot be held responsible for providing protection against every negative effect on human health, according to General Comment No. 14, action is required regarding the provision of health facilities, services,[463] and—explicitly—the protection of environmental conditions.[464] The right's object and purpose thus include the prevention of health risks caused by the environment.[465] This explains its close connection to the right to a healthy environment,[466] but does not clarify in how far it depends on natural resources. For this reason, it will be considered as well when analyzing the right to a healthy environment and the rights together later on. Regarding the scarcity of resources, the interrelationship with the right to health tends to be low: While the right to health includes necessary

---

[460] Human Rights Committee, General Comment No. 36: Article 6 of the International Covenant on Civil and Political Rights, the Right to Life, para. 2.

[461] The Office of the High Commissioner for Human Rights, "Human Rights, Poverty Reduction and Sustainable Development: Health, Food and Water—A Background Paper," 6.

[462] Leib (2011), 78.

[463] Committee on Economic, Social and Cultural Rights, "General Comment No. 14: The Right to the Highest Attainable Standard of Health," E/C.12/2000/4 § (2000), para. 9.

[464] Committee on Economic, Social and Cultural Rights, General Comment No. 14: The Right to the Highest Attainable Standard of Health, para. 11.

[465] Committee on Economic, Social and Cultural Rights, General Comment No. 14: The Right to the Highest Attainable Standard of Health, para. 15.

[466] Committee on Economic, Social and Cultural Rights, General Comment No. 14: The Right to the Highest Attainable Standard of Health, para. 4.

goods as food, water, and shelter,[467] which are based on natural resources, the direct connections can be better retraced to the rights to food, water and housing than to health. The right to health moves into focus, when considering environmental threats and health hazards.[468] Since the extraction process itself does not fall within the scope for this part, these consequences relate more to the management of waste, which will be analyzed in the next chapter. The direct connections between the right to health and the availability of resources remain too vague to derive any form of obligation to safeguard resources therefrom. Their indirect relation will be considered when examining the right to a healthy environment.

2.2.2.3 Right to Adequate Food

From the general right to health, the next logical step consists in its concretization to a more specific basic need: food. The right to adequate food, vested in Art. 11 (1) ICESCR and accompanied by the fundamental right to freedom from hunger and malnutrition in Art. 11 (2) ICESCR, predominately aims for ending hunger by providing enough food for everyone. Its wording emphasizes the focus on the issues of hunger and malnutrition, which do not constitute the main objective of a circular economy. However, from a teleological point of view, the right to food incorporates the availability of food for present and future generations and its safety as well.[469] Hence, it touches on an intergenerational aspect of food security, which contains parallels to the objective of circular economy. Food thus represents a natural resource that is vital for human life. Nonetheless, its availability cannot be directly compared to the resources safeguarded by a circular economy. The characteristic of the resource food is that it will be consumed. Although food also forms part of a natural cycle, its usage cannot follow the same path as that of components which can be recycled and introduced in the production process again. The benefits of the resource-saving effect of circular economy thus only apply to e.g. the soil, the food is cultivated on. Fertile ground is the natural resource, which can be safeguarded for future generations, not the food

[467] Human Rights Committee, General Comment No. 36: Article 6 of the International Covenant on Civil and Political Rights, the Right to Life, para. 26.

[468] Committee on Economic, Social and Cultural Rights, General Comment No. 14: The Right to the Highest Attainable Standard of Health, para. 15.

[469] The Office of the High Commissioner for Human Rights, "Human Rights, Poverty Reduction and Sustainable Development: Health, Food and Water—A Background Paper," 10; Committee on Economic, Social and Cultural Rights, "General Comment No. 12: The Right to Adequate Food," E/C.12/1999/5 § (1999), para. 7.

itself. For this reason, humanity needs another way of using farmland and conducting agriculture.[470] Systems like acroecology, which are—similarly to circular economy—based on sustainable use, address this issue. Even if a circular economy would also involve the "recycling" of soil, its relation to the right to food remains on an indirect and loose level. The other aspect of food safety, which includes the quality of food and the prevention of a contamination by adverse substances like toxins,[471] rather relates to the consequences of waste than to the use of resources and will be treated in the following chapter. On these grounds, the right to food shows only a distant relation to the issue of depleting resources and cannot lead to any further findings at this point.

2.2.2.4 Right to Adequate Housing

The next relevant right under Art. 11 (1) ICESCR is the right to adequate housing, integral component of an adequate standard of living.[472] A range of issues relating to the housing process are incorporated in the term "housing".[473] This is the case because of its fundamental relevance to human living conditions and its close connections to the other rights under Art. 11 (1) ICESCR addressing basic human demands.[474] If the right to housing provides further findings on the research question, depends on its relation to resource depletion. Therefore, its content, especially its object and purpose will be regarded more in detail. Generally, it does not comprise a comprehensive obligation to construct houses for everyone.[475] The object of this right rather encompasses a duty to create the conditions that everyone has the possibility and access to adequate housing.[476] In terms of resource management, that includes the sufficient availability of working

---

[470] Beyerlin (2005), 535.

[471] Committee on Economic, Social and Cultural Rights, General Comment No. 12: The Right to Adequate Food, para. 10.

[472] Committee on Economic, Social and Cultural Rights, "General Comment No. 4: The Right to Adequate Housing," E/1992/23 § (1991), para. 1.

[473] United Nations Human Settlements Programme and United Nations, eds., *Housing Rights Legislation: Review of International and National Legal Instruments*, Series of Publications in Support of the Global Campaign for Secure Tenure, no. 05 (Nairobi: United Nations Human Settlements Programme: Office of the High Commissioner for Human Rights, 2002), 15.

[474] Saul, Kinley and Mowbray (2014), 926.

[475] United Nations Human Settlements Programme and United Nations, *Housing Rights Legislation*, 18.

[476] United Nations Human Settlements Programme and United Nations, *Housing Rights Legislation*, 19.

material.[477] Hence, the obligation to provide adequate housing involves ensuring that working material, e.g. wood and sand as the most basic materials, will be available. Naturally, this duty does not comprise every brick or screw for the construction of a house. However, its fundamental character implies that this right shall not be interpreted in a narrow way, e.g. only providing a roof.[478] Since the wording includes the term "adequate" and its connections with other rights involve the right to live in security and dignity, a state must ensure that everyone has the opportunity to live under these conditions.[479] Applying the principle of effectiveness, this right must not only exist in a theoretical manner, but needs to be practically feasible. If a lack of basic materials like sand (which is the main component of concrete) leads to the impossibility to construct houses, this unavailability of resources renders the right ineffective. Due to lacking resources and other obstacles, there is even today a "gap between the standards set in article 11 (1) of the Covenant and the situation prevailing in many parts of the world"[480]. A depletion of these resources in the future even aggravates this problem. It has thereby been clarified in how far the right to adequate housing is dependent from resources. Now, it needs to be revealed what kind of obligation can be derived therefrom. For this reason, Art. 2 (1) ICESCR must be taken into consideration, giving further information about the sort of possible obligations in the ICESCR: Like already stated above, the ICESCR rights need to be realized progressively, dependent from a state's available resources. Again, Art. 11 (1) ICESCR speaks of taking "appropriate steps to ensure the realization of this right". Regarding the provision of building materials, states need to take steps to ensure their availability.[481] These steps obviously vary from one state to another dependent from that state's resources,[482] but also dependent from the needs and concerns of the residents. At this point, the special affection of

[477] Committee on Economic, Social and Cultural Rights, General Comment No. 4: The Right to Adequate Housing, E/1992/23 (1991), para.1, 8 (b).

[478] Committee on Economic, Social and Cultural Rights, General Comment No. 4: The Right to Adequate Housing, para. 7.

[479] Committee on Economic, Social and Cultural Rights, General Comment No. 4: The Right to Adequate Housing, para. 7.

[480] Committee on Economic, Social and Cultural Rights, General Comment No. 4: The Right to Adequate Housing, para. 4.

[481] Committee on Economic, Social and Cultural Rights, General Comment No. 4: The Right to Adequate Housing, para. 8 (c).

[482] Committee on Economic, Social and Cultural Rights, General Comment No. 4: The Right to Adequate Housing, para. 12.

indigenous people, often relying on natural resources,[483] must be highlighted. Particularly, their right to housing is closely interrelated with their right to land and its natural resources.[484] Conserving natural resources is thus even more crucial for their enjoyment of the right to adequate housing.[485] For that reason, it can be assumed that states are obliged to make greater efforts in providing materials for the construction of houses in this case. Besides this special affection of indigenous communities, it needs to be clarified, what steps a state must generally undertake in order to fulfil its duty. As it is widely accepted, the rights under the ICESCR involve minimum core requirements: The UN Human Settlement Programme assumes an immediate state action, "if any significant number of individuals are deprived of basic shelter and housing"[486]. As a consequence, the urgency of residents' needs can imply an immediate provision of materials in order to fulfil their right to housing. On top of that, the Human Rights Council emphasizes that also environmental degradation interferes with the right to housing and must be addressed by states.[487] Hence, the right to housing involves various connections to resource use and other environmental issues. The first result at this point is that the fulfillment of the human right to housing is not possible without natural resources. The provision of materials to build houses is thus demanded by states in order to fulfil this right. In what exactly an obligation to safeguard resources—especially for future generations—consists in, has to be determined together with the other rights and the potential implications of the environmental law principles and concepts in the next part.

2.2.2.5 Right to Water

Speaking of natural resources, one important resource shall not be neglected: the resource water. Neither in the text of the ICCPR nor in that of the ICESCR there exists an explicit right to water. However, the UN General Assembly has already recognized the right to safe and clean drinking water and sanitation as a

483 Human Rights Council, "Guidelines for the Implementation of the Right to Adequate Housing," A/HRC/43/43 § (2019), para. 72 (d).

484 UN General Assembly, "Adequate Housing as a Component of the Right to an Adequate Standard of Living, and the Right to Non-Discrimination in This Context," A/74/183 § (2019), para. 4.

485 UN General Assembly, Adequate housing as a component of the right to an adequate standard of living, and the right to non-discrimination in this context, para. 4.

486 United Nations Human Settlements Programme and United Nations, *Housing Rights Legislation*, 21.

487 Human Rights Council, Guidelines for the Implementation of the Right to Adequate Housing, para. 28 (c).

human right in its resolution in 2010.[488] Although the right is not reflected in a written agreement, its content has been concretized. One important aspect of the right to water is—according to the Human Rights Council—the availability of water and a prevention of water shortages due to its fundamental significance for human life.[489] Currently, the use of water increases.[490] With the major impacts of a water scarcity on human well-being including other human rights like the right to life or health in mind, the need to save and restore water is evident.[491] The right to water thus involves to safeguard this sort of resource. Regarding water, its limited comparability to solid resources needs to be taken into consideration: Similar to the issue with food, water is used and follows its own cycle. Nonetheless, for many types of its usage, it is not consumed but rather used for production processes. Although water cannot be recycled in the same sense as e.g. cell phones, it can be cleaned or reused.[492] Therefore, a circular economic system can also be applied to water in many parts. The Human Rights Council recommends its implementation in order to reuse and recycle water and wastewater.[493] Besides that, a circular economy reducing material use can help to safeguard a huge amount of water used in extraction processes.[494] Thereby, water is linked

[488] UN General Assembly, "Resolution Adopted by the General Assembly on 28 July 2010, 64/292. The Human Right to Water and Sanitation," A/RES/64/292 § (2010), 2.

[489] Human Rights Council, "Human Rights and the Global Water Crisis: Water Pollution, Water Scarcity and Water-Related Disasters—Report of the Special Rapporteur on the Issue of Human Rights Obligations Relating the Enjoyment of a Safe, Healthy and Sustainable Environment," A/HRC/46/28 § (2021), para. 14.

[490] Human Rights Council, Human Rights and the Global Water Crisis: Water Pollution, Water Scarcity and Water-Related Disasters—Report of the Special Rapporteur on the Issue of Human Rights Obligations Relating the Enjoyment of a Safe, Healthy and Sustainable Environment, para. 8.

[491] Human Rights Council, Human Rights and the Global Water Crisis: Water Pollution, Water Scarcity and Water-Related Disasters—Report of the Special Rapporteur on the Issue of Human Rights Obligations Relating the Enjoyment of a Safe, Healthy and Sustainable Environment, para. 25.

[492] Human Rights Council, Human Rights and the Global Water Crisis: Water Pollution, Water Scarcity and Water-Related Disasters—Report of the Special Rapporteur on the Issue of Human Rights Obligations Relating the Enjoyment of a Safe, Healthy and Sustainable Environment, para. 89 (i).

[493] Human Rights Council, Human Rights and the Global Water Crisis: Water Pollution, Water Scarcity and Water-Related Disasters—Report of the Special Rapporteur on the Issue of Human Rights Obligations Relating the Enjoyment of a Safe, Healthy and Sustainable Environment, para. 89 (i).

[494] See https://www.umweltbundesamt.de/themen/abfall-ressourcen/ressourcennutzung-ihre-folgen accessed 4 April 2024.

to the exploitation to other resources and can be saved by a reduced extraction of those. Hence, the right to water is also connected to the use of resources and the need to safeguard them for present and future generations.

2.2.2.6 Right to a Healthy Environment

Central in the debate about human rights and the use of resources is the right to a healthy environment. With due regard to its unwritten nature and its relatively recent application, its development and current state of implementation will be set out, before evaluating its connection to resource depletion.

2.2.2.6.1 Development of the Right to a Healthy Environment

First of all, its evolution and the reason for its development will be regarded. As already emphasized above, a functioning environment providing all the necessary conditions for a human life builds the foundation of enjoying human rights.[495] Especially the right to life and the right to health are closely connected to a healthy environment.[496] This strong relation between human life and the environment shows the dependence of economic and social development on the ecosystem.[497]Resulting from these interconnections and the growing awareness of our ecosystem's fragility, the right to a healthy environment has evolved.[498] Its first reflections go back to the 1970 s Stockholm Declaration, referring in Principle 1 to "an environment of quality that permits a life of dignity and well-being" and the "responsibility to protect and improve the environment for present and future generations". Until now, it has only been expressly incorporated in regional human rights law, i.a. in the African Charter on Human and Peoples' Rights[499] or the Arab Charter on Human Rights[500]. With due regard to the recognition of the environmental crisis and its consequences for humanity *after* the adoption of the main UN human rights treaties, it does not explicitly form part of the

---

[495] Shelton (2011), 265.

[496] UN General Assembly, "Report of the Special Rapporteur on the Issue of Human Rights Obligations Relating to the Enjoyment of a Safe, Clean, Healthy and Sustainable Environment," A/73/188 § (2018), para. 12.

[497] Human Rights Council, "Report of the Special Rapporteur on the Issue of Human Rights Obligations Relating to the Enjoyment of a Safe, Clean, Healthy and Sustainable Environment," A/HRC/34/49 § (2017), para. 8; Francioni (2010), 44.

[498] Kotzé (2021), 89.

[499] Art. 24 of the African Charter on Human and Peoples' Rights (adopted on 27 June 1981, entered into force on 21 October 1986) UN Treaty Series 1520, 217.

[500] Art. 38 of the Arab Charter on Human Rights (adopted on 22 May 2004, entered into force on 15 March 2008) reprinted in 12 Int'l Hum. Rts. Rep. 893 (2005).

universal human rights regime.[501] Nonetheless, it is reflected in many environmental treaties and constitutions by now.[502] Hence, "at least 155 states already are legally obligated, through treaties, constitutions, and legislation, to respect, protect, and fulfil the right to a healthy environment"[503]. Alternative formulations to "healthy" are i.a. "clean", "favourable", "ecologically balanced" or "sustainable".[504] For reasons of simplification it will be only referred to it as the right to a healthy environment, without evaluating the other circumscriptions.

Furthermore, human rights bodies have contributed to the understanding and definition of a right to a healthy environment.[505] This development culminated in the UN General Assembly Resolution recognizing the right to a clean, healthy and sustainable environment as a human right in 2022.[506] Naturally, the recognition in such a resolution does not substitute the adoption of an international treaty in terms of legal bindingness. Its realization and enforcement would clearly benefit from a uniform implementation in a global agreement. However, this resolution supports the general and nearly universal acceptance of this right and its development towards customary law. Pointing to the regional human rights treaties and the prominence of this matter in legal discussions, *Peters* accurately describes that the question "is not whether the right should be acknowledged, but how"[507]. This can be best answered by taking a look at the regional level, particularly regional human rights courts' decisions, which have made the principal contribution to its actual recognition.[508]

2.2.2.6.2 Scope and Content of the Right to a Healthy Environment

Most far-reaching concretizations of the right to a healthy environment are made by the African Commission concerning the Ogoni Case[509]. The Commission

---

[501] Boyd (2019), 31.

[502] Boyd (2019), 31.

[503] Boyd (2019), 33.

[504] Boyd (2019), 32.

[505] UN General Assembly, Report of the Special Rapporteur on the issue of human rights obligations relating to the enjoyment of a safe, clean, healthy and sustainable environment, para. 13.

[506] UN General Assembly, "The Human Right to a Clean, Healthy, and Sustainable Environment," A/76/L.75 § (2022), 3.

[507] Peters (2021), para. 3.

[508] Boyd (2019), 31.

[509] African Commission on Human and Peoples' Rights, Communication 155/96: Social and Economic Rights Action Center (SERAC) and Center for Economic and Social Rights (CESR)/Nigeria, Ogoni Case, No. 155/96 (2001).

derives specific obligations from this right, namely "to take reasonable and other measures to prevent pollution and ecological degradation, to promote conservation, and to secure an ecologically sustainable development and use of natural resources"[510]. It thereby concretizes different aspects of environmental protection like preventing pollution and sustainable development, specifying different fields of necessary action. This goes together with the required responsibility "for protecting and conserving their environment and natural resources and for using them in a sustainable manner with the aim to satisfy human needs"[511] in the African Convention on the Conservation of Nature and Natural Resources. Referring to the right to a satisfactory environment in the African Charter on Human's and People's Rights, it supports the inclusion of resource conservation through this right and its connection to human needs.[512] Moreover, the Inter-American System is said to involve the preservation of natural ecosystems for present and future generations as well.[513] The Inter-American Court's Advisory Opinion in 2017[514], and later decisions such as the Case of the Indigenous Communities of the Lhaka Honhat (Our Land) Association v. Argentina[515] describe the right to a healthy environment as protecting the components of the environment like forests and rivers due to its benefits for humanity but also for its own sake. The focus on preservation is seconded by *Sands*, pointing to an enforceable obligation for states to take action in order to protect and preserve the environment.[516]

In turn, the European region is more reluctant in recognizing a right to a healthy environment: In fact, the Parliamentary Assembly of the Council of Europe recognized a human right to a healthy, viable and decent environment in 2003.[517] In 2009 an additional protocol to the ECHR recognizing such a right

---

[510] African Commission on Human and Peoples' Rights, *Ogoni Case* para. 52.

[511] Preamble of the African Convention on the Conservation of Nature and Natural Resources (adopted on 11 July 2003, entered into force on 23 July 2016) available at https://au.int/sites/default/files/treaties/41550-treaty-Charter_ConservationNature_NaturalResources.pdf accessed 26 March 2024.

[512] Chenwi (2018), 63, 64.

[513] Leib (2011), 76.

[514] Advisory Opinion OC-23/17, No. OC-23/17 (Inter-American Court of Human Rights November 15, 2017).

[515] Case of the Indigenous Communities of the Lhaka Honhat (Our Land) Association v. Argentina, Jugment (Inter-American Court of Human Rights February 6, 2020).

[516] Sands et al. (2012), 781.

[517] Council of Europe, Parliamentary Assembly, "Recommendation 1614 (2003), Environment and Human Rights," 1614 § (2003), para. 9.2.

was even recommended—results without any effect.[518] The most recent try of establishing a "legal framework—domestically and at European level—to anchor the right to a safe, clean, healthy and sustainable environment, based on the UN guidance on this matter"[519] in 2021 still did not lead to an explicit incorporation in the ECHR. Anyhow, the European Court of Human Rights itself states that despite of its lacking incorporation in the ECHR it "has been called upon to develop its case-law in environmental matters on account of the fact that the exercise of certain Convention rights may be undermined by the existence of harm to the environment and exposure to environmental risks"[520]. Therefore, even on the European level environmental matters have played an important role in the decisions concerning human rights for a long time.

The question remains, in how far these regional perspectives are able to influence the content and scope of the right to a healthy environment beyond their jurisdiction. It needs to be noted that the communication of a regional commission like that of the African Commission is not legally binding.[521] However, this assessment of a commission has a strong indicative effect for the perception of this right: Firstly, because of the fact that the African Charter was the first multilateral treaty involving the right to a healthy environment and thereby laid the foundation of the right's development. Secondly, the progressive implementation of this right in the African human rights system inspired its now advancing acceptance. Hence, the commission's reasoning can also have signal effect regarding its concretization.

At the UN level, the Human Rights Council explicitly refers to the overexploitation of the natural ecosystem as thwarting the enjoyment of human rights in one of its reports relating to the human right to a healthy environment.[522] Similarly to the African Commission's communication, it thereby directly links this right to the conservation of the ecosystem including natural resources. These

[518] European Council, "Recomendation 1885 (2009), Drafting an Additional Protocol to the European Convention on Human Rights Concerning the Right to a Healthy Environment," 1885 § (2009), para. 10.1.

[519] Council of Europe, Parliamentary Assembly, "Resolution 2396 (2021), Anchoring the Right to a Healthy Environment: Need for Enhanced Action by the Council of Europe," 2396 § (2021), para. 14.1.

[520] European Court of Human Rights, Press Unit, "Factsheet—Environment and the European Convention on Human Rights," October 2022, 1.

[521] Beyerlin (2005), 531.

[522] Human Rights Council, Report of the Special Rapporteur on the issue of human rights obligations relating to the enjoyment of a safe, clean, healthy and sustainable environment, 2017, para. 8.

examples show that on a substantive level, the different institutions are united with respect to the necessity of conserving the environment and its resources in order to fulfil the right to a healthy environment. The sustainable use of resources thus forms an integral component of this right.

In consequence, the next question deals with the character of an obligation addressing resources. The African Commission refers to an "appropriate legislation and effective enforcement"[523] which also protects from damages caused by private stakeholders. The UN General Assembly demands to adopt standards and an effective enforcement and monitoring of private parties as well.[524] The required positive action, therefore, incorporates to strengthen and amend environmental and other laws towards a focus on environmental protection.[525] In summary, the right to a healthy environment, which has not gained the status of customary law yet, but is strongly anchored in the regional human rights systems and recognized by the UN General Assembly, demands for positive state action with respect to protect and preserve the environment including its components such as natural resources. The duty to legislate respective rules, however, remains unspecific regarding how exactly the ecosystem and its resources shall be safeguarded. In order to specify such an obligation, it is necessary to apply an overarching interpretive approach, making use of the previous findings in international environmental law. With help of the environmental principles and concepts analyzed before, it will be determined in how far human rights can oblige states to safeguard resources and if a certain way is prescribed. Whether this combined interpretation is possible and if it leads to further insights on an obligation which addresses the states' economic systems, will be set out in the next part.

2.3 Human Rights and International Environmental Law

Can human rights together with the aforementioned environmental principles and concepts lead to an obligation to safeguard natural resources or even to apply a circular economy? To answer this question, it must firstly be determined if

[523] African Commission on Human and Peoples' Rights, *Ogoni Case* para. 57.

[524] UN General Assembly, Report of the Special Rapporteur on the issue of human rights obligations relating to the enjoyment of a safe, clean, healthy and sustainable environment, para. 17.

[525] Boyd (2018), 26.

environmental principles and concepts play a role in the interpretation of human rights.

In order to clarify the general possibility of analyzing human rights and environmental principles and concepts together, the human rights analyzed before will be considered together. As proven above, the right to life, the right to adequate housing, the right to water and particularly the right to a healthy environment depend on the availability of resources and thus demand to safeguard the ecosystem and natural resources. Their interdependence with the environment and its resources roots in their focus on basic human needs,[526] which are closely connected to a functioning ecosystem and a sufficient supply of resources.[527] Sharing the same core, they must be considered together rather than regarding every right separately. These rights are not only connected to natural resources, but are also linked to each other: As the right to life builds the foundation of all other rights, it informs other rights and can be informed by them as well.[528] The right to a healthy environment, itself derived from the right to life and health,[529] also forms a prerequisite for other rights, since the enjoyment of human rights cannot be guaranteed in a destroyed environment.[530] Therefore, environmental protection provides a functioning ecosystem, building the basis for the fulfillment of human rights.[531] The separate analysis of these rights before was helpful to determine their concrete content regarding the use of resources. However, in order to reveal a specific obligation, these rights must be seen as a unit, reinforcing each other. These different but interrelated implications on resource use must be discussed together. Besides that, a degrading environment and depleting resources have an impact on more than just one right.[532] Hence, a comprehensive consideration is regarded appropriate.

[526] Human Rights Council, Report of the Special Rapporteur on the issue of human rights obligations relating to the enjoyment of a safe, clean, healthy and sustainable environment, 2017, para. 6.

[527] Office of the High Commissioner of Human Rights and UN Environment Programme, "Human Rights and the Environment—Rio + 20: Joint Report OCHR and UNEP," 20.

[528] Human Rights Committee, General Comment No. 36: Article 6 of the International Covenant on Civil and Political Rights, the Right to Life, para. 2.

[529] Leib (2011), 74.

[530] Shelton (2011), 265.

[531] Office of the High Commissioner of Human Rights and UN Environment Programme, "Human Rights and the Environment—Rio + 20: Joint Report OCHR and UNEP," 20.

[532] Grant (2015), 159.

2.3.1 Legitimacy of their Combined Interpretation

The central methodological question relates to the discussion whether environmental law principles and concepts play a role in the interpretation of human rights. First of all, the multiple connections and interdependencies between both human rights and international environmental law argue in favor of their joint interpretation. *Schabas and Nowak* refer to the close relationship between the right to life and environmental degradation, demanding that the obligations under human rights law shall also inform the obligations under international environmental law and vice-versa, paying attention to international environmental law principles and concepts.[533] In addition, *Boyle* votes for involving environmental concerns in the interpretation of human rights.[534] This strong relation between environmental law and human rights could not be proven better than by the existence of a human right to a healthy environment. The evolvement of this right marks a visible connection between both fields of law. As a direct intersection between the human rights regime and environmental concerns, it unifies issues of the environment and humanity and thereby builds a bridge between both fields of international law.

From a methodological perspective, the legitimacy of their uniform interpretation must be answered by taking a look at Art. 31 (3) (c) VCLT. This interpretation rule extends the interpretation material to any relevant rules of international law applicable in the relations between the parties. What is then to be understood by "rules of international law"? Naturally, international agreements and customary international law fall within the scope of that provision.[535] This would only encompass binding law, excluding soft law principles or concepts.[536] Regional interpretation rules and case law, however, apply a more extensive approach: In the African human rights system, Art. 60 of the African Charter of Human and People's Rights includes "provisions of various instruments adopted within the Specialised Agencies of the United Nations" into the interpretation of human rights, while Art. 61 of the Charter also encompasses "general principles of law". The reference to instruments, rather than to the narrower term of treaties, as well as the inclusion of principles show that the interpretation of human rights is not limited to binding treaty and customary law. Furthermore, the European Court of Human Rights enlarges the perception of rules under Art. 31

---

[533] Schabas and Nowak (2019), 127.

[534] Boyle (2012), 640.

[535] Fitzmaurice (2013), 749.

[536] Fitzmaurice, (2013), 765.

(3) (c) VCLT towards general principles.[537] In the Case of Golder v. The United Kingdom, it explicitly refers to "general principles of law and especially 'general principles of law recognized by civilized nations'"[538] according to Art. 38 (1) (c) of the Statute of the ICJ. Moreover, the European Court acknowledges that the ECHR does not represent the only framework for the interpretation of human rights but enlarges it by rules and principles of international law in the Case of Demir and Baykara v. Turkey.[539] In this case, it furthermore concretizes these rules and principles by also referring to evolving norms,[540] non-binding instruments,[541] and common international and domestic law standards[542]. The inclusion of evolving norms is rooted in the necessity to interpret these rights "in the light of present-day conditions"[543] due to the character of the Convention as a living instrument. Common international and domestic law standards "reflect a reality that the Court cannot disregard when it is called upon to clarify the scope of a Convention provision"[544]. Hence, both binding and non-binding instruments are considered relevant for the interpretation of human rights.[545] These regional approaches of course cannot be applied directly to the international level. Since they form a crucial part in the development of environmental human rights, their interpretive approaches, however, can be used as leading examples in the interpretation of human rights connected to the environment. *Grant* speaks of a mutual reinforcement of the regional jurisprudence leading to the general acceptance of environmental protection as a relevant component of human rights interpretation.[546]

On top of that, the regional case law, arguing in favor of involving commonly accepted standards, principles and non-binding instruments in the interpretation of human rights, is not contradicted on an international level: *Gilbert* points to the fact that human rights and international environmental law "are increasingly

---

537 Fitzmaurice (2013), 769.

538 Case of Golder v. The United Kingdom, Judgment, No. Application no. 4451/70 (European Court of Human Rights February 21, 1975).

539 Case of Demir and Baykara v. Turkey, Judgment, No. Application no. 34503/97 (European Court of Human Rights November 12, 2008).

540 Case of Demir and Baykara v. Turkey, Judgment para. 67.

541 Case of Demir and Baykara v. Turkey, Judgment para. 74.

542 Case of Demir and Baykara v. Turkey, Judgment para. 76.

543 Case of Demir and Baykara v. Turkey, Judgment para. 68.

544 Case of Demir and Baykara v. Turkey, Judgment para. 76.

545 Fitzmaurice (2013), 769.

546 Grant (2015), 176.

cross-fertilizing" and that UN institutions already acknowledged the connection between human rights and environmental protection.[547] This acceptance was recently proven by the recognition of the human right to a healthy environment by the UN General Assembly. Concerning international jurisprudence, it is Judge *Weeramantry* again, who emphasized that environmental protection represents a "vital part of contemporary human rights doctrine"[548]. Although the incorporation of environmental standards and principles in the human rights interpretation is not uncontested,[549] the jurisprudential development, particularly on a regional level, shows that the term "rules" in Art. 31 (3) (c) VCLT incorporates more than just hard law provisions.

Another aspect, the European Court of Human Rights emphasized is the "premise that no treaty exists in a legal vacuum, but instead has to be interpreted within the wider background of international law"[550]. This is rooted in constitutionalist approaches, opposing the separate consideration of different legal regimes.[551] Especially the non-reciprocal character of human rights supports the idea of constitutionalism, since the state parties obliged themselves to various duties benefitting individuals without any reciprocity.[552] The special nature of the human rights system deviates from the classic reciprocal duties between states and resembles a national constitution. Constitutionalism contradicts the separate interpretation of different fields of international law and rather promotes their uniform consideration. Acknowledging the transdisciplinary nature of environmental issues, the concept of common concern seconds the constitutionalist approach by summarizing the affection of both the environment and humanity in one concept. As a framework concept, it unifies objectives and measures regarding environmental protection and human well-being,[553] and thus builds a bridge between those fields of international law. With its overarching character addressing the international community,[554] it therefore argues in favor of interpreting both regimes together as well.

---

[547] Gilbert (2018), 148.

[548] Gabčikovo-Nagymaros Project (Hungary v Slovakia), Judgement (Separate Opinion of Vice-President Weeramantry), ICJ Rep 7 at 88.

[549] Cf. Atapattu (2002), 71.

[550] Fitzmaurice (2013), 749.

[551] Fitzmaurice (2013), 741.

[552] Fitzmaurice (2013), 742.

[553] See 2.1.3.2.

[554] Boyle, (2012), 635.

Furthermore, the principle of effectiveness is derived from the focus on the object and purpose of human rights.[555] Rendering the human rights guarantees practical and effective can be achieved best by opening their interpretation to the standards of environmental law. Thereby, both can mutually support each other and reinforce their realization. While a separate analysis would possibly leave gaps, a joint interpretation can make use of their strength by concretizing human rights with the measures and standards laid down in the aforementioned principles and concepts.

In summary, the arguments in favor of a uniform interpretation of human rights and international environmental law underscored by the existing case law prevail the possible doubts and thus provide the basis for further findings. Incorporating standards and principles in the interpretation of human rights thus means that the preventive and precautionary principle as well as the concepts of sustainable development and common concern of humankind will be interpreted together with the analyzed rights. Whether this joint interpretation leads to further insights on the potential obligation to transform the economy will be examined in the following sections.

2.3.2 Implications of their Joint Interpretation

Analyzing the human rights already examined with regard to the depletion of resources led to the result that a fulfillment of these rights depends on a sufficient supply of natural resources. The crucial point relates to the sort of obligation which can be derived therefrom. In order to determine such an obligation, the findings on the previously analyzed concepts and principles under international environmental law will be used for the interpretation of human rights.

2.3.2.1 Overexploitation and Sustainable Development

First of all, the connection between human rights and the concept of sustainable development needs to be set out to determine the relevance of the latter in

[555] See 2.2.1.3.

the interpretation. Sustainable development and human rights are closely interrelated.[556] The recognition of a right to a healthy and sustainable environment[557] alone shows their close relation. Several human rights are linked to the concept of sustainable development,[558] since the social component of this concept is said to incorporate human rights.[559] Furthermore, its inherent purpose of safeguarding ecosystems and their natural resources also impedes the violation of human rights, suffering from an overexploitation of resources and a degrading environment.[560] Achieving an effective realization of human rights is, therefore, conditioned by environmental protection.[561] Hence, moving away from treating environmental law and human rights as completely separate regimes towards acknowledging their uniform objectives will reveal their joint potential to encounter these problems. Sustainable development with its capability to modify the application of norms thus represents an appropriate tool for bringing both regimes together and providing a holistic concept for realizing their intertwining goals.

Concerning the overuse of natural resources, its sub-notion of sustainable use requires to safeguard resources for future generations but must be combined with other norms in order to provide concrete legal obligations.[562] Applied to the human rights depending on the continuing availability of resources, it enforces the states' duties to fulfil them by concretizing the aspect of resource conservation. Since this concept is able to influence on the development of treaties and human rights treaties in turn are to be interpreted to present-day conditions (see their character as a "living instrument") such a concretization through the concept of sustainable use is assumed to be legitimate. It follows that the resource-related

---

[556] The Office of the High Commissioner for Human Rights, "Human Rights, Poverty Reduction and Sustainable Development: Health, Food and Water—A Background Paper," 3.

[557] Human Rights Council, Report of the Special Rapporteur on the issue of human rights obligations relating to the enjoyment of a safe, clean, healthy and sustainable environment, 2017, para. 7.

[558] Kerri Woods, *Human Rights and Environmental Sustainability* (Cheltenham, UK; Northampton, MA: Edward Elgar, 2010), 4.

[559] Stellina Jolly, "The Vedanta (Niyamgiri) Case: Promoting Environmental Justice and Sustainable Development," in *The Cambridge Handbook of Environmental Justice and Sustainable Development*, ed. Sumudu A. Atapattu, Carmen G. Gonzalez, and Sara L. Seck, 1st ed. (Cambridge University Press, 2021), 294, https://doi.org/10.1017/9781108555791.022.

[560] Human Rights Council, Report of the Special Rapporteur on the issue of human rights obligations relating to the enjoyment of a safe, clean, healthy and sustainable environment, 2017, para. 8.

[561] Leib (2011), 114.

[562] See 2.1.1.5.

human rights incorporate an obligation to safeguard natural resources including a sustainable strategy for their management.

2.3.2.2 Intertemporal Human Rights Duties

Ensuring the sustainable use of resources benefits present and particularly future generations with due regard to a threatening scarcity.[563] The human rights of future generations, however, entail an intertemporal perspective on human rights and lead to the question if states are responsible *now* for saving resources for future generations. If building materials are not lacking now, but are predicted to be depleted, which action of states is required at the moment? The answer can be found by referring back to the findings of the preventive and precautionary principle and implementing them in the interpretation of human rights, as well as considering case law dealing with the intertemporal aspects of human rights.

Generally, human rights concentrate on the actual generations, not drafting states' obligation towards individuals that are not born yet.[564] However, the effects on present and future generations cannot always be divided strictly,[565] keeping in mind the fluent transitions between generations and the hardly predictable occurrence of environmental consequences. Especially children—already addressees of the human rights system—will face various environmental issues and the depletion of many resources. This is highlighted in the Oposa Case before the Supreme Court of the Philippines, in which children were fighting against forest destruction.[566] They referred to the right to a healthy environment and the intergenerational responsibility to preserve the environment for future generations.[567] Such an example before a national court can also be found in the recent climate change litigation, confirming the relation between human rights and climate protection: The Dutch Supreme Court decided that human rights oblige

[563] Human Rights Committee, General Comment No. 36: Article 6 of the International Covenant on Civil and Political Rights, the Right to Life, para. 62.

[564] Human Rights Council, "Report of the Special Rapporteur on the Issue of Human Rights Obligations Relating to the Enjoyment of a Safe, Clean, Healthy and Sustainable Environment," A/HRC/37/58 § (2018), para. 67.

[565] Human Rights Council, Report of the Special Rapporteur on the issue of human rights obligations relating to the enjoyment of a safe, clean, healthy and sustainable environment, 2018, para. 68.

[566] Minors Oposa v Secretary of the Department of Environmental and Natural Resources, 33 ILM 173 (1994) (Supreme Court of the Philippines 1993).

[567] Minors Oposa v Secretary of the Department of Environmental and Natural Resources, 33 ILM 173 (1994).

states to reduce their greenhouse gas emissions[568] and derived a state's duty to prevent its citizens from the adverse effects of climate change from the rights under the ECHR.[569] Additionally, the German Federal Constitutional Court in its decision about the Federal Climate Change Act holds that "Basic Law imposes an obligation to safeguard fundamental freedom over time and spread the opportunities associated with freedom proportionally across generations"[570]. It points out the aspect of the intertemporal dimension of these rights.[571] Hence, the intergenerational conflict is already represented in actual case law. Especially the issue raised about a "budget" of emissions, caused by one generation, can be transferred to the budget of natural resources. Therefore, the intertemporal debate, if state action is necessary for future problems, is already developing concerning climate change and the courts' approaches can be regarded as path-breaking regarding the role of human rights in light of future environmental degradation. *Kotzé* describes this as an "encouraging trend [...] extend[ing] the intergenerational reach of human rights and their protective reach to future [...] generations"[572]. Since sustainable development involves the *continuous* fulfillment of human needs,[573] it supports the intertemporal application of human rights, when interpreting both together.

Moreover, state action regarding the future violation of human rights becomes necessary when applying the precautionary and preventive principle. As already stated above, both principles demand for anticipatory action in order to prevent irreversible future harm. While the precautionary principle is applicable to uncertain risks and, therefore, to the unpredictable factors of resource depletion, the preventive principle applies to certain hazards and thus to the fact that several resources will be overexploited. The application of the precautionary principle and the necessity for preventive action with regard to the right to a healthy

568 Urgenda Foundation v. State of the Netherlands, Hoge Raad, December 20 2019, 19/00135, available at https://www.urgenda.nl/wp-content/uploads/ENG-Dutch-Supreme-Court-Urgenda-v-Netherlands-20-12-2019.pdf (English translation) https://uitspraken.rechtspraak.nl/inziendocument?id=ECLI:NL:HR:2019:2006 (original Dutch version) accessed 12 January 2022.

569 Urgenda Foundation v State of the Netherlands: para.5.

570 German Federal Constitutional Court, Order of 24 March 2021, 1 BvR 2656/18, 1 BvR 288/20, 1 BvR 96/20, 1 BvR 78/20, headnote 4, available at https://www.bundesverfassungsgericht.de/SharedDocs/Entscheidungen/DE/2021/03/rs20210324_1bvr265618.html (also available in English) accessed 12 January 2022.

571 German Federal Constitutional Court, Order of 24 March 2021, headnote 4.

572 Kotzé (2021), 97.

573 Mies and Gold (2021), 2.

environment is expressly seconded by UN General Assembly.[574] In the jurisprudence, the case of Lhaka Honhat v. Argentina before the Inter-American Court of Human Rights explicitly recognizes the obligation to prevent violations as a duty under the right to a healthy environment.[575] It further concretizes the obligation of prevention by the duty of implementing necessary measures ex ante.[576] Demanding for preventive action as an obligation under human rights law has thus already been applied on different levels. Accordingly, the precautionary and preventive principle concretize the intertemporal duties of human rights by requiring anticipatory action to prevent their future violations.

2.3.2.3 Concretizing the States' Obligation Regarding Resource Depletion & Interim Conclusion

What sort of an obligation thus results from the joint interpretation? Even though the character of prevention and precaution as principles impedes to derive concrete obligations therefrom, their incorporation in the interpretation of human rights leads to considering preventive action in fulfilling human rights. As the preventive principle prescribes an obligation of due diligence, a duty to take the future depletion into account and implement effective measures to encounter this issue can be derived therefrom applied to resource depletion. In terms of concrete measures, this means legislating strict rules and establishing a system of monitoring and enforcement.[577] Furthermore a due diligence obligation involves standards for detecting a violation of human rights[578]—in the case of resource depletion environmental standards regarding the exploitation of natural resources. Similarly, the sustainable use of natural resources requires such standards and environmental impact assessment.[579] With concrete standards states can adapt their behavior towards a sustainable extraction of resources and environmental impact assessments serve to avoid an overexploitation or risks for the environment. How strict those standards are and if they entail specific limits to the extraction of the respective resource depends on the extraction level and the risk

574 UN General Assembly, "Human Rights Obligations Relating to the Enjoyment of a Safe, Clean, Healthy and Sustainable Environment," A/77/284 § (2022), para. 40.

575 Case of the Indigenous Communities of the Lhaka Honhat (Our Land) Association v. Argentina, Jugment para. 207.

576 Case of the Indigenous Communities of the Lhaka Honhat (Our Land) Association v. Argentina, Jugment para. 208.

577 UN General Assembly, Human rights obligations relating to the enjoyment of a safe, clean, healthy and sustainable environment, 2022, para. 38.

578 Biermann (1996), 447.

579 Schabas and Nowak (2019), 127.

of a scarcity. Since such an obligation is mainly derived from economic, social and cultural rights, it must be kept in mind that these obligations may be realized progressively rather than immediately. Furthermore, the states' financial and institutional resources and their capability to take action must be considered in the light of Art. 2 (1) ICESCR. While the differentiated obligations of states, especially those of less developed countries will be considered more closely in the later chapter about sovereignty, it needs to be highlighted at this point that the obligation to safeguard resources and apply standards in their extraction is a global one. Although the concept of common concern of humankind rather represents a framework concept than offering concrete measures, it can structure obligations in treaties.[580] Its significance lies in its capability to subsume the different measures under a global context. The concept of common concern demands for global action and cooperation. As the Special Rapporteur on human rights obligations concerning the right to a healthy environment states, the achievement of human rights relies on the joint action of states to encounter global environmental risks for human rights.[581] Putting aside the individual duties of states at the moment, this concept elevates the obligation to safeguard resources to an international level, demanding cooperation and a joint implementation of standards in the exploitation of resources.

New standards in the resource extraction are, however, conflicting with the current economic systems, relying on an unsustainable exploitation of natural resources.[582] Can these required standards be further specified with regard to their effects on the economy? The preventive principle concretizes these standards to applying the best available technology.[583] As clarified above, a circular economic system would drastically reduce resource use and therefore can serve to safeguard resources. Whether this comprehensive concept can be subsumed under the best available technology standard, is questionable. What is more important, is that these findings only concentrate on depleting resources, rather than providing results applicable to the whole production process. Safeguarding resources

[580] Brunnée (2003), 55.

[581] UN General Assembly, Report of the Special Rapporteur on the issue of human rights obligations relating to the enjoyment of a safe, clean, healthy and sustainable environment, para. 19.

[582] Sumudu A. Atapattu, "The Paris Agreement and Human Rights: Is Sustainable Development the New Human Right," *Journal of Human Rights and the Environment*, no. 9 (March 2018): 77.

[583] UN General Assembly, Report of the Special Rapporteur on the issue of human rights obligations relating to the enjoyment of a safe, clean, healthy and sustainable environment, para. 16.

does not necessarily need to go together with a comprehensive economic transformation. Standards for a reduced resource exploitation prescribe adapting this extraction to a sustainable level but leave the way to achieve this open.

In summary, the previous findings cannot lead to an obligation to transform the economy alone. Nonetheless, the joint interpretation of human rights and the concepts and principles under international environmental law leads to an obligation to adopt binding standards to reduce the exploitation of natural resources in order to prevent their future scarcity. Whether the whole economic process must be changed can only be determined by looking at the further stages in a product's life cycle. The obligation to safeguard natural resources for future generations, however, builds the first pillar for a different approach to the use of resources.

Waste Management

3

Thinking about a transition to a circular economy, most relevant besides the use of resources is the stage after the product's usage.[1] Consequently, the next relevant step in a product's life cycle, which deserves a comprehensive analysis, is waste management.

In a chronological order of the product's life cycle, the production process would need to be thematized firstly. However, requirements for an adapted production process or product design cannot be determined without concentrating on the current end-product in the linear economy. The production process builds the bridge between resource use and waste management and thus represents the consequence of a different approach for using natural resources and handling waste. For this reason, questions about the production process and product design will complete this chapter after clarifying the topic around waste management.

Accordingly, the necessity of analyzing waste management will be set out first, followed by framing the concrete scope of this chapter. Second, the current legal waste framework will be scrutinized in light of the overall research question. Hereafter, the influence of human rights on actual waste and implications thereof will be examined in order to complete the picture of affected regimes. Potential findings will then be combined with the previous results of the chapter about resource depletion to derive implications on a circular economy therefrom.

---

[1] Schulze (2020), 180.

V. Wefringhaus, *Circular Economy and International Law*, Juridicum—Bochumer Schriften zur Friedenssicherung und zum Humanitären Völkerrecht I Bochum Studies on the International Law of Peace and Armed Conflict 70,
https://doi.org/10.1007/978-3-658-49936-5_3

3.1 Waste Framework

Waste management represents a broad field, not only in legal, but also in technical and political terms. It must therefore be set out, in how far waste management relates to the overall topic of circular economy. This will be illuminated by providing an overview of the practical consequences of current waste management in order to determine the relevance of this issue. Secondly, the current legal waste framework will be briefly set out in pursuance of potential shortcomings and development areas, which will result in narrowing down this chapter's scope towards a central research focus. This leads over to the central analysis of the waste framework in light of the research focus.

3.1.1 Consequences of Current Waste Management

Growing piles of garbage as well as their multifaceted consequences show the necessity of considering the way we actually deal with products at the end of their lifetime. Shifting the focus on the aggravating issues of current waste management will reveal the practical relevance of changing the actual conception of waste management and illuminating this field of law with regard to the concept of circular economy. Before summarizing the main consequences of current waste streams, it is indispensable to bear in mind the huge discrepancies between waste management systems in different states. May it be the full lack of an adequate waste management or problems regarding hazardous shipments from other countries, it is to notice that every state faces divergent problems concerning waste. Even reputed leading states in waste management with e.g. advanced recycling systems are confronted with major hurdles concerning the adequate treatment of waste. Since these differences will be considered in the next chapter in detail, this part will focus on the general issues in the sector of waste management. The main commonality consists in the global negative consequences of waste on the environment and humanity, as will be shown in the following: Waste, and especially hazardous waste, leads to a range of different consequences during its transportation, disposal, or its general management, including irreparable environmental harm.[2] These damages on the local environment consist in air pollution through incineration of wastes, groundwater and surface pollution through landfills, and on top of that in contamination of the oceans through illegal disposal.[3]

---

[2] Parrish (2005), 9.

[3] Wilson (2015), 27.

Resulting environmental damages are best illustrated by taking a closer look at the visible consequences of plastic and electronic waste. With its annual 8,3 billion tons, plastic waste marks one of the fastest rising waste streams.[4] Particularly in the ocean, plastic debris causes severe threats to the marine ecosystem,[5] by representing a threat for sea mammals or birds as well as by contributing to the degradation of coral reefs.[6] The second major threat by waste is rooted in its toxic substances, leaching into the environment. Besides the toxins from plastic waste, the emerging issue of electronic waste demands solutions for toxic waste streams. Electronic waste (shortly e-waste) contains hazardous components and thus contaminates areas in which it is disposed of.[7] Recognizing the amount of up to fifty million metric tons of e-waste with its harmful components such as mercury or lead, the dimension of resulting threats becomes tangible.[8] Not only the environment, but also residents near waste processing sites or landfills and workers in the waste management business suffer from these severe damages. While the danger of mercury and other toxic substances from e-waste is already known, the threat of microplastics on ecosystems or human health is not entirely explored.[9] Nonetheless, it can be stated at this point that waste in its various forms poses a significant threat to the local and global environment as well as to human health and their living conditions. The practical urgence to examine this topic from the perspective of international law is thus given. For this reason, the international framework relating to waste management is to be examined.

3.1.2 Overview of the Waste Framework

International law does not remain silent on the topic of global waste streams. Within the different conventions and principles, touching upon the issue of waste, it needs to be set out in how far statements regarding a circular economy are implemented in the current framework. In order to introduce the actual waste legislation, a short overview about the international and regional waste system

---

[4] See https://www.dw.com/en/there-are-83-billion-tons-of-plastic-in-the-world/a-39765670 accessed 26 March 2024.

[5] See for more information on plastic waste in the ocean Cortat Simonetti Goncalves and Faure (2019), 882.

[6] See https://www.encyclopedie-environnement.org/en/zoom/plastic-a-danger-to-coral-reefs/ accessed 26 March 2024.

[7] Khan (2021), 245.

[8] Bogale (2011), 236.

[9] Khan (2021), 244.

will be provided, followed by revealing its focus and potential shortcomings. A detailed interpretation of the different norms will be conducted hereafter in the main analysis. An overview of the written rules concerning waste management will show which sort of rules about managing waste are already incorporated in the international framework and in what the focus of this framework consists. It is necessary to detect actual gaps therein to disclose fields of development and shape the scope and the research question within this chapter. Starting with the basic documents of international environmental law, the Stockholm Declaration does not offer explicit prerequisites for the treatment of waste.[10] It generally touches upon waste by calling for the discharge of toxic and other substances, similar to the Rio Declaration, which demands to prevent the relocation or transfer of hazardous substances to other states in its Principle 14.[11] Without mentioning the term "waste", both declarations involve the problem of toxic substances in the environment, but refrain from directly addressing the source of this problem, which lies in the generation of waste.

Moving over to explicit agreements surrounding waste management, there is a range of treaties addressing different parts of the issue with waste. In the field of international waste management, the Basel Convention represents an internationally accepted base for the treatment of (hazardous) waste, due to its high ratification. In contrast to its title, the convention also covers the treatment of other wastes like household wastes, listed in Annex II.[12] As the title suggests, its main focus lies on the *movement* of hazardous waste. By addressing the global trade with waste and establishing a prior informed consent procedure, it does not prohibit the movement of waste, but rather regulates it.[13] This procedure serves to reinforce the transparency in international shipments of waste.[14] Concerning the disposal of waste, the 1996 Protocol to the Convention on the Prevention of Marine Pollution by Dumping of wastes and Other Matter[15] (London Protocol) as well as the International Convention for the Prevention of Pollution from Ships[16] (MARPOL) restrict the discharge of garbage into the ocean. These

[10] Sands et al. (2012), 554.

[11] Sands et al. (2012), 555.

[12] Rublack (1989), 370.

[13] Sands et al. (2012), 569.

[14] Khan (2021), 251.

[15] Convention on the Prevention of Marine Pollution by Dumping of Wastes and Other Matter 1972 (adopted on 13 November 1972, entered into force on 30 August 1975) UN Treaty Series vol. 1046, 120.

[16] International Convention for the Prevention of Pollution from Ships (adopted on 2 November 1973, entered into force on 2 October 1983) UN Treaty Series vol. 1340, 184.

specialized treaties offer concrete regulation regarding the disposal of waste. Together with the provisions of the UNCLOS about the protection of the marine environment (Part XII), they build the framework about marine pollution through the disposal of waste, which constitutes an important area due to the increased dumping of waste into the ocean.[17] Focusing on toxic substances, the Stockholm Convention on Persistent Organic Pollutants[18] (Stockholm Convention) aims for protecting humanity and the environment from persistent organic pollutants[19] and thus addresses one facet of toxic waste streams. Similarly, the Rotterdam Convention on the Prior Informed Consent Procedure for Certain Hazardous Chemicals and Pesticides in International Trade[20] (Rotterdam Convention) shares the objective of protecting the environment and human beings from the adverse affects of hazardous chemicals[21]. Waste may consist of a range of these toxic components that are addressed by these conventions. However, waste as such does not constitute their focus since they only address one aspect of waste.

These examples of current international waste legislation show that waste regulation involves three main focal points: The first area of focus lies in the disposal of waste into the ocean (London Protocol, MARPOL, UNCLOS). The second major focus is the trade with waste (Basel Convention), and the third one covers the use of toxic substances (Stockholm Convention, Rotterdam Convention). Although every aspect, currently regulated, is important for avoiding negative consequences to the (marine) environment or human health, they fail to address the source of the issue, which lies in the generation of waste itself. With respect to the annually increasing amount of waste, scholars regard the international framework surrounding waste as inconsistent and developing.[22] The main critique relates to the incident regulation of waste within a framework aiming for other goals like marine protection.[23] Waste is said to be regulated only peripherally, rather than being part of a comprehensive waste management strategy,

---

[17] NOAA, "Ocean pollution and marine debris", available at https://www.noaa.gov/education/resource-collections/ocean-coasts/ocean-pollution accessed 13 January 2022.

[18] Stockholm Convention on Persistent Organic Pollutants (adopted on 22 May 2001, entered into force on 17 May 2004) UN Treaty Series vol. 2256, 119.

[19] Art. 1 Stockholm Convention.

[20] Rotterdam Convention on the Prior Informed Consent Procedure for Certain Hazardous Chemicals in International Trade (adopted on 10 September 1998, entered into force on 24 February 2004) UN Treaty Series vol. 2244, 337.

[21] Art. 1 Rotterdam Convention.

[22] Barsalou and Picard (2018), 887.

[23] Sands et al. (2012), 554.

incorporating especially its reduction.[24] Additionally, *Sands* criticizes the lacking uniform institutional responsibility for waste and classifies the current waste framework as fragmented.[25] *Barsalou and Picard* second this by remarking that environmental protection is only relegated to a secondary role in actual waste law.[26] The growing amount of garbage affecting humanity and the environment proves them right regarding the ineffectiveness of the current regulation vis-à-vis the huge problems within the waste management systems. Since regulation about the disposal and movement of waste only covers the symptoms rather than the roots of the problem, it is not capable of enabling a long-term improvement. What does help to conquer the negative effects of waste is the sustained reduction and prevention of waste generation. Representing one of the core requirements of a circular economy,[27] only waste prevention and minimization will reduce the environmental impacts and risks for human beings effectively. These measures directly deal with the source of the problem and are thus considered the most crucial component of a circular economy. Waste prevention and minimization represent a promising approach for solving the pressing issues with waste altogether in theory. If or to what extent current international legislation incorporates the idea of waste prevention and minimization, is to be examined in order to reveal, if this theory has already been put into practice. Therefore, the current waste regulation—written agreements as well as soft law—will be analyzed regarding its statements about waste prevention and minimization.

3.1.3 Analysis of the Waste Framework

3.1.3.1 Definition of Waste

Before starting with the core analysis about the current waste framework, the term "waste" needs to be clarified. With due regard to the fragmented international waste framework and its different treatment under the respective regimes, a uniform definition of waste is lacking and—unsurprisingly—its "legal nature and juridical qualification changes across sovereign jurisdictions"[28]. Current definitions adhere to the respective treaty's subject and do not draw a comprehensive

---

[24] Barsalou and Picard (2018), 888.

[25] Sands et al. (2012), 554.

[26] Barsalou and Picard (2018), 889.

[27] See 1.4.3.

[28] Barsalou and Picard (2018), 888.

picture about the legal value of waste.[29] The Basel Convention, as the most ratified and thus accepted treaty concerning waste speaks of waste as "substances or objects which are disposed of or are intended to be disposed of or are required to be disposed of by the provisions of national law"[30]. The definition's focus, such as the whole convention's focus, lies on the disposal and therefore on one possible activity, which applies after the product's usage.[31] An alternative handling like recycling is not included, which can be explained by the scope of this convention, only covering the disposal and movement of waste. Regarding the overall research question, treating a different approach of an *economy*, the so-called economic definition may shed light on the unclear perception of waste in legal terms. It describes waste as "the disposable residue or our activities having a negative value to be externalized by the market, which in turn converts it into a positive value"[32]. Highlighting its economic value, this definition thereby moves closer to the understanding of waste under a circular economy, which does not speak about a useless object to be disposed of, but rather about a valuable basis for secondary resources.[33] Besides its varying definitions, also the general perception of waste has evolved in the recent period. A product after its end of usage is not considered as an object to be thrown away anymore. Valuable components (especially in electronic products) and its different recycling options have transformed it into a "global commodity"[34], which already arrived in the business world.[35] Further developed in a circular economy, the term "waste" in its common sense will be outdated, since the traditional disposal will only play a subordinate role. Nonetheless, this terminology is still established in international documents and treaties and this thesis must, therefore, deal with this term and its current meaning.

Wiprächtiger is striking the right balance between the traditional understanding and underscoring its various utilization possibilities by defining waste as a "moveable object thrown in a waste bin or transferred to a waste collector by a third party and subsequently recycled, incinerated, or landfilled"[36]. One might

[29] Barsalou and Picard (2018), 889.

[30] Art. 2 (1) Basel Convention.

[31] Sands et al. (2012), 557.

[32] Barsalou and Picard (2018), 890.

[33] See https://ellenmacarthurfoundation.org/topics/circular-economy-introduction/overview accessed 26 March 2024.

[34] Barsalou and Picard (2018), 888.

[35] Rayfuse (2016), 12.

[36] Wiprächtiger et al. (2021), 105742.

question, if it starts with throwing the product in a waste bin or already directly after its last usage, but generally this definition combines the necessary steps at the end of a product's life. For this reason, it can be seen as the lowest common denominator between traditional and more advanced approaches and as adequately describing the current perception of waste. If waste as the basis for secondary resources can also be traced in the current legislation, will need to be examined in the main analysis.

On the grounds of the frequent reference to "hazardous" wastes, the categorization of hazardous wastes is to be elucidated briefly. Such as in the Basel Convention, waste is categorized along its qualities (hazardous or other wastes).[37] Although the term "hazardous" is part of the Convention's title, the Basel Convention equally covers other wastes. The reason for this differentiation or particular reference to hazardous wastes lies in the more severe consequences of toxic wastes on the environment and human health. Naturally, hazardous and toxic wastes demand for a special handling, like specialized incineration or protected landfills.[38] However, non-hazardous waste, also called municipal waste, generated by households or shops, leads to air or groundwater pollution as well, when incinerated or stored on landfills.[39] For these reasons, both types of waste need to be part of this chapter, since waste in all its forms leads to negative consequences. With this working definition and clarifications around the term as well as different categorizations of waste, its legal treatment will be analyzed in detail in the following.

3.1.3.2 Framework on Waste Prevention and Minimization

Whether the current framework on waste management can build a pillar for a general obligation of establishing a circular economy depends on its commitment to waste prevention and minimization. Reducing waste streams marks the core concern of circular economy and it is, therefore, to be examined to what extent the actual waste legislation incorporates the idea of preventing and minimizing waste. Firstly, international agreements will be analyzed regarding their implications on waste prevention and minimization. This will be followed by an examination of the pioneering role of regional legislation towards waste prevention. Thirdly, the principles under international environmental law will be illuminated again, in light of their capability to concretize or enhance the hard law framework.

---

37 Sands et al. (2012), 557.

38 Sands et al. (2012), 558.

39 Sands et al. (2012), 558.

3.1.3.2.1 Hard Law on Waste Prevention and Minimization

Starting again with the Basel Convention as the leading agreement concerning waste, its focus on disposal and transboundary trade of waste appears to exclude the idea of addressing the previous step of waste generation. On the contrary, this treaty contains the goals of waste prevention and minimization in its preamble as well as in the main text. In its preamble, the Basel Convention states that "the most effective way of protecting human health and the environment from the dangers posed by such wastes is the reduction of their generation to a minimum"[40] and thereby explicitly recognizes the importance of reducing waste to achieve its overall objective.[41] Connecting the protection of human health and the environment with the need for minimizing waste, highlights that despite its focus on disposal, it acknowledges the importance of addressing the roots of the waste problem. This commitment of minimizing the generation of waste is also reflected in the obligations set out in Art. 4 (2) (a), explicitly demanding for reducing the generation of waste to a minimum, and Art. 10 (2) (c),[42] which calls for cooperation "in the development and implementation of new environmentally sound low-waste technologies and the improvement of existing technologies with a view to eliminating, as far as practicable, the generation of hazardous wastes and other wastes". *Parrish*, therefore, rightly assumes that this convention aims for a minimization of hazardous waste generation.[43] Although the Basel Convention has implemented this aim of waste prevention and minimization, it fails to provide concrete measures how states could achieve this goal.[44] Rather than obliging states to implement concrete targets for waste reduction, including detailed measures to reach these targets, the convention limits itself to a periodic review of possibilities for reducing waste.[45] *Rublack* explains this hesitance by clarifying that the reduction of waste generation falls within national jurisdictions and a detailed regulation would have exceeded the mandate for the Basel Convention.[46] According to the core issue of this convention, concrete regulation only relates to the prevention of waste *movement*. Certainly, the reduction of waste shipments represents a facet of preventive action, since it protects the environment and local

[40] Preamble of the Basel Convention.

[41] Rayfuse (2016), 23.

[42] Rayfuse (2016), 23.

[43] Parrish (2005), 10.

[44] Sands et al. (2012), 561.

[45] Rublack (1989), 380.

[46] Rublack (1989), 379.

residents of receiving countries.[47] Therefore, it establishes the prior informed consent procedure and promotes the disposal of waste at its source.[48] These measures will surely positively contribute to the environmentally sound management of waste.[49] Nonetheless, the reduction of waste movements is not equal to the reduction of waste generation itself. The clear focus on the transboundary movement of waste only leaves little room for concrete obligations towards waste prevention and minimization. However, with its overall goal regarding the reduction of waste generation it provides a first step in this direction.

The idea of prevention is also reflected in the UNCLOS, especially in its Art. 192 demanding for preventing the pollution of the marine environment. Although incorporating a detailed regulation about preserving the marine environment in Part XII, its focus lies primarily on shipping and maritime jurisdiction.[50] The search for rules concerning the prevention of waste *generation* remains unsuccessful. Similarly, the CBD does not offer further rules about waste prevention, although waste threatens biodiversity as the main object of protection under this convention.[51] This summary of hard law agreements shows that waste is already recognized as a threat for the environment and human health in international treaties and first attempts to address the source of the problem have been made by now. However, their focus on the symptoms rather than on the roots of these different issues dominates the current international hard law legislation.

3.1.3.2.2 Regional Regulation as a Leading Example?

Again, the development at the regional level concerning waste will be considered in order to trace the actual implementation of waste prevention and minimization and to draw conclusions as to what extent potential findings can be transferred to the international level. Although the Bamako Convention[52] as well as the Waigani Convention[53] incorporate the idea of minimizing the generation of hazardous

---

[47] Khan (2021), 251.

[48] Parrish (2005), 10; Khan (2021), 251.

[49] Sands et al. (2012), 561.

[50] Cortat Simonetti Goncalves and Faure (2019), 893.

[51] Cortat Simonetti Goncalves and Faure (2019), 901.

[52] Bamako Convention on the Ban of the Import into Africa and the Control of Transboundary Movement and Management of Hazardous Wastes within Africa (adopted on 30 January 1991, entered into force on 22 April 1998) UN Treaty Series vol. 2101, 177.

[53] Convention to Ban the Importation of Hazardous and Radioactive Wastes into Forum Island Countries and to Control the Transboundary Movement and Management of Hazardous Waste within the South Pacific Region (Waigani Convention) (adopted on 16 September 1995, entered into force on 21 October 2001) UN Treaty Series vol. 2161, 91.

waste, a special focus will lie on the EU legislation due to its further advances concerning waste prevention.

Starting with the Waigani Convention, which constitutes the regional implementation of the international waste regime for the Pacific Islands Forum countries,[54] its Art. 4 (4) aims for the minimization of waste, leaving open how to achieve this goal. Moving one step further, the Bamako Convention concretizes the duty of encouraging waste generators to minimize their waste production in its preamble,[55] by explicitly dedicating itself to the application of the precautionary principle.[56] Within the application of the precautionary principle,[57] states "shall promote clean production methods applicable to entire product life cycles, including raw material selection [...] product conceptualization, design, manufacture and assemblage [...] reintroduction of the product into industrial systems or nature when it no longer serves a useful function"[58]. Thereby, the Bamako Convention directly links the precautionary principle to the goal of waste prevention and provides more concrete measures of how to achieve this, addressing the whole product life cycle. It culminates in the imposition of an unlimited liability on hazardous waste generators.[59] Despite these far-reaching measures, their enforcement fails due to lacking data about the amount and location of waste as well as missing organizational structure because of gaps in the financing.[60]

The most developed framework concerning waste prevention and minimization is conducted at the EU level: Already in 1975, the regulation on waste in Directive 75/442/EEC subscribed to the goal of protecting the environment and human health,[61] followed by a continuous advancement of the measures concerning waste management.[62] A clear priority for waste prevention was then implemented in the Waste Framework Directive (2008/98/EC) in 2008.[63] This directive created a hierarchy of different measures regarding the treatment of waste in its Art. 4 (1): "(a) prevention; (b) preparing for re-use; (c) recycling;

[54] See https://www.sprep.org/convention-secretariat/waigani-convention accessed 26 March 2024.

[55] Preamble of the Bamako Convention.

[56] Bogale (2011), 247.

[57] Art. 4 (3) (f) Bamako Convention.

[58] Art. 4 (3) (g) Bamako Convention.

[59] Art. 4 (3) (b) Bamako Convention.

[60] Bogale (2011), 248.

[61] Bartl (2014), 3.

[62] Sands et al. (2012), 556.

[63] Zhang et al. (2022), 3.

(d) other recovery, e.g. energy recovery; and (e) disposal"[64]. In contrast to the highest priority on prevention, the common measure of disposal shall only be chosen as the last option.[65] This hierarchy is flanked by different measures: The most important one is that of an extended producer responsibility in Art. 8 (1), which entails the mandatory acceptance of returned products by the manufacturing enterprises. Through this responsibility of the manufacturing industries, the prevention of waste generation shall be encouraged.[66] Additionally, it encompasses the obligation to develop and adopt waste management plans as well as waste prevention programs in Art. 29 of the Directive. With the more recent Directives 30/5/2018 and 2018/852, the EU picked up on the goal of waste prevention and focused on reducing packaging as well as enhancing recycling and recovery of products.[67] Besides the objective of waste prevention, the EU also focuses on the issue of waste minimization and, therefore, concentrates on reducing landfilled waste through targets for recycling and restricting the waste which is accepted on a landfill.[68] Certainly, the action by the EU does not stop at this point. However, the most recent developments at the European level, including the Circular Economy Action plan will be analyzed in the following section about product design, which constitutes the connecting link between waste management and resource use.

The primary reason, why this ambitious legislation does not lead to reduced waste streams lies in inadequate compliance and control mechanisms.[69] *Wiprächtiger* adds that clear targets and indicators are still missing in this framework.[70] Furthermore, the current system including enterprises and infrastructure does not provide the necessary requirements for higher rates of reuse and recycling.[71] On top of that, there are conflicting interests of the industry, which aims for an increased production due to higher profits of new product sales.[72] For these reasons, the EU framework on waste prevention can be described as a leading

---

64 European Parliament and European Council, "Waste Framework Directive," 2008/98/EC § (2008).

65 Bartl (2014), 5.

66 Chioatto and Sospiro (2023), 254.

67 Chioatto and Sospiro (2023), 254.

68 See Art. 5 (3) Council Directive 1999/31/EC of 26 April 1999 on the Landfill of Waste (OJL 182, 16.7.1999, 1–19).

69 Gottberg et al. (2006), 40.

70 Wiprächtiger et al. (2021), 105742.

71 Bartl (2014), 14.

72 Bartl (2014), 13.

example, not in terms of bindingness and enforceability, but in establishing an explicit priority for waste prevention and minimization.

3.1.3.2.3 Soft Law on Waste Prevention and Minimization

The international waste framework is said to be based on principles of international environmental law.[73] Therefore, the analysis of this framework must include the pertinent soft law principles as well in order to reveal their implications regarding waste prevention and minimization. For determining the relevance of these principles concerning waste management, the relation between hard law regulation and soft law principles will be illuminated, followed by applying the relevant principles to the issue of waste generation.

In contrast to the international legal framework on resource depletion, there exists a range of international treaties directly addressing the issue of waste. Why is then a consideration of the soft law principles relevant? Sometimes soft law is only regarded as an intermediate step towards hard law,[74] and it is thus denied being an independent category of law. According to this view, there would be no room for soft law principles next to the hard law agreements on waste. *Abbott and Snidal*, however, argue in favor of a separate significance of these principles, which are often chosen for reasons of flexibility and lower risk in contrast to a binding agreement.[75] According to them, "soft law is sometimes designed in a way station to harder legalization, but often it is preferable on its own terms"[76], being able to establish new norms that affect political and legal discourses.[77] *Rayfuse* seconds this by highlighting their guiding character in the interpretation of legal norms and their "valuable role in integrating various legal, economic, social and political considerations into various fields of international law"[78]. She mentions treaties, customary law, and principles as independent components of the international legal system and—in terms of environmental law—as a foundation for international environmental standards.[79] Consequently, they form a separate group of international legal bases and have to be considered apart from the hard law framework concerning waste management.

---

[73] Rayfuse (2016), 11.

[74] Abbott and Snidal (2000), 422.

[75] Abbott and Snidal (2000), 435.

[76] Abbott and Snidal (2000), 423.

[77] Abbott and Snidal (2000), 456.

[78] Rayfuse (2016), 13.

[79] Rayfuse (2016), 13.

After this clarification of the equal importance of soft law principles in the framework surrounding waste, it needs to be determined which principles must be included into the analysis. *Rayfuse* describes i.a. the preventive and the precautionary principle, the concept of sustainable development and the principle of cooperation as relevant in the waste context.[80] As stated above, the focus of this chapter lies in the prevention and minimization of waste. Hence, the principles of prevention and precaution will build the main focus within the field of soft law principles. The concept of sustainable development and the duty of cooperation will form part of the next parts. Since the general content and application of these principles were already analyzed in the previous chapter, this chapter will illuminate their connections to waste prevention and minimization. On these grounds, the implications of these principles on waste management will be revealed by analyzing the respective documents which cover the application of prevention and precaution to the treatment of waste.

Main objective of both the preventive and the precautionary principle is the minimization of environmental harm and their proposed measure to achieve this consists in action in advance.[81] As already examined above, their difference lies in the degree of certainty regarding the probability of the occurring harm[82] as well as in the concreteness of their legal consequences.[83] The precautionary principle primarily involves the negligence of scientific certainty in case of threatening irreversible damage,[84] whereas the preventive principle leads to more concrete measures like the necessity to use the best available technology and specific environmental standards depending on the type of the potential harm.[85] *Sands* even derives a regulation or prohibition of harmful activities and substances from the precautionary principle.[86] Generally, its capability to guide environmental decisions and enabling precautionary action is widely accepted. The preventive principle incorporates a due diligence obligation of minimizing and preventing environmental risks and entails positive action to encounter them.[87] In the context of waste management, it needs lesser justification for determining that waste constitutes a huge environmental risk than in case of depleting resources. As

80 Rayfuse (2016), 11.

81 See 2.1.2.

82 See 2.1.2.

83 See 2.1.2.2.

84 See 2.1.2.1.

85 See 2.1.2.2.

86 Sands et al. (2012), 222.

87 See 2.1.2.2.

stated in the introductory part of this chapter, the negative impacts of waste on the ground, the air quality, the water reserves, and even the marine environment represent visible examples of the environmental damage resulting from waste. Especially its toxic components fulfil the prerequisite of certain environmental hazards under the preventive principle. Since the indirect effects of waste pollution and its impacts on the environment and human health are not entirely explored, there is also room for the application of the precautionary principle in this context. On these grounds, both principles are closely related to the effects of waste.[88] The question is thus not *if* waste can be subsumed under the preventive or precautionary principle, but rather *what* implications and consequences these principles generate concerning the treatment of waste and in how far these possible legal consequences can be translated into binding state obligations.

Rayfuse concludes from the application of the preventive and precautionary principle in the waste context the development of more concrete principles like this of waste minimization.[89] If such a principle can be derived from applying these principles on waste management and in how far waste minimization constitutes an accepted principle or sub-category must be traced in legal documents, which cover the principles of prevention and precaution in the field of waste management. In that regard, the following documents deserve a closer investigation. They serve as illustrative examples for the implementation of these principles, which make the development of these principles in the field of waste management visible and shall not be seen as a comprehensive collection of documents in that field.

First of all, a clear commitment to waste minimization can be found in the Cairo Guidelines and Principles for the Environmentally Sound Management of Hazardous Waste[90]. Within their overall goal of protecting human health and the environment from the adverse affects of waste, they give priority to that method of waste management which entails the lowest environmental impact.[91] Ultimate goal is thus reducing waste generation to a minimum.[92] This objective of waste minimization is flanked by a commitment to applying low-waste technologies as

[88] See for their application concerning plastic waste UN General Assembly, Report of the Special Rapporteur on the implications for human rights of the environmentally sound management and disposal of hazardous substances and wastes, Marcos Orellana, para. 92.

[89] Rayfuse (2016), 11.

[90] UN Environment Programme, "Cairo Guidelines and Principles for the Environmentally Sound Management of Hazardous Wastes," Decision 14/30 § (1987).

[91] Sands et al. (2012), 556.

[92] UN Environment Programme, Cairo Guidelines and Principles for the Environmentally Sound Management of Hazardous Wastes, 6.

well as employing the recycling and reuse of unavoidable wastes.[93] The Cairo Guidelines also address the common responsibility of the states for environmental protection and demand for cooperation concerning the management of waste.[94] What is particularly reformative is their approach of covering the treatment of waste from its generation to its disposal.[95] This priority on waste minimization including the need for cooperation and considering a holistic approach to waste treatment represents a strong relation between the general principle of prevention and waste legislation. These guidelines—although non-binding—constitute an early reference to the treatment of hazardous wastes and following agreements in the field of waste law, since e.g. the Basel Convention or the Bamako Convention referenced them as one of their foundations.[96] Nonetheless, this clear focus on waste minimization has not found entry into the written treaties. Does that involve a final renunciation to the approach of waste prevention and minimization? In the case of the Basel Convention, the reason why this approach is only reflected incidentally, lies in the mandate, which only covers the international movement of waste and leaves the issue of waste generation to be nationally regulated.[97] A more detailed engagement with waste prevention and minimization would have exceeded the mandate of Basel.[98] Therefore, it is to be noted that the current written treaties are not intended to negate the need for waste prevention and minimization, but were rather drafted with another focus. For this reason, the Cairo Guidelines shall be viewed as a first attempt to integrate waste minimization into the international waste framework by connecting the idea of prevention to the issue of waste. However, these guidelines alone cannot serve as a basis for the assumption that international waste law is developing towards an incorporation and application of the principle of prevention.

As a second document, the Decision V/33 by the Conference of Parties to the Basel Convention from 1999 establishes a priority for i.a. the prevention and minimization of hazardous wastes as objectives for future action.[99] This decision

---

[93] UN Environment Programme, Cairo Guidelines and Principles for the Environmentally Sound Management of Hazardous Wastes, 6.

[94] UN Environment Programme, Cairo Guidelines and Principles for the Environmentally Sound Management of Hazardous Wastes, 5.

[95] UN Environment Programme, Cairo Guidelines and Principles for the Environmentally Sound Management of Hazardous Wastes, 3.

[96] See Preamble of the Basel Convention and Preamble para. 11 of the Bamako Convention.

[97] Rublack (1989), 379.

[98] Rublack (1989), 379.

[99] Sands et al. (2012), 561.

speaks of a "principle of hazardous waste minimization"[100] and declares waste prevention and minimization as priority goals for the next decades.[101] Thereby, it lays down a pathway for a focus on these objectives within the Basel Convention and even describes them as principles.

This prediction of waste prevention and minimization as future goals condensed in a more recent document, namely the Cartagena Declaration on the Prevention, Minimization and Recovery of Hazardous Wastes and Other Wastes[102]. Adopted by the parties to the Basel Convention in 2011, the Cartagena Declaration thus provides insights on the actual implementation of the preventive principle in the field of waste management: Firstly, it incorporates the acknowledgement that the "most effective way of protecting human health and the environment from the dangers posed by such wastes is the reduction of their generation to a minimum in terms of quantity and/or hazard potential"[103]. Secondly, the declaration underscores that Art. 4 (2) (a) Basel Convention can be best met by preventing and minimizing the *generation* of waste,[104] and therefore puts the focus on the production process rather than on the later movement of waste. This is supported by its acknowledgement, that environmental impacts are not only related to hazardous waste shipments but directly to its generation.[105] Moreover, the waste hierarchy with the priority on waste prevention and minimization, which is similarly addressed in the EU framework,[106] was explicitly mentioned in this declaration.[107] Hence, the idea of a hierarchy in waste management is also reflected at the international level. Furthermore, the Cartagena

---

[100] UN Environment Programme, "Conference of the Parties to the Basel Convention on the Control of Transboundary Movements of Hazardous Wastes and Their Disposal," UNEP/CHW.5/29 § (1999), para. 76.

[101] UN Environment Programme, Conference of the Parties to the Basel Convention on the Control of Transboundary Movements of Hazardous Wastes and their Disposal, para. 13.

[102] Conference of the Parties to the Basel Convention, "Cartagena Declaration on the Prevention, Minimization and Recovery of Hazardous Wastes and Other Wastes" (2011).

[103] Conference of the Parties to the Basel Convention, Cartagena Declaration on the Prevention, Minimization and Recovery of Hazardous Wastes and Other Wastes, 1.

[104] Conference of the Parties to the Basel Convention, Cartagena Declaration on the Prevention, Minimization and Recovery of Hazardous Wastes and Other Wastes, 1.

[105] Conference of the Parties to the Basel Convention, Cartagena Declaration on the Prevention, Minimization and Recovery of Hazardous Wastes and Other Wastes, 2 para. 2.

[106] See 2.1.3.2.

[107] Conference of the Parties to the Basel Convention, Cartagena Declaration on the Prevention, Minimization and Recovery of Hazardous Wastes and Other Wastes, 2.

Declaration offers more concrete claims concerning waste prevention and minimization such as an "active promotion and implementation of more efficient strategies to achieve prevention and minimization of the generation of hazardous waste"[108] as well as reports of progress in waste reduction at the national level.[109] The development towards a broader recognition of waste prevention and minimization as a vital part of the Basel Convention is highlighted by the reaffirmation that the "Basel Convention is the primary global legal instrument for guiding the environmentally sound management of hazardous and other wastes and their disposal, including efforts to prevent and minimize their generation"[110]. Lastly, the Cartagena Declaration stretches the arc between waste prevention and minimization and the concept of sustainable development by characterizing them as pillars of this concept and emphasizing the Basel Convention's contribution to the goals of sustainable development.[111] The role of sustainable development, although already linked to waste prevention and minimization at this point, will be illuminated in a following section. Hence, the Cartagena Declaration shows the embedment of waste minimization and prevention in the Basel Convention—not only as a supporting role, but with its growing importance for waste management in general. As a Conference of the Parties Decision, it remains a non-binding document. However, it describes the development of Basel in terms of application and improvement. The fact that a declaration with a focus on waste prevention and minimization has evolved within the Basel framework, which—on top of that—describes them as principles, suggests that their importance for waste management is now widely accepted.

This recognition of waste prevention and minimization as priority goals within the waste framework has been carried forward until a relatively young document under Basel, which is the Draft Guidance to Assist Parties in Developing Efficient Strategies for Achieving the Prevention and Minimization of Hazardous and Other Wastes and their Disposal[112]. As its name suggests, it offers guidelines on how

[108] Conference of the Parties to the Basel Convention, Cartagena Declaration on the Prevention, Minimization and Recovery of Hazardous Wastes and Other Wastes, 2 para. 1.

[109] Conference of the Parties to the Basel Convention, Cartagena Declaration on the Prevention, Minimization and Recovery of Hazardous Wastes and Other Wastes, 2 para. 4.

[110] Conference of the Parties to the Basel Convention, Cartagena Declaration on the Prevention, Minimization and Recovery of Hazardous Wastes and Other Wastes, 2 para. 3.

[111] Conference of the Parties to the Basel Convention, Cartagena Declaration on the Prevention, Minimization and Recovery of Hazardous Wastes and Other Wastes, 3 para. 13.

[112] UN Environment Programme, "Draft Guidance to Assist Parties in Developing Efficient Strategies for Achieving the Prevention and Minimization of the Generation of Hazardous and Other Wastes and Their Disposal," UNEP/CHW.13/INF/11 § (2017).

protection of individual human beings requires its provisions to be interpreted and applied in such a way as to make its safeguards practical and effective"[137]. Secondly, it supports the recognition of a positive obligation under the right to life to protect the life of human beings,[138] also "in the case of industrial activities, which by their very nature are dangerous, such as the operation of waste-collection sites"[139], and thereby directly derives a duty of protection in the field of waste management.[140] Ultimately, the judgment highlights the protection in advance, mentioning preventive measures in the context of the right to life.[141] Bearing in mind the regional character of this case, it nonetheless shows that prevention constitutes a necessary measure for states in order to fulfill their positive obligations under the right to life effectively. Since there does not exist any contradicting case law at the international level, it can serve as a guidance in interpreting the right to life in the context of waste treatment. The judgment acknowledges that waste collection sites can create life-threatening situations. In those situations, the right to life imposes positive obligations for states to protect the affected persons and establish preventive measures. What both the regional and the international legislation and their interpretation share is the lacking incorporation of more concrete consequences of such a threat to the right to life. They do not entail a direct statement regarding the prevention of waste *generation*, but only concerning generally preventing those hazards. Waste prevention and minimization could be subsumed under those preventive measures, which are demanded, but are not embedded in the statements by the UN institutions or regional case law. What can be derived from the right to life, however, is its inherent positive duty to protect human beings from life-threatening situations in advance and the applicability of the right to life in the context of waste management.

3.2.2.2 Right to Health

Next, the right to the highest attainable standard of health under Art. 12 ICESCR is to be analyzed regarding its implications on waste management. The fact that even the right to life is affected by the consequences of waste, facilitates the justification of the applicability of the right to health in this context. Similarly, the

[137] Case of Öneryildiz v. Turkey, Judgment para. 69.

[138] Case of Öneryildiz v. Turkey, Judgment para. 89.

[139] Case of Öneryildiz v. Turkey, Judgment para. 71.

[140] Case of Öneryildiz v. Turkey, Judgment para. 65.

[141] Case of Öneryildiz v. Turkey, Judgment para. 90.

contamination of soil and water such as the pollution of air through waste management practices affect human health and invoke the application of the right to health. People in the vicinity of waste treatment sites or landfills get in touch with hazardous substances from waste or the pollution caused by its processing.[142]

Again, the crucial question deals with the legal obligations of states regarding these health issues. According to the General Comment, states need to protect the health of affected persons by refraining "from unlawfully polluting air, water and soil, e.g. through industrial waste from State-owned facilities"[143] as well as by preventing third parties like companies in the waste management sector from causing the same.[144] The Human Rights Council complements this by specifying the protection from contamination and pollution to preventing and reducing "the population's exposure to hazardous substances and wastes that have a direct or indirect impact on human health"[145], thereby explicitly involving waste. The Committee on Economic, Social and Cultural Rights seconds this by subsuming preventive measures including the prevention of exposure to hazardous substances under Art. 12 (2) (b) ICESCR,[146] which addresses the environmental and industrial hygiene and thus directly refers to the industrial processes surrounding waste management. This shall be conducted by the adoption of appropriate legislative, administrative, and other measures.[147] Although states are not obliged to "provide protection against every possible cause of human ill health"[148], the required

---

[142] UN General Assembly, Report of the Special Rapporteur on the implications for human rights of the environmentally sound management and disposal of hazardous substances and wastes, Marcos Orellana, para. 2.

[143] Committee on Economic, Social and Cultural Rights, General Comment No. 14: The Right to the Highest Attainable Standard of Health, para. 34.

[144] Committee on Economic, Social and Cultural Rights, General Comment No. 14: The Right to the Highest Attainable Standard of Health, para. 33.

[145] Human Rights Council, Report of the Special Rapporteur on the implications for human rights of the environmentally sound management and disposal of hazardous substances and wastes, 2017, para. 9.

[146] Committee on Economic, Social and Cultural Rights, General Comment No. 14: The Right to the Highest Attainable Standard of Health, para. 15.

[147] Committee on Economic, Social and Cultural Rights, General Comment No. 14: The Right to the Highest Attainable Standard of Health, para. 33.

[148] Committee on Economic, Social and Cultural Rights, General Comment No. 14: The Right to the Highest Attainable Standard of Health, para. 9.

measures must be effective.[149] In that sense, the prevention of pollution and contamination by (waste) industries[150] plays a decisive role, since preventing hazards constitutes the most effective way of protection. The link between the consequences of waste on the right to health and preventive measures is embedded in the Case of San Mateo de Huanchor v. Peru, in which precautionary measures towards the pollution by a toxic waste sludge were adopted in order to protect the affected residents.[151] However, those statements in documents and case law only refer to the prevention of hazards in general, not explicitly involving the prevention or minimization of waste itself. The focus lies on the outcomes of waste disposal and does not include earlier steps like waste generation. From these documents concerning the right to health, a further developing duty to prevent waste generation cannot be derived alone. The fact that the right to health is closely linked to the other rights under Art. 11 ICESCR,[152] especially the right to food, is shown by its core obligation of ensuring access to adequate and safe food.[153] More detailed findings are thus to be revealed by taking a closer look at the following rights under Art. 11 ICESCR.

3.2.2.3 Right to Food

The right to adequate food, laid down in Art. 11 (1) ICESCR, involves the absence from dangerous substances,[154] to ensure the core content of guaranteeing safe and sufficient food.[155] Mismanagement of waste can directly and indirectly impact on food in various ways: Contamination of the soil leads to toxins which may accumulate in plants that are destined for food.[156] Microplastics or toxic

---

[149] Human Rights Council, Report of the Special Rapporteur on the implications for human rights of the environmentally sound management and disposal of hazardous substances and wastes, 2017, para. 9.

[150] Committee on Economic, Social and Cultural Rights, General Comment No. 14: The Right to the Highest Attainable Standard of Health, para. 51.

[151] Inter-American Commission on Human Rights, "Community of San Mateo de Huanchor and Its Members v. Peru," October 15, 2004, para. 12.

[152] Committee on Economic, Social and Cultural Rights, General Comment No. 14: The Right to the Highest Attainable Standard of Health, para. 3.

[153] Committee on Economic, Social and Cultural Rights, General Comment No. 14: The Right to the Highest Attainable Standard of Health, para. 43 (b).

[154] Committee on Economic, Social and Cultural Rights, General Comment No. 12: The Right to Adequate Food, para. 10.

[155] Committee on Economic, Social and Cultural Rights, General Comment No. 12: The Right to Adequate Food, para. 8.

[156] UN General Assembly, "Human Rights Obligations Relating to the Enjoyment of a Safe, Clean, Healthy and Sustainable Environment," A/76/179 § (2021), para. 26.

substances in the ocean or rivers do not only harm the marine wildlife including fish, but get back into the food chain through the consumption of fish.[157] Waste thus finds its way through a range of different possibilities to contaminate food, which affects the right to food such as the right to health again. The adverse affects of waste are thus covered by the right to food as well. Since the states' duty consists in providing adequate and safe food,[158] it also entails to protect the population from this contamination.[159] Prevention is, hence, embedded as a necessary measure in the right to food.

3.2.2.4 Right to Housing

The connections between the right to housing and the negative consequences of waste are less obvious at first sight: Their relation is strongly determined by its reference to the right to health, since the requirement of habitability under the right to housing involves i.a. the protection against threats to health.[160] Further defined by the General Comment, "housing should not be built on polluted sites nor in immediate proximity to pollution sources that threaten the right to health of the inhabitants"[161]. As pollution sources are not concretized further, this broad term can also be applied to the pollution caused by waste treatment sites such as landfills or waste processing industries. But does that involve any more far-reaching aspects than those under the right to health? This can be answered by taking a look at the regional level, which provides case law regarding a similar situation. In European human rights law, not the right to housing, but the right to respect for his private and family life, his home and his correspondence under Art. 8 ECHR plays an important role in this context. Although a similar formulation can be found at the international level in Art. 17 (1) ICCPR, which prohibits the interference with his privacy, family, home or correspondence, the regional level offers more concrete interpretive guidance led by a range of judgments, which rely upon that right when considering the consequences of waste dumps. Art. 8 ECHR incorporates references to both the right to housing and

[157] UN General Assembly, Human rights obligations relating to the enjoyment of a safe, clean, healthy and sustainable environment, 2021, para. 26.

[158] Committee on Economic, Social and Cultural Rights, General Comment No. 12: The Right to Adequate Food, para. 15.

[159] Committee on Economic, Social and Cultural Rights, General Comment No. 12: The Right to Adequate Food, para. 10.

[160] Committee on Economic, Social and Cultural Rights, General Comment No. 4: The Right to Adequate Housing, para. 8 (d).

[161] Committee on Economic, Social and Cultural Rights, General Comment No. 4: The Right to Adequate Housing, para. 8 (f).

Art. 17 (1) ICCPR and is, therefore, to be included into this section. The right to private and family life, home and correspondence under Art. 8 ECHR entails a duty of protection such as positive obligations to ensure that private actors do not interfere with the guarantees set out by this right.[162] Additionally, the state's duty refers to the decision-making process regarding measures of interference, which must be fair and involve the inhabitants' interests.[163] Applied to the concrete Case of López Ostra v. Spain[164], this balance between the interests of the residents affected by a waste plant and the community's economic interest for this plant must be fair.[165] The judgment explicitly refers to the negative effects of air pollution on the local population by a waste treatment plant,[166] and thereby highlights the significance of pollution caused by waste for human rights. Moreover, the court also clarifies that "severe environmental pollution may affect individuals' well-being and prevent them from enjoying their homes in such a way as to affect their private and family life adversely, without, however, seriously endangering their health"[167]. Hence, the violation of human rights by a nearby waste treatment plant does not necessarily require a negative impact on human health. The right to private and family life, home and correspondence thus applies a lesser benchmark for an affection by pollution or contamination caused by waste. With its recognition of a violation of Art. 8 ECHR by a waste treatment plant, this judgment marks an important cornerstone in acknowledging the severe consequences of waste on human beings and highlights the state's duty of not only taking positive measures to prevent such an interference, but also of taking the individual's interests into consideration when deciding upon the establishment of such industries. Although not involving a waste processing site, but a chemical

---

[162] European Court of Human Rights, "Guide on Article 8 of the European Convention on Human Rights" (2022), para. 5; see the similar formulation ini Human Rights Committee, "CCPR General Comment No. 16: Article 17 (Right to Privace) The Right to Respect of Privacy, Family, Home and Correspondence, and Protection of Honour and Reputation" (1988), para. 1.

[163] European Court of Human Rights, Guide on Article 8 of the European Convention on Human Rights, para. 4.

[164] Case of López Ostra v. Spain, No. Application no. 16798/90 (European Court of Human Rights December 9, 1994).

[165] Case of López Ostra v. Spain para. 58.

[166] Case of López Ostra v. Spain para. 8.

[167] Case of López Ostra v. Spain at 51.

factory, the Case of Guerra and Others v. Italy[168] treats the effect of toxic emissions on the right to respect for his private and family life under Art. 8 ECHR as well.[169] While recognizing the positive obligation to secure this right, the court characterizes severe environmental pollution caused by hazardous substances as an interference with Art. 8 ECHR again.[170] Concerning waste treatment, the Case of Giacomelli v. Italy[171] also deals with the adverse affects of waste on Art. 8 ECHR.[172] While reaffirming the aforementioned judgments, the court considers the term "home" more closely: It is described not only as a "physically defined area, where private and family develops"[173] but also involves enjoying this area without any interference.[174] Equivalently, violations of this right cannot only consist in physical breaches, but also in non-physical forms like noise or emissions.[175] It thereby focuses on the interfering character of toxic emissions and underscores that Art. 8 ECHR does not only apply with pollution directly caused by states, but also with cases of failing regulation of private actors.[176] This series of cases treating Art. 8 ECHR in the context of hazardous pollution is completed by the Case of Di Sarno and Others v. Italy.[177] Again, dealing with environmental threats by a waste disposal site,[178] this decision provides a detailed consideration of the negative impacts of waste management activities in the light of human rights obligations.[179] Firstly, it introduces the obligation of adopting "all necessary measures to ensure that waste was recovered or disposed of without endangering human health and without using processes or methods which could harm the environment"[180]. Secondly, it reiterates that Art. 8 ECHR

[168] Case of Guerra and Others v. Italy, No. 116/1996/735/932 (European Court of Human Rights February 19, 1998).

[169] Case of Guerra and Others v. Italy para. 57.

[170] Case of Guerra and Others v. Italy para. 60.

[171] Case of Giacomelli v. Italy, No. Application no. 59909/00 (European Court of Human Rights November 2, 2006).

[172] Case of Giacomelli v. Italy para. 11.

[173] Case of Giacomelli v. Italy para. 76.

[174] Case of Giacomelli v. Italy para. 76.

[175] Case of Giacomelli v. Italy para. 76.

[176] Case of Giacomelli v. Italy para. 78.

[177] Case of Di Sarno and others v. Italy, No. Application no. 30765/08 (European Court of Human Rights January 10, 2012).

[178] Case of Di Sarno and others v. Italy para. 7.

[179] Case of Di Sarno and others v. Italy para. 104.

[180] Case of Di Sarno and others v. Italy para. 54.

entails the positive obligation of effectively securing private and family life.[181] What is new, is the particular consideration of dangerous activities, for which states must establish rules that take into account the special risks thereof.[182] The court explicitly refers to measures which "ensure the effective protection of citizens whose lives might be endangered by the inherent risks"[183] and which cover the whole process from licensing to supervision. Despite the missing affection of the inhabitants' lives or health, their deteriorated quality of life through the maladministration of a waste treatment site and resulting emissions is considered sufficient for the application of Art. 8 ECHR.[184] Its violation consists in the authorities' failure of taking appropriate steps in order to contribute to a well-functioning waste treatment site,[185] and "more generally, to [...] a safe and healthy environment"[186].

Within this range of regional case law, it becomes clear that lacking or insufficient state action against toxic emissions from waste processing sites constitutes—even without a direct impact on human health—a violation of human rights regarding their private and family life as well as their home. Although these cases refer to the European human rights regime, their underlying principles can be transferred to the equivalent rights at the international level, such as Art. 17 ICCPR and Art. 11 ICESCR due to their similar scope of protection. Preventive and precautionary action against threatening hazards from waste is thus incorporated in the aforementioned rights to private and family life as well as to living in security under the right to adequate housing. Which specific measures of prevention are required neither follows from case law nor from other regional or international statements. However, a general duty of preventing these hazards can be subscribed to these rights as well.

3.2.2.5 Right to Water

Since the toxic emissions from landfills or other waste sites contaminate water areas such as rivers or even the groundwater, the right to water plays an important role.[187] Besides the adverse affects for marine wildlife, water pollution directly

---

[181] Case of Di Sarno and others v. Italy para. 105.

[182] Case of Di Sarno and others v. Italy para. 106.

[183] Case of Di Sarno and others v. Italy para. 106.

[184] Case of Di Sarno and others v. Italy para. 108.

[185] Case of Di Sarno and others v. Italy para. 109.

[186] Case of Di Sarno and others v. Italy para. 110.

[187] Human Rights Council, Human Rights and the Global Water Crisis: Water Pollution, Water Scarcity and Water-Related Disasters—Report of the Special Rapporteur on the Issue

impacts on drinking water and thus on human health.[188] The right to water is considered to ensure the quality of water, free from toxic substances.[189] In the Case of Zander v. Sweden before the European Court of Human Rights, the contamination of water by cyanide from a waste disposal site was negotiated,[190] seconding that water contamination by waste constitutes a human rights issue.

Pollution caused by waste is explicitly mentioned in the General Comment: A state's obligation consists in "refraining from [...] unlawfully diminishing or polluting water, for example through waste from State-owned facilities"[191]. In order to preserve the quality of water, states must adopt measures to reduce contamination[192]—not only by the negative duty of not polluting water themselves, but also via programs that inhibit such contamination by third parties.[193] Insofar the states' obligations resemble those under the right to health and food.[194] More ambitiously, the Human Rights Council demands in this context for accelerating "efforts to shift to a circular economy—which includes the safe reuse and recycling of water and wastewater, and redesigning products and processes to phase out water pollution"[195]. It explicitly refers to the principle of waste reduction and precaution[196], thus building a connection between those principles and

---

of Human Rights Obligations Relating the Enjoyment of a Safe, Healthy and Sustainable Environment, para. 25; Sands et al. (2012), 780.

[188] Committee on Economic, Social and Cultural Rights, "General Comment No. 15: The Right to Water (Arts. 11 and 12 of the Covenant)," E/C.12/2002/11 § (2003), para. 12 (b).

[189] Committee on Economic, Social and Cultural Rights, General Comment No. 15: The Right to Water (Arts. 11 and 12 of the Covenant), para. 10.

[190] Case of Zander v. Sweden, No. Application no. 14282/88 (European Court of Human Rights November 25, 1993).

[191] Committee on Economic, Social and Cultural Rights, General Comment No. 15: The Right to Water (Arts. 11 and 12 of the Covenant), para. 21.

[192] Human Rights Council, Human Rights and the Global Water Crisis: Water Pollution, Water Scarcity and Water-Related Disasters—Report of the Special Rapporteur on the Issue of Human Rights Obligations Relating the Enjoyment of a Safe, Healthy and Sustainable Environment, para. 57.

[193] Committee on Economic, Social and Cultural Rights, General Comment No. 15: The Right to Water (Arts. 11 and 12 of the Covenant), para. 23.

[194] See 2.2.2.2.

[195] Human Rights Council, Human Rights and the Global Water Crisis: Water Pollution, Water Scarcity and Water-Related Disasters—Report of the Special Rapporteur on the Issue of Human Rights Obligations Relating the Enjoyment of a Safe, Healthy and Sustainable Environment, para. 89 (i).

[196] Human Rights Council, Human Rights and the Global Water Crisis: Water Pollution, Water Scarcity and Water-Related Disasters—Report of the Special Rapporteur on the Issue

human rights in the context of waste. As this connection will be diligently examined in the following sections, these advanced ideas are only to be captured at this point, leaving open their legal relevance for the later analysis. In conclusion, even the right to water on its own involves a clear reference to the pollution by waste processing sites or landfills and reinforces the states' duty of preventing such contamination.

3.2.2.6 Right to a Healthy Environment

As the connecting right between human health and the environment, the right to a healthy environment, which is now widely accepted,[197] complements the separate analysis of human rights in the context of waste management. Since it aims for environmental preservation as the foundation of human health and well-being, the right to a healthy environment requires the protection against environmental damages such as pollution and contamination of air, water, and soil.[198] Within this objective, the disposal and management of toxic and hazardous wastes are explicitly mentioned by the Human Rights Council[199] as well as in the Joint Report of the Office of the High Commissioner of Human Rights and the UNEP.[200] Regarding the special affectedness of communities in the vicinity of waste dumps, the Special Rapporteur on human rights obligations relating to the right to a healthy environment particularly acknowledges these dumps as a source of pollution and environmental harm.[201] On these grounds, the negative consequences by waste directly touch upon the connection between human rights and the environment[202] and thus invoke the applicability of the right to a healthy environment.

The question is, which implications follow from the application of the right to a healthy environment on the topic of waste management. *Shelton* ascribes the

---

of Human Rights Obligations Relating the Enjoyment of a Safe, Healthy and Sustainable Environment, para. 89 (f).

[197] See 2.2.2.6.

[198] Leib (2011), 78.

[199] Human Rights Council, "Resolution Adopted by the Human Rights Council—The Human Right to a Clean, Healthy and Sustainable Environment," A/HRC/RES/48/13 § (2021), 2.

[200] Office of the High Commissioner of Human Rights and UN Environment Programme, "Human Rights and the Environment—Rio + 20: Joint Report OCHR and UNEP," 13.

[201] UN General Assembly, Report of the Special Rapporteur on the issue of human rights obligations relating to the enjoyment of a safe, clean, healthy and sustainable environment, para. 24 (f).

[202] Human Rights Council, Resolution adopted by the Human Rights Council—The human right to a clean, healthy and sustainable environment, 2.

establishment of environmental standards for the restriction of pollution to the right to a healthy environment.[203] She considers it necessary to implement such minimum substantive standards in order to ensure the prevention of such pollution to render this right effective.[204] This spotlight on the necessity of preventive action is seconded by the UN General Assembly, which highlights the important role of prevention relating to human rights violations and refers to the objective of "zero pollution and zero waste"[205]. Since the Inter-American Commission on Human Rights subsumes the duty of prevention as one of the obligations under the right to a healthy environment,[206] it only needs further concretization of this duty in order to derive the obligation of waste prevention therefrom. Similarly, the African Commission on Human and Peoples' Rights demands for measures to prevent pollution and environmental degradation, including industrial hygiene.[207] The Committee on Social, Economic and Cultural Rights specifies this duty of prevention by requiring the "prevention and reduction of the population's exposure to harmful substances such as radiation and harmful chemicals or other detrimental environmental conditions"[208]. Although referring to the right to health, these maxims can be transferred to the right to a healthy environment due to its close relation. The duty of prevention in the context of waste management can thus be derived from the right to healthy environment as well. What remains difficult, is the specification to a duty of prevention of waste *generation* due to the lacking statements in documents or judgments relating to this right. Nonetheless, the right to a healthy environment shows a strong connection to the duty of prevention and is applicable in the context of waste management.

3.2.2.7 Conclusion on Human Rights and Waste Management

In order to clarify which obligation follows from the analysis of human rights in the context of waste management, their separate analysis provides a first insight. However, for revealing the complete picture, these rights must be regarded altogether. With due regard to their interrelation and interdependence, the separate

---

[203] Shelton (2006), 163, 164.

[204] Shelton (2006), 163, 164.

[205] UN General Assembly, Human rights obligations relating to the enjoyment of a safe, clean, healthy and sustainable environment, 2022, para. 38.

[206] See Case of the Indigenous Communities of the Lhaka Honhat (Our Land) Association v. Argentina, Jugment para. 207.

[207] African Commission on Human and Peoples' Rights, *Ogoni Case* para. 52.

[208] Committee on Economic, Social and Cultural Rights, General Comment No. 14: The Right to the Highest Attainable Standard of Health, para. 15.

consideration only shows a fragmented result and must be enhanced by conducting a joint interpretation, as it is done in the chapter about resource depletion.[209] The foregoing analysis of the rights has proven their applicability in the context of waste management and their incorporation of a duty to prevent environmental hazards. In this regard, the aforementioned rights share the objective of preventive environmental protection in order to fulfill the guarantees set out in the respective right. *Gilbert* clarifies that "not the pollution [...] per se, but the impact of such pollution on the enjoyment of protected human rights"[210] builds the rationale of this obligation. In terms of the necessary effectiveness of human rights, this obligation involves the establishment of environmental standards.[211] A general obligation to prevent environmental hazards caused by waste can thus be derived from the human rights regime.

As already mentioned above, states must adopt certain measures to impede or at least reduce the pollution caused by waste.[212] In the case of state-owned facilities, the state's responsibility to adopt preventive measures is clear.[213] What needs to be justified is the state's responsibility regarding third parties. Refraining from causing pollution builds one aspect of a state's obligation. Pollution by waste is, however, also released by private companies that are dealing with waste. *Shelton*, hence, derives a due diligence obligation towards non-state actors regarding the protection of human rights in this field.[214] The Inter-American Court speaks of a "duty to prevent third parties from violating the protected rights in the private sphere"[215] as well. As already touched upon above,[216] an effective protection thus demands for a state's duty of prevention towards third parties in order to meet its obligation under human rights law regarding waste pollution. The Inter-American Court, nevertheless, limits the state's responsibility to foreseeable hazards by stating that the authorities must "knew or should have known of the existence of a situation of real and imminent danger for the life of a specific individual or group of individuals and failed to take the necessary

[209] See 2.2.3.

[210] Gilbert (2018), 154.

[211] Cf. Advisory Opinion OC-23/17 para. 115.

[212] Committee on Economic, Social and Cultural Rights, General Comment No. 14: The Right to the Highest Attainable Standard of Health, para. 36.

[213] See Committee on Economic, Social and Cultural Rights, General Comment No. 14: The Right to the Highest Attainable Standard of Health, para. 34.

[214] Shelton (2006), 130.

[215] Advisory Opinion OC-23/17 para. 118.

[216] See considerations under the right to health, 2.2.2.2.

measures within their area of responsibility that could reasonably be expected to prevent or to avoid that danger" in order to avoid a disproportionate burden.[217] The state's obligation, hence, does not equate state-owned facilities with those operated by private parties, but entails a due diligence obligation towards preventing human rights violations by those companies through effective legislation and policies.

Another issue relates to the attribution of the responsibility over the negative consequences of waste, especially in the transboundary sphere. The impacts of waste do not only take place in its country of origin. Waste from one country may lead to human rights violations in another, which invokes questions about the extraterritorial applicability of human rights. While the state's responsibility regarding the protection of its own population is definite, the extraterritorial responsibility is disputed. Relating to the right to water, the Committee on Economic, Social and Cultural Rights speaks of an international obligation to "respect the enjoyment of this right in other countries [...] [and to] refrain from actions that interfere, directly or indirectly, with the enjoyment of the right to water in other countries"[218]. Thereby, the Committee extends the obligation of protection to areas outside national jurisdiction. The principles developed by the Special Rapporteur on the implications for human rights of the environmentally sound management and disposal of hazardous substances and wastes, equally constitute a state's responsibility for cross-border cases of exposure to toxic substances.[219] Whereas the respective responsibility of a state in terms of causation as well as concerning the different situations in more and less developed countries will be analyzed in the following chapter, it can be stated at this point, that an effective protection of human rights vis-à-vis waste pollution cannot stop at a country's border. Whether the states are obliged to address the issue with waste outside their national jurisdiction can only be clarified if the exact scope of such an obligation is determined. Therefore, it is firstly to be analyzed what sort of obligation is demanded in regard of the prevention of the negative impacts by waste, before elucidating questions of attribution.

In conclusion, states are obliged under human rights law to prevent human rights violations by waste pollution from their own facilities, as well as by private actors. What that obligation consists in concretely and through which measures

---

[217] Advisory Opinion OC-23/17 para. 120.

[218] Committee on Economic, Social and Cultural Rights, General Comment No. 15: The Right to Water (Arts. 11 and 12 of the Covenant), para. 31.

[219] See Human Rights Council, "Report of the Special Rapporteur on the Implications for Human Rights of the Environmentally Sound Management and Disposal of Hazardous Substances and Wastes," A/HRC/39/48 § (2018), para. 114.

this duty can be fulfilled, will be revealed by a joint interpretation of human rights and the principles under international environmental law in the context of waste management.

3.2.3 Human Rights and Environmental Law Regarding Waste

The question whether human rights also contain a duty to waste prevention must be answered by interpreting the human rights obligations regarding its implications on waste management together with the findings of international environmental law. It will be set out firstly, why a joint interpretation of both regimes in the context of waste management is useful to answer the above question, followed by the actual analysis of the environmental law principles together with human rights.

3.2.3.1 Reasons for their Joint Interpretation

Such as in the Chapter of Resource Depletion, the results of both international environmental law and human rights law in the context of waste management will be considered together in order to develop further findings on the question of concrete obligations. The methodological legitimacy of interpreting human rights together with principles under international environmental law has already been proven above.[220] The reasons for analyzing both regimes together are twofold: Firstly, the separate analysis of human rights in the context of waste management has led to the result that there does exist a general duty of prevention. A concrete obligation of how to prevent these consequences, however, could not be derived from those rights alone. Therefore, it is necessary to combine the further concretized duties under the environmental law principles of prevention and precaution in order to reveal if an obligation of waste prevention and minimization is embedded in the human rights regime. With due regard to the adverse affects of waste on human rights, that are set out above, the Human Rights Council also supports the idea of a "human rights-based approach that emphasizes the duty and responsibility of States and businesses to prevent and minimize exposure"[221].

---

[220] See 2.2.3.1.

[221] Human Rights Council, Report of the Special Rapporteur on the implications for human rights of the environmentally sound management and disposal of hazardous substances and wastes, 2018, para. 10.

International environmental law with its more specific but non-binding principle of waste prevention and minimization may, hence, shed light on a concrete duty.

Furthermore, a range of regional judgments already connect human rights with environmental law principles and thereby highlight the acceptance of their joint interpretation, as the following examples show: First, the Case of Tatar v. Romania[222] before the European Court of Human Rights shows the importance of environmental law principles in the human rights interpretation: By holding that the exposure of residents to sodium cyanide[223] must be prevented by the authorities to effectively protect their human rights, the court explicitly refers to the principle of precaution as a principle of environmental law and makes use of it by invoking a human rights violation.[224] The principle of precaution was thereby used as a legal foundation for assuming the violation of human rights. *Shelton* rightly states that the court "relied on international environmental law as a basis for determining the adequacy of measures taken by the respondent government"[225] and notes the court's recognition that the state's inaction regarding industrial operations, which harm human health, represents a violation of the precautionary principle.[226] This can also be traced in the Case of Lhaka Honhat v. Argentina before the Inter-American Court of Human Rights, in which the court directly connects human rights violations with lacking anticipatory action, laid down in the obligation of prevention.[227]

Hence, the connection between human rights law and the principles of prevention and precaution under international environmental law has already found entry into the jurisprudence. The principles' reinforcing and specifying nature will thus be used in order to derive concrete obligations from the human rights regime in the field of waste management.

3.2.3.2 Joint Analysis

After highlighting the importance and acceptance of environmental law principles in the interpretation of human rights, the analysis will combine the previous

---

[222] Tâtar v. Romania, No. No. 67021/01 (European Court of Human Rights January 27, 2009).

[223] Tâtar v. Romania para. 104.

[224] Tâtar v. Romania para. 109.

[225] Shelton (2018), 119.

[226] Shelton (2018), 115.

[227] Case of the Indigenous Communities of the Lhaka Honhat (Our Land) Association v. Argentina, Jugment para. 207.

findings from the principles of prevention and precaution under the waste framework as well as the results from the human rights section concerning waste management.

First of all, a priority for waste prevention and minimization has developed within the waste framework.[228] Regarding the soft law principles of prevention and precaution, their applicability to environmental risks from waste collecting and processing sites can be identified.[229] Their legal implications, which can be traced in a range of legal documents like the Cartagena Declaration, consist in demanding for preventing and minimizing the generation of waste.[230] What can be derived from the general principle of prevention is thus the concrete principle of waste prevention and minimization, which is also reflected in the hard law framework, e.g. as a goal in the Basel Convention.[231] As already set out in the chapter about resource depletion, international environmental law principles are not offering concrete binding rules, but serve as interpretational guidelines and help to concretize other rules, such as the duties under human rights law. With due regard to human rights in the context of waste management, they entail positive measures and demand for an effective protection of environmental threats from waste management.[232] Both international environmental law and human rights law, therefore, share the objective of preventing environmental hazards of waste. Under the right to health, the necessary prevention refers to the exposure to toxic substances from waste that needs to be encountered by an effective prevention of pollution by waste in general.[233] Following from this, the UN General Assembly states that human rights obligations cannot be met "without preventing human exposure to hazardous substances"[234], directly referring to a resulting obligation. Even below the threshold of an affection of human health, the right to private and family life, home, and correspondence involves living undisturbed

228 See 3.1.3.2.

229 See 3.1.3.2.

230 See 3.1.3.2.

231 See 3.1.3.2.

232 See 3.2.2.1.

233 See 3.2.2.2.

234 UN General Assembly, "Implications for Human Rights of the Environmentally Sound Management and Disposal of Hazardous Substances and Wastes," A/75/290 § (2020), para. 51.

by pollution caused by waste treatment.[235] Moreover, the prevention from contamination of food through waste can be derived from the right to food.[236] The right to water with its necessity for preventing the pollution of water from the toxic substances from waste explicitly refers to waste reduction and precaution and thereby entails one of the most concrete obligations.[237] The Human Rights Council's document regarding the global water crisis even suggests the application of "the waste management hierarchy to wastewater"[238], directly linking the human rights obligations to the developments under the waste framework. In terms of concrete obligations, the right to science—although not mentioned before due to its lacking applicability as a substantive right in the context of waste management—explicitly highlights the need to adopt preventive and precautionary measures for an effective protection of the population, by requiring that states must "adopt measures to prevent exposure to hazardous substances on the basis of the best available science".[239] Lastly, the prevention of environmental hazards by waste pollution is also incorporated in the right to a healthy environment.[240] Relating to this right, the Human Rights Council acknowledges the "principle of waste reduction"[241] and thereby connects both fields of law. The general obligation of preventing the exposure to toxic substances by waste is thus embedded in the human rights regime.[242] In order to protect these human rights from the adverse affects of waste effectively, preventive action is necessary.[243]

This general obligation must then be concretized with the help of the principle of waste prevention and minimization. As the general principle of prevention

---

235 See 3.2.2.4.

236 See 3.2.2.3.

237 See 3.2.2.5.

238 Human Rights Council, Human Rights and the Global Water Crisis: Water Pollution, Water Scarcity and Water-Related Disasters—Report of the Special Rapporteur on the Issue of Human Rights Obligations Relating the Enjoyment of a Safe, Healthy and Sustainable Environment, para. 89 (h).

239 Human Rights Council, "Right to Science in the Context of Toxic Substances," A/HRC/48/61 § (2021), para. 10.

240 See 3.2.2.6.

241 Human Rights Council, Human Rights and the Global Water Crisis: Water Pollution, Water Scarcity and Water-Related Disasters—Report of the Special Rapporteur on the Issue of Human Rights Obligations Relating the Enjoyment of a Safe, Healthy and Sustainable Environment, para. 89 (f).

242 UN General Assembly, "Implications for Human Rights on the Environmentally Sound Management and Disposal of Hazardous Substances and Wastes," A/74/480 § (2019), para. 6.

243 See 3.2.2.7.

entails a due diligence obligation of taking "all appropriate measures to achieve, progressively, the full effectiveness of the corresponding rights"[244], this kind of obligation can also be ascribed to its concretization, which is the principle of waste prevention and minimization. Furthermore, the duty of prevention also involves the use of the best available technology in order to encounter environmental hazards in advance.[245] What follows from these statements is that the duty of prevention requires the most effective protection of the rights through the best available technology. Most effective for preventing the exposure to the adverse affects from waste is to ensure that waste is not generated in the first place. Reducing waste streams and minimizing the amount of waste in general can only be conducted effectively by addressing this issue at its source, which is waste generation. Only the prevention and minimization of waste will serve as a long-term solution for preventing the exposure to toxic substances and environmental hazards caused by waste. Conversely, this means that starting at a later point like the trade with waste does not correspond to the most effective protection. Therefore, applying the principle of waste prevention and minimization to the necessity of prevention embedded in the aforementioned human rights, leads to a concretized duty of waste prevention and minimization under human rights law. Additionally, the principle of effectiveness supports this argumentation by demanding for the most effective way of human rights protection, which involves a long-term solution that addresses the source of the problem.

This development towards a priority for waste prevention and minimization does not only take place in the European sphere but is also visible at the international level.[246] It is the Human Rights Council again, who provides one example for this by referring to eliminating hazards as the best practice for preventing the exposure to them and explicitly mentioning the reduction of hazardous waste generation in this context.[247] Moreover, the Council subsumes the regulation of i.a. waste management industries under the duty of prevention and refers to the goals of "zero pollution and zero waste".[248] In its report on the implications for human rights of the environmentally sound management and disposal of hazardous and toxic wastes, the Special Rapporteur *Orellana* seconds this by demanding for

---

[244] Advisory Opinion OC-23/17 para. 123.

[245] See 2.1.2.2.

[246] See 3.1.3.2.

[247] Human Rights Council, Report of the Special Rapporteur on the implications for human rights of the environmentally sound management and disposal of hazardous substances and wastes, 2017, para. 47.

[248] Human Rights Council, "The Right to a Clean, Healthy and Sustainable Environmnet: Non-Toxic Environment," A/HRC/49/53 § (2022), para. 55.

"reducing plastics production"[249]. In addition, the UN Environment Assembly of the UNEP argues in favor of national reduction targets and design standards in order to achieve the aim of waste reduction.[250]

These examples underscore that the need for reducing waste generation has arrived in the international human rights discussion. While they show that hard law regulation on such a duty is still missing, these statements support the acceptance of thinking waste prevention and human rights together. Lacking treaties on this issue, however, do not exclude the existence of a legal foundation for deriving a duty of waste prevention and minimization under human rights law. As the previous findings have demonstrated, an effective prevention of human rights violations from the negative consequences of waste can only consist in preventing and minimizing waste generation. The soft law principle of waste prevention and minimization is thus capable of concretizing the general duty of prevention under human rights law into a specific obligation of waste prevention and minimization.

In conclusion, the combination of international environmental law and human rights law in the context of waste management leads to a duty to prevent and minimize waste generation in order to prevent human rights violations from the adverse affects of waste management.

3.3 Combination of the Findings About Resource Depletion and Waste Management

With this result of a duty of waste prevention and minimization under the human rights regime, the question arises in how far such a duty leads to a mandatory economic shift towards a circular economy in the end. Although waste prevention and minimization represent two of the key objectives of a circular economy,[251] they do not directly entail an obligation for a holistic economic transition. In order to find out whether such an obligation can also be derived from international law, the results from the chapter about waste management must be considered together with the findings from the previous chapter about resource depletion. Therefore, the findings from both chapters must be combined in a first step,

[249] UN General Assembly, Report of the Special Rapporteur on the implications for human rights of the environmentally sound management and disposal of hazardous substances and wastes, Marcos Orellana, para. 110 (k) (iii).

[250] UN Environment Assembly of the UNEP, "Report on the Work of the Ad Hoc Open-Ended Expert Group on Marine Litter and Microplastics at Its Fourth Meeting," UNEP/AHEG/4/7 § (2020), para. 141.

[251] See 1.4.2.

followed by illuminating the question of how these duties can be achieved and if the solution lies in a shift towards a circular economy. Within this analysis, the crucial element of product design deserves a closer look as the connective stage between the exploitation of resources and the management of waste.

3.3.1 Separate or Joint Consideration of the Previous Results?

Recalling the main findings from the chapter about resource depletion, it is firstly to state that the concept of sustainable development in its special emanation of the sustainable use of natural resources can be described as a normative concept, resolving conflicts between environmental and economic concerns.[252] It serves as a modifying norm and, hence, is capable of influencing other rules.[253] Together with the preventive and the precautionary principles, which demand for anticipatory measures to facilitate safeguarding natural resources, it builds a strong argument for an alternative resource management.[254] Since the depletion of resources and the concept of common concern of humankind are closely interrelated,[255] this concept provides a framework for the aforementioned international environmental law principles and concepts, highlighting their reinforcing power.[256]

Since the analyzed human rights depend on the availability of natural resources and demand to safeguard the ecosystem as the basis for fulfilling those rights,[257] their underlying obligations can be concretized by the concept of sustainable development to an obligation of safeguarding natural resources including a sustainable strategy for their management.[258] Together with the preventive and precautionary principle, which shed light on the intertemporal dimension of human rights, this duty also relates to future generations.[259] An effective realization of human rights thus incorporates a due diligence obligation including

[252] See 2.1.1.5.

[253] See 2.1.1.5.

[254] See 2.1.2.3.

[255] See 2.1.3.1.

[256] See 2.1.3.3.

[257] See 2.2.3.

[258] See 2.2.3.2.

[259] See 2.2.3.2.

binding standards to safeguard natural resources for actual and future generations, building the first pillar of a potential obligation regarding an economic transformation.[260]

As examined in the previous chapter, the analysis of waste management leads to a binding duty of waste prevention and minimization under human rights law, concretized by the environmental law principle of preventing and minimizing waste generation, derived from the general preventive and precautionary principle.

The duty of safeguarding natural resources on the one side, and the duty to prevent and minimize waste generation on the other can be regarded separately, demanding for the legislation of specific measures to pursue each objective on its own. However, this separate treatment would disregard the interdependence of both the issue of resource depletion and the consequences of the enormous waste generation as well as the chance of considering both problems together. Addressing these issues individually also ignores the fact that the use of resources and the generation of waste are both inseparable parts of a product's life cycle. It follows the question, if such a consideration of the entire product's life cycle is embedded in international law and what such a holistic approach consists in in terms of concrete measures.

3.3.2 Considering the Whole Product's Life Cycle

In order to examine, in how far the approach of considering the whole product's life cycle is displayed in a legal context and what it consists in, the product's life cycle must be reflected more in detail. In general, regarding the life cycle of a product entirely means considering the connection of the different stages from the exploitation of resources, the production process including the design and manufacturing, until its usage and the end of a product's life.[261]

This development from a focus on waste law towards a comprehensive consideration of the entire product's life cycle on a legal level is best visible in the EU context: *Zhang et al.* aptly set out that the "EU waste hierarchy also considered matters beyond waste management, taking into account the resource use at product scale to reduce waste"[262]. The waste hierarchy, which is already examined above, does not only involve the aim of reducing waste, but is also interconnected with the supply and value of resources. *Maitre-Ekern* seconds this

---

[260] See 2.2.3.2.

[261] See 1.4.2.

[262] Zhang et al. (2022), 5.

observation and speaks of waste law as the "key element in efforts to develop a sustainable and resource-efficient economy"[263]. At an early step in its development from waste law towards a plan for a circular economy, the EU recognizes waste prevention not only as an end in itself, but also acknowledges its benefits for the availability of materials.[264] The regulation of waste management is thus viewed as an important aspect of achieving a cyclical use of resources.[265]

At the international level, the connection between the different stages and a comprehensive consideration of the product's life cycle are conducted as well: First of all, the Human Rights Council links the protection of human rights from hazardous substances by eliminating them throughout the life cycle of products to the transformation towards a circular economy,[266] thereby acknowledging the importance of considering the whole product's life cycle. Moreover, it highlights that in every stage of a product's life not only the exposure to hazardous substances can be reduced but also the input of raw material can thereby be minimized.[267] Likewise, the Special Rapporteur *Orellana* refers to the plastic cycle and mentions a circular economy as the key factor for an effective protection.[268] The idea of regarding the entire life cycle is thus already taken into consideration by human rights bodies. Hence, it must be determined what exactly is meant by a life-cycle approach in the legal context and what is involved therein.

Chioatto and Sospiro highlight the importance of creating resource cycles and thereby tying together the treatment of waste and the recovery of resources as the main aim of considering the entire product's life cycle.[269] They correctly note that the EU framework concerning waste has developed towards "strengthening the link between waste treatment and resource recovery"[270]. This can be achieved by thinking both concerns together and putting a focus on the production process

[263] Maitre-Ekern (2021), 1.

[264] Wilson (2015), 275.

[265] Maitre-Ekern (2021), 13.

[266] Human Rights Council, Report of the Special Rapporteur on the implications for human rights of the environmentally sound management and disposal of hazardous substances and wastes, 2017, para. 47.

[267] Human Rights Council, Report of the Special Rapporteur on the implications for human rights of the environmentally sound management and disposal of hazardous substances and wastes, 2017, para. 49.

[268] UN General Assembly, Report of the Special Rapporteur on the implications for human rights of the environmentally sound management and disposal of hazardous substances and wastes, Marcos Orellana, para. 78.

[269] Chioatto and Sospiro (2023), 251.

[270] Chioatto and Sospiro (2023), 253.

phase and manufacturing phase.[285] In order to reintegrate waste in the production process, a product's design must consider the later treatment of a used product like reuse, repairment and recycling. On that account, *Pouikli* links the necessity of a life-cycle approach to binding standards regarding product design.[286] Since the development towards a circular economy is already conducted at the EU level, e.g. with the Circular Economy Action Plan,[287] this regional legislation regarding the production phase will be regarded first, followed by referring back to the international level. It will eventually answer the question of what sort of duty is embedded in international law.

3.3.2.1.1 EU Regulation Regarding Product Design

Taking a look at the EU regulation in order to find concrete measures of how to achieve a cyclical flow of materials, the waste hierarchy only provides general and flexible guidelines,[288] except the goals of recycling and reuse under Art. 29 of the Waste Framework Directive.[289] Since product design marks the crucial phase, in which resource use and waste treatment are interconnected, already existing written agreements regarding the design of products must be taken into consideration in a holistic examination. First insights of how such regulation can look like can be found in the Waste Electrical and Electronic Equipment Directive 2012/19/EU (WEEE).[290] Addressing the issue around the treatment of electronic waste, it provides a detailed example regarding product design at the EU level. It involves rules concerning the whole product life cycle from product design to its recovery.[291] Although it is regarded ineffective due to the huge part of electronic waste that disappears on the informal market,[292] it involves future-oriented norms such as binding rules about product design, "encouraging cooperation between producers and recyclers and measures to promote the design and production of EEE, notably in view of facilitating re-use, dismantling and recovery of WEEE, its components and materials"[293]. Together with its objective

[285] Pouikli (2020), 492.

[286] Pouikli (2020), 492.

[287] Wiprächtiger et al. (2021), 105742.

[288] Zhang et al. (2022), 9.

[289] European Parliament and European Council, Waste Framework Directive.

[290] European Parliament, "Directive 2012/19/EU of the European Parliament and of the Council on Waste Electrical and Electronic Equipment," 2012/19/EU § (2012).

[291] Bogale (2011), 242.

[292] Barsalou and Picard (2018), 904.

[293] See Art. 4 WEEE.

of a rationale resource use, it includes binding targets for a separate collection and explicitly mentions economic incentives in order to put the waste hierarchy into practice.[294] Despite its shortcomings, the WEEE represents a good example of how concrete rules on product design may look like in a broader context.

Moreover, the amended Waste Framework Directive 2018/851, which forms part of the circular economy package, includes measures for waste prevention that encompass "sustainable production and consumption models" and "encourage the design, manufacturing and use of products that are resource-efficient, durable [...] repairable, re-usable and upgradable"[295], likewise focusing on the design phase.

Coming to more specific measures, European legislation regarding a circular economy brought one measure forward that serves as a concretization of a general rule for adapted product design into a tool for the implementation of a company's responsibility: the Extended Producer Responsibility. An enforceable regulation must directly address those stakeholders that are responsible for product design. Therefore, a concrete measure needs to refer to the companies and industries involved in the production process. Already embedded in the Waste Framework Directive, Art. 8 foresees this extended producer responsibility, which consists in the "acceptance of returned products and of the waste that remains after those products have been used"[296] by the respective producer. This responsibility for a post-consumer product[297]—with its roots going back to the 90's—shall provide "incentives to producers to improve product design and ultimately save waste management costs"[298]. Additionally, it aims for achieving resource-efficiency and high recycling rates.[299] It does not represent a legal mechanism itself, but rather serves as a political tool to implement binding standards for product design.[300] This far developed framework at the EU level shows how a concrete elaboration of standards for an adapted product design under a circular economy may look like. Questionable is, whether such measures for an adapted product design and this link to a circular economy can also be traced in international law.

---

[294] See 5 (1) and 16a WEEE.

[295] European Parliament, "Directive (EU) 2018/851 of the European Parliament and of the Coucil Amending Directive 2008/98/EC on Waste," 2018/851 § (2018), art. 9 (a) and (b).

[296] European Parliament and European Council, Waste Framework Directive, para. 8 (1).

[297] UN General Assembly, Report of the Special Rapporteur on the implications for human rights of the environmentally sound management and disposal of hazardous substances and wastes, Marcos Orellana, para. 98.

[298] Maitre-Ekern (2021), 2.

[299] Pouikli, (2020), 495.

[300] Pouikli (2020), 495.

3.3.2.1.2 Rules on Product Design under International Law

European law explicitly incorporates plans for a circular economy and represents a first mover in specifying goals for achieving such an economic transformation. The main question, however, is whether these conclusions can also be drawn at the international level. Written rules and plans directly addressing a circular economy or an adapted product design are missing at a global scale.[301] Nonetheless, on the foundation of the demanded action towards a life-cycle approach, a basis for an adapted product design can also be found in the principles of international environmental law together with human rights law.

First of all, it has already been highlighted that human rights violations must be prevented effectively.[302] Applying the rule of waste prevention and that of safeguarding resources for future generations effectively means that states must implement measures which protect human rights best possible. *Rylander*, therefore, deems it necessary to start with the production process for conducting effective waste prevention.[303] Taking the life-cycle approach into account, it is most effective to not only establish measures for waste prevention but also to apply methods for a better resource-efficiency. The obligation of safeguarding natural resources can be conducted more efficiently if a product can be reintroduced in the production process as a secondary resource at the end of its lifetime. In other words: When waste prevention and safeguarding resources are thought together as two sides of the same coin, their joint implementation involves benefits for both goals. Since the design and manufacturing phase connects both duties, the production process is the stage in which measures have the biggest effect. Hence, thinking the duties of waste prevention and safeguarding resources together as parts of a life cycle and addressing product design as their connective stage leads to the most effective implementation of both obligations.

On top of this application of the principle of effectiveness, the general preventive principle, which condensed in the rules of waste prevention and safeguarding resources, involves a duty of due diligence including the use of the best available technology.[304] The best available technology for both preventing waste generation and safeguarding natural resources consists in an adapted product design and production processes, which allow the reduced resource input, product reuse and

301 See 1.1.

302 See 2.2.1.3.

303 Rylander (2019), 84.

304 See 2.1.2.2.

its recycling.[305] The necessity for focusing on product design including reusability, repairability and recycling in order to mitigate the consequences by waste is also shared by *Maitre-Ekern.* Fulfilling both duties thus does not only demand for thinking them together and addressing the whole product's life cycle, but also calls for using the best available technology regarding product design. Besides these voices of scholars, also the Special Rapporteur *Orellana* calls for "urgent and robust measures [...] and an emphasis on product design"[306]. Additionally, he builds the bridge to the necessity of applying a circular economy.[307] The UNEP supports this approach by underscoring the importance of addressing the issue of waste prevention at its source and mentioning concrete measures like eco-design and resource-efficient manufacturing.[308] At last, the Human Rights Council argues in favor of a shift towards a circular economy in the context of the right to a healthy environment and waste,[309] seconded by the UN General Assembly.[310] These statements by scholars and UN bodies in favor of measures concerning product design and towards establishing a circular economy support the argumentation that an effective implementation of both the duty of waste prevention and the obligation of safeguarding resources can only be achieved by measures for an adapted product design and considering the whole product's life cycle.

Moreover, this argumentation is reinforced by the implications of the concept of sustainable development, as will be demonstrated in the following: Sustainable development does not only play an important role concerning the use of natural resources. Its significance for the duty of waste prevention is, however, less obvious and only visible when thinking both duties together. *Rayfuse* locates the connection between waste prevention and sustainable development in

---

[305] Cf. Wilson (2015), 41.

[306] UN General Assembly, Report of the Special Rapporteur on the implications for human rights of the environmentally sound management and disposal of hazardous substances and wastes, Marcos Orellana, para. 92.

[307] UN General Assembly, Report of the Special Rapporteur on the implications for human rights of the environmentally sound management and disposal of hazardous substances and wastes, Marcos Orellana, para. 96.

[308] UN Environment Programme, Draft guidance to assist Parties in developing efficient strategies for achieving the prevention and minimization of the generation of hazardous and other wastes and their disposal, para. 11.

[309] Human Rights Council, "Issue of Human Rights Obligations Relating to the Enjoyment of a Safe, Clean, Healthy and Sustainable Environment," A/HRC/40/55 § (2019), para. 116 (d).

[310] UN General Assembly, Human rights obligations relating to the enjoyment of a safe, clean, healthy and sustainable environment, 2022, para. 83 (c).

the need for a sustainable resource use.[311] The concept of sustainable development with its sub-notion of sustainable use of natural resources primarily refers to a sustainable production and consumption.[312] Although some of the SDGs are interrelated with the goal of waste prevention,[313] demanding for waste generation through prevention, reduction, recycling, and reuse,[314] and addressing illnesses from contamination and pollution,[315] the concept is only loosely connected to the consequences of current waste management practices. Its linkage to the duty of waste prevention becomes clear when considering the whole product life cycle and "waste management as a recovery of resources and environmental impact prevention"[316]. *Gottberg et al.*, therefore, regard sustainable development as the concept calling for sustainable production and consumption and supporting resource efficiency and the minimization of pollution.[317] Since waste prevention and minimization are interconnected with minimizing the use of resources[318] and this connection relates to the way a product is designed, this concept, therefore, addresses the intersection between both goals. It thus refers directly to the production phase as the link between resource use and waste management. Sustainable development can, hence, be regarded as being the connective element between both stages in the product's life cycle. The way in which sustainable development addresses both objectives is best described by *Rayfuse*, speaking about its function of integration.[319] According to her, this concept builds the foundation of implementing recycling and other waste treatment strategies that minimizes the exploitation of natural resources through providing a source of secondary resources.[320] Sustainable development with its character as an interpretive, modifying norm, which reconciles different interests, incorporates the function of integrating the duties of waste prevention and that of safeguarding natural resources. Its main task consists, therefore, in requiring the joint consideration of both pollution by waste and resource efficiency and integrating both

[311] Rayfuse (2016), 28.
[312] Wilson (2015), 299.
[313] Wilson (2015), 299.
[314] SDGs Target 12.5.
[315] See SDGs Target 3.9.
[316] Brunnée (2003), 56.
[317] Gottberg et al. (2006), 39.
[318] Ghisolfi et al. (2017), 28.
[319] Rayfuse (2016), 30.
[320] Rayfuse (2016), 30.

obligations in one phase. This integration brings these two duties in an interdependence: It is not about preventing waste *and* safeguarding resources, but about preventing waste *in order to* safeguard resources. On these grounds, it builds the third argument that both obligations must be pursued together. As examined above, this can only be achieved by legislating measures concerning product design. The crucial phase is thus the design and production phase, in which concrete standards for a product design that entails reusability, repairability and recyclability, must be implemented.

3.3.2.1.3 Interim Conclusion on their Joint Fulfillment

The analyzed principles and concepts under international environmental together with the findings under human rights law do not only involve separate duties of waste prevention and safeguarding resources, but rather demand for their joint fulfillment. This includes the obligation of implementing rules that address both goals, which can only be conducted effectively when focusing on the production phase. Such a duty of enabling a circular flow of materials necessitates an adapted product design that allows reuse, repairment and recycling in order to obtain secondary resources. Therefore, the analysis results in an obligation of a joint fulfillment of both duties, which must take place in the production phase through standards for an adapted product design for the objective of enabling a cyclical use of natural resources.

Such an obligation directly influencing on the production process may lead alone to huge economic changes. Nonetheless, a duty regarding an adapted product design is not equivalent to an obligation to transform the economy, although it builds the core lever of a circular economy. The concept of circular economy encompasses—next to the crucial product design—a range of changes at different levels and addressing various stakeholders besides the important companies.[321] It needs organizational and institutional adaptations beyond the production process.[322] Whether this duty to implement standards for product design, therefore, involves a mandatory economic transformation towards a circular economy cannot be answered without taking the other side of the coin into consideration: the state's sovereignty. Therefore, the assumption of an obligation to establish a circular economy can only be made after illuminating the requirements and implications of the state's sovereignty. Balancing the previous findings vis-à-vis the state's sovereignty will be part of the following chapter.

---

[321] See 1.4.3.

[322] See 1.4.3.

Sovereignty 4

After clarifying the demands of international environmental law and human rights law concerning resource depletion and waste management, it is now the task to examine the opposite side of a potential obligation which is the state's sovereignty. An obligation of transforming the economy into a circular one represents a huge interference with a state's opportunity to decide upon its economic system. Decisions about the national economy are generally seen as directly intertwined with the state's sovereignty. In how far a mandatory economic transformation and sovereignty converge in the first place, and whether or how they can be reconciled will be examined in this chapter.

Therefore, it is first to analyze what the concept of sovereignty consists in and which implications it entails on a potential obligation. Second, the findings from Part 1 will be balanced vis-à-vis the prerequisites of sovereignty. To complete the picture, the disparate situations of less developed countries will be regarded in order to take the different obstacles on a way towards an economic transformation into account. With this perspective, a final conclusion can be drawn.

4.1 Concept of Sovereignty Regarding Implicit Obligations

Sovereignty is an ambiguous[1] and broad term whose multiple facets fill libraries. Hence, it is necessary to define this analysis' scope concerning this concept. This chapter does not include an in-depth examination of the history and relevance

---

[1] Kelsen (1944), 207.

V. Wefringhaus, *Circular Economy and International Law*, Juridicum—Bochumer Schriften zur Friedenssicherung und zum Humanitären Völkerrecht I Bochum Studies on the International Law of Peace and Armed Conflict 70,
https://doi.org/10.1007/978-3-658-49936-5_4

of sovereignty, but rather aims for clarifying the concept regarding implicit obligations in the complex area between economic decisions and demands of the environment and human rights. Nonetheless, this analysis must be built on the actual understanding of sovereignty in order to trace its development and concretize it to its implications on implicit obligations. Therefore, it will be started with its general perception as the basis for determining how this concept relates to economic decisions, to the use of resources and waste management, in other words to a mandatory economic transformation towards a circular economy.

Starting with a short overview of this concept's nature, it is first to be scrutinized how economic decisions and sovereignty are interlinked and whether this concept encompasses a state's right to freely decide upon its economic system. Since Part 1 has revealed that human rights together with international environmental law argue in favor of an implicit obligation, it must be clarified by referring to the development of sovereignty in how far states can be bound by rules which are not codified in treaties or which do not form part of customary international law. In order to trace the development of sovereignty vis-à-vis implicit obligations, its evolution from the early Lotus Case until its modern perception will be briefly introduced, coming to a conclusion of the legitimacy of implicit obligations. After framing the notion of sovereignty concerning implicit obligations in the field of economic decisions, the result will build the basis for the following balancing process with the findings from the previous chapters.

4.1.1 Overview of the Concept of Sovereignty

Generally, sovereignty is described as the "supreme authority within a territory or the ultimate power within that territory"[2]. Still lacking a uniform definition, this concept forms a crucial foundation of the international order, although it has an ambivalent relation to international law,[3] which will be scrutinized in the following. For a better understanding of its legal notion, it is conceptualized into an internal and external dimension: Regarding its internal dimension, sovereignty entails rights and duties of a state, granting it "competence over all people and all things within its territory"[4]. The latter refers to the state's position within the international community, including the rights and duties vis-à-vis other

[2] Besson (2011), para. 56.

[3] Besson (2011), para. 1.

[4] Besson (2011), para. 70.

states.[5] The question about an implicit obligation concerning the economic system touches upon both dimensions. On the one hand, the duty per se is located in the international relations as it is derived from international law. On the other hand, however, the implications of such a duty directly concern people and companies and thus permeate into the internal dimension. Moreover, there exists a discussion, if the concept of sovereignty shall be described as the basis of international law or rather as a crucial part of it.[6] Apart from its theoretical classification inside or outside the international legal order, it is important to answer the thesis' question, in how far this relation to international law leaves room for the adaption of an implicit obligation regarding economic decisions. As *Hertogen* highlights, the growing interdependence of states challenges the free determination of a state's domestic affairs.[7] Therefore, it needs to be examined, whether these economic decisions that are affected by a mandatory economic transition, are part of the domestic affairs and in how far they are protected by the concept of sovereignty.

4.1.1.1 Economic Decisions as Part of a State's Internal Affairs?

When speaking about obligations intruding the free determination of a national economy, it is quickly insisted on the protection of the internal or domestic affairs, derived from sovereignty. In order to reveal whether an obligation—may it concern product design or the entire economic transformation—referring to economic decisions is consistent with the concept of sovereignty, it must be determined first, to what extent economic decisions fall under the scope of sovereignty.

Besson subsumes next to the organizational autonomy including self-determination and territorial jurisdiction the protection of a state's *domaine réservé* under rights derived from sovereignty.[8] The Case of Nicaragua concretizes these affairs to the "freedom of choice of the political, social, economic

[5] Fassbender (2003), 116.

[6] Besson (2011), para. 86.

[7] Hertogen (2015), 901.

[8] Besson (2011), para. 118.

> "International law governs relations between independent States. The rules of law binding upon States therefore emanate from their own free will as expressed in conventions or by usages generally accepted as expressing principles of law and established in order to regulate the relations between these co-existing independent communities or with a view to the achievement of common aims. Restrictions upon the independence of States cannot therefore be presumed."[27]

With this well-known formulation, the judgment constitutes first the significance of international law for the relations between legally equal states. Second, it underscores the states' free will to decide upon their law. Third and most important, it suggests that "a state's freedom to exercise its sovereignty is only limited by prohibitive rules to which the state in question has consented"[28], which has evolved to the Lotus principle. This principle has developed to the main tool for defending sovereignty against international rules and was treated as a *carte blanche* for states regarding any action that was not explicitly prohibited by a consensual rule.

Support for this prominent importance of consent is also read into the Nuclear Weapons Advisory Opinion, which describes the principles of sovereignty and consent as the basis of international law and refers back to the Lotus Case, while judging on a potential prohibition concerning the use of nuclear weapons.[29] Applying the Lotus principle to this chapter's main question would lead to the clear result that the state's freedom regarding its economy cannot be limited by obligations, to which the state has not explicitly consented. Deriving obligations from human rights law and environmental principles would not suffice to build a rule which is capable to bind a state according to this still advocated approach.

However, as the further development will show, this classical approach only represents one potential approach to the relation between international law and sovereignty regarding implicit obligations.[30]

4.1.1.2.2 Modern Perception of Sovereignty

Completing the picture about implicit obligations in the interplay between sovereignty and international law, the development towards a modern perception of sovereignty must be included in the analysis. Since sovereignty constitutes a concept without a uniformly agreed content and with a still evolving character,

---

[27] The Case of the S.S. "Lotus," Publications of the Permanent Court of International Justice 18 (Permanent Court of International Justice 1927).

[28] Hertogen (2015), 902.

[29] Hertogen, (2015), 902.

[30] Ruiz Fabri (2008), 36.

it leaves room for interpretation and divergent characterizations.[31] A range of recent approaches challenges the classical understanding based on different reasons,[32] which can be summarized in four categories and will be illuminated in the following:

4.1.1.2.2.1 Different Approach to the Lotus Case

First of all, there exist doubts of whether the judgment in the Lotus Case in fact intended to create the Lotus principle as it is used by the classical approach. *Hertogen* disassembles the judgement piece by piece in her article and provides an extensive argumentation that the Lotus principle is diametrically opposed to the goals of the judgment, which rather aims for the co-existence of independent states and for ensuring their cooperation for common aims.[33] To not repeat the entire course of her arguments, the main points will be identified to show that the still often cited Lotus principle is not the only possible reading of this judgment, challenging the basis of the classical approach. First, *Hertogen* points out that the judgment did not expressly follow Turkey's claim, that a state is free to act in case of any doubt.[34] In contrast, the majority is said to acknowledge limits to sovereignty even without an explicit rule.[35] Second, she classifies "a system based on permissions [...] [as] unrealistic"[36], referring to the fact that such a legal system, which foresees every issue and thus provides a complete set of fitting rules for any possible conflict, cannot exist.[37] In case of a new and therefore not suitable problem a state could then only decide between passivity or violating international law due to the non-existence of a permission.[38] Such a system would be counterproductive for the judgment's goal of joint action for common aims. Furthermore, *Hertogen* criticizes that the above cited paragraph of the Lotus judgment is only read in isolation, neglecting the following sections that are essential for a proper understanding.[39] In contrast to the restrictive Lotus principle, she argues in favor of an "alternative reading that centres on the

[31] Ruiz Fabri (2008), 37.

[32] Ruiz Fabri (2008), 36.

[33] Hertogen (2015), 903.

[34] Hertogen (2015), 908.

[35] Hertogen (2015), 908.

[36] Hertogen (2015), 915.

[37] Hertogen (2015), 915.

[38] Hertogen (2015), 915.

[39] Hertogen (2015), 907.

judgment's reference to the 'co-existence of independent communities'"[40]. Ultimate objective of international law, according to the wording of the judgment, is to "regulate the relations between these co-existing independent communities or with a view to the achievement of common aims"[41]. This aim cannot be achieved if state action intending to improve cooperation by legislating international law, that regulates areas of global interest, is restricted by the Lotus principle, insisting on an express consent for every rule. As it will be demonstrated in the following, this argument is embedded in the broader context of modern demands in a globalized world and will be concretized in the next section. At this point, it underscores the approach of an alternative reading of the Lotus Case. *Hertogen*, therefore, assumes that in case of no explicit rule, the Lotus judgment does not argue in favor of the state's freedom to act, but rather in favor of an exercise of sovereignty in order to safeguard co-existence and cooperation between states.[42] This last point leads over to the second argument in favor of a modern perception of sovereignty in relation to international law, which is the progressing globalization and related changes in the international legal order.

4.1.1.2.2.2 The Effects of Globalization

Together with a more and more interconnected world, which evolved throughout the second half of the 20th century, the interdependence between states increased and mere co-existence has been replaced through cooperation.[43] Globalization and cooperation form diverging demands to international law and sovereignty. Rather than only protecting the domestic sphere, this growing interconnection requires the states to open their shield and pave the way for joint regulation. State action becomes more likely of affecting other states in a globalized world, which demands for a limitation of sovereignty[44] and at the same time for upscaling the significance of international law.[45] As the basis for regulating relations between states,[46] the role of international law rises due to this development. Besides the necessity of international regulation for cooperation, it becomes relevant for protecting the sovereignty of states as well, since it constitutes accountability for

[40] Hertogen (2015), 904.

[41] The Case of the S.S. "Lotus," Publications of the Permanent Court of International Justice at 18.

[42] Hertogen (2015), 917.

[43] Besson (2011), para. 44.

[44] Ruiz Fabri (2008), 36.

[45] Hertogen (2015), 901.

[46] Nolte (2005), 289.

violations.[47] Accordingly, this evolution—not only in economic and societal, but also in legal terms—builds the basis for a reorganization of international law.[48]

This approach can also be traced in case law, e.g. in the Wimbledon Case of 1923.[49] Already before globalization has become tangible, the judgment described sovereignty as inherently limited[50] Therefore, *Nolte* describes it as "the liberty of states within the limits of international law [which] is open for the development of international law in the process of globalization"[51]. Moreover, it shows that even if the Lotus principle was the correct reading of the Lotus judgment, this perception of sovereignty is challenged by the further developments. With due regard to the increasing interdependence of states, a principle which provides an extensive leeway for states and thereby minimizes accountability for their actions, works against efforts for more cooperation.[52] Hence, this approach to sovereignty vis-à-vis international law is no longer suitable to the modern international community and has become outdated. This argument is supported by Judge *Weeramantry* in its dissenting opinion to the ICJ's Nuclear Weapons Advisory Opinion: "In the half century that has elapsed since the Lotus case, it is quite evident that international law [...] [has] developed considerably, imposing additional restrictions on State sovereignty over and above those that existed at the time of the Lotus case"[53].

These examples show that a focus on a consent-based approach is rather obstructive and does not meet the demands of a modern globalized world. Globalization and the recent developments thus notably influenced the relation between sovereignty and international law[54] and vote in favor of acknowledging limits to the liberty without explicit consent.[55]

---

[47] Besson (2011), para. 30.

[48] Fassbender (2003), 118.

[49] Case of the S.S. Wimbledon, ICGJ 235 (Permanent Court of Justice 1923).

[50] Case of the S.S. Wimbledon, ICGJ 235 at 24.

[51] Nolte (2005), 389.

[52] Hertogen (2015), 914.

[53] Advisory Opinion on the Legality of the Threat or Use of Nuclear Weapons, Dissenting Opinion Judge Weeramantry, 1996 I.C.J. Reports 226, 495 (International Court of Justice 1996).

[54] Orrego Vicuña (2004), 4.

[55] Nolte (2005), 289.

4.1.1.2.2.3 Individualism and the Role of Human Rights

International law is not only developing in terms of an economic interconnection, but the evolution likewise refers to the relation between sovereignty and individuals. Especially with the rise of human rights, international law further intruded upon matters which are traditionally considered to pertain to the state's internal affairs.[56] Human rights obligations significantly impact upon the traditional understanding of sovereignty,[57] since states have limited their freedom benefitting the role of individuals.[58] Accountability for ensuring human rights thus leads to a further limitation of the state's sovereignty.[59] In how far those obligations influence the modern perception of sovereignty with regard to economic decisions will be revealed in the following balancing process. At this point, it is rather to be noted that the increasing individualization *did* reshape the legal notion of sovereignty in terms of a higher significance of international law, building a further stage of its development. Notwithstanding the fact that states continue to be the main subjects under international law, the increasing importance of individuals challenge the monopoly of them as the only actors in the international legal order.[60]

Moving beyond this state-centric approach paved the way for discussions surrounding constitutionalism in international law.[61] Not only the expansion of human rights, but also the existence of global remedies as well as the emergence of jus cogens rules are seen as indicators of a new form of the international legal order.[62] Especially the existence of jus cogens norms, which themselves are consent-based but can override written agreements that violate these rules, as well as erga omnes rules have transformed international law in a significant way.[63] These new forms of rules create an objective legal order, in which explicit consent is partly dispensable and derogation from rules is not entirely possible.[64] Thereby, the international legal order evolves towards a global system, which does not rely exclusively on consent-based rules anymore. This transformation goes along with a change of legal sources and the creation of new forms

---

56 Fassbender (2003), 139.

57 Orrego Vicuña (2004), 4.

58 Orrego Vicuña (2004), 7.

59 Cohen (2012), 75.

60 Cohen (2012), 21.

61 Cohen (2012), 21.

62 Cohen (2012), 22.

63 Cohen (2012), 22.

64 Besson (2011), para. 44.

of law.[65] That is why some scholars consider constitutionalist approaches—or at least aspects thereof—as suitable for describing the current state of international law.[66] Although the assumption of a global constitution is still premature,[67] the development of law follows this direction in some respects. These systemic changes indicate an evolution of sovereignty, which opens its shield more and more towards the intrusion by international law. Its development is, moreover, an indicator for the legitimacy of implicit obligations without explicit consent, even in the area of internal affairs. This transformation does not deny the relevance of sovereignty, on the contrary, it suggests a renegotiation of this concept in the light of these developments.[68]

In conclusion, the development of international law regarding the increasing importance of individuals has led to an adapted understanding of sovereignty, away from the narrow classical approach of absolute power towards a further limited idea of this concept. With the recent shift of its main objective towards protecting individuals,[69] international law is now seen as the source of sovereignty,[70] providing the legal basis as well as limitations for the execution of a state's power. Accordingly, sovereignty develops from a supreme and unlimited authority towards an inherently limited concept, in which international law does not only affect the external dimension but also regulates the internal elements of a state's competence.[71] International law thus transcends the shield of sovereignty in an increasing range of matters and thereby overcomes the traditional requirement of explicit consent.[72] Rather than consent-based treaties, limitations of the state's sovereignty originate from customary law and even from general principles as the reflection of minimal common standards of the international community.[73] With due regard to this developing legal order, it is to be determined that there does not exist a closed entity of domestic affairs which cannot be touched upon without the state's consent. On the contrary, this development supports the argument that rules under international law—whether explicit

[65] Orrego Vicuña (2004), 6.

[66] Hertogen (2015), 903.

[67] Cohen (2012), 55.

[68] Cohen (2012), 24.

[69] Besson (2011), para. 49.

[70] Besson (2011), para. 46.

[71] Besson (2011), para. 46.

[72] Besson (2011), para. 45.

[73] Besson (2011), para. 51.

or implicit—are capable of limiting the free determination of states regarding traditionally internal affairs such as economic decisions. Nevertheless, this evolution does not mean that sovereignty loses its significance. The independence of states is not challenged since the subordination to international law is not equivalent to the subordination to the authority of other states.[74] Sovereignty as a concept remains relevant as it protects this independence and individuals within the international community. The state's liberty and independence, although limited by rules of international law, is not denied through these developments.

4.2 Balancing Previous Findings with Implications of Sovereignty

Balancing the results from international environmental law and human rights law vis-à-vis the state's sovereignty in the concrete context of depleting resources and increasing waste generation builds the core task to examine in how far international law can oblige states to transform their economies in order to safeguard resources and minimize waste. Contrasting environmental and human rights demands and their development with the actual perception of sovereignty applied to the thesis' main issue will lead to further insights on the character of a potential obligation. At the same time, it is to consider their mutual dependence, since the principles and rules of international law are based on sovereignty,[75] and the compliance with human rights and environmental demands does not permit the non-compliance with other concepts such as the requirements of sovereignty.[76] Therefore, this weighing process does not only involve sovereignty on one side and the claims of environmental law and human rights on the other side, but also aims for reconciling both dimensions to derive a well-balanced conclusion on a potential obligation. Before starting with the weighing process, it must first be determined which parameters are guiding this process. Afterwards, the balancing process will be conducted within both the fields of environmental law and human rights.

[74] Customs Régime Between Germany and Austria Advisory Opinion, Individual Opinion Judge Anzilotti, No. 41 (Permanent court of International Justice September 5, 1931).

[75] Besson (2011), para. 2.

[76] Advisory Opinion OC-23/17 para. 90.

4.2.1 Guidelines for the Balancing Process

Balancing these different findings requires parameters which guide the analysis of in how far international law can limit the states' right to decide freely upon their economy. As long as the legitimacy of international law intruding into the state's internal affairs is debated,[77] its exact reach must be discussed. Behind that lies the question of who or what prescribes if a limitation is legitimate. In the light of the modern perception of international law, it is assumed that there is no area that remains completely internal and thus cannot be influenced by rules of international law.[78] Nonetheless, *Ruiz Fabri* questions if there must be a limit to the increasing internationalization in order to secure the existence of a core content of sovereign matters.[79] The Permanent Court of International Justice Advisory Opinion on the Nationality Decrees Issued in Tunis and Morocco sheds light on this question by holding that if a matter solely belongs within a state's jurisdiction "depends upon the development of international relations"[80]. Its jurisdiction itself is again limited by international law.[81] Therefore, this case refers back to international law as the source of prescribing which matter can be influenced and to what extent. This simple answer seems to circle around the topic on the one hand as it gives international law the power to determine in how far international law can intrude into the state's sovereignty. On the other hand, international law is considered as the source of sovereignty, and it is the logic conclusion that it can therefore describe its limits itself. Hence, rules of international law define the reach of sovereignty and provide the basis for balancing the different interests within the international community.[82] Since there are no express norms of in how far international law may influence on economic decisions in the context of international environmental law and human rights, these parameters must be found in the respective field of law. On that account, it will be started by defining a parameter in the field of resource management, followed by analyzing the relationship between environmental law and state sovereignty regarding the issue of waste. The balancing process will be finalized by weighing the demands of

[77] Besson (2011), para. 52.

[78] Ruiz Fabri (2008), 36.

[79] Ruiz Fabri (2008), 36.

[80] Nationality Decrees Issued in Tunis and Morocco, Advisory Opinion, No. 4 (Permanent Court of International Justice February 7, 1923).

[81] Nationality Decrees Issued in Tunis and Morocco, Advisory Opinion at 23.

[82] Besson (2011), para. 109.

human rights vis-à-vis state sovereignty applied to the concrete demands which are already set out in the Chaps. 2 and 3.

4.2.2 Balancing Sovereignty and Resource Management

Regarding the field of resource management, the principle of permanent sovereignty over natural resources including its further evolution represents an important interface between resource law and sovereign rights. Consequently, it marks the starting point for determining a balancing parameter concerning this field of law. As a broad principle, it entails different aspects and is thus suitable for a range of issues like i.a. questions surrounding self-determination or decolonization.[83]However, the focus will lie on resources and their scarcity with regard to environmental matters and human needs, rather than concerning conflicts of distribution. Its analysis will, nonetheless, start with a brief general introduction about its history and its current status in order to illuminate its capability to serve as a benchmark in the balancing process. Subsequently, its development will be scrutinized and the principle will be applied to the concrete context of depleting resources.

4.2.2.1 Development of the Principle of Permanent Sovereignty

The principle of permanent sovereignty over natural resources, applicable to both living and non-living resources, is rooted in the 1950s and was established to strike a balance between the states' rights over their own resources vis-à-vis the interests of foreign companies regarding investments.[84] According to the UN General Assembly, states are entitled "to dispose of their natural wealth and resources in accordance with their national interests, and on respect for the economic independence of States"[85]. Although this principle initially only imposed few limitations upon the states' right to freely dispose of their resources, once it fell under their exclusive sovereignty,[86] it was quickly recognized that further limitations on that right are necessary for different reasons: First, the resolution itself stated that this right must be exercised not only in favor of the state's

[83] Schrijver (2008), para. 1.

[84] Rayfuse (2016), 16.

[85] UN General Assembly, "Resolution on Permanent Sovereignty over Natural Resources," A/RES/1803(XVII) § (1962).

[86] Birnie, Boyle, and Redgwell (2009), 191.

development but must serve for the well-being of the people as well.[87] Second, with the growing awareness of environmental issues like overexploitation and their transboundary impacts[88] in the 1970s, the need for restricting the unlimited use of natural resources became clear.[89] Hence, the interest of people and environmental concerns fueled the limitation of this principle.

Although the first resolutions did not entail references to resource conservation,[90] they already acknowledged the need of international cooperation and of limitations of sovereignty.[91] With its further development towards cooperation of the international community and the recognition of resource conservation as a common interest,[92] *Birnie et al.* argue in favor of a "redefinition of sovereignty itself, so that it is no longer a basis for exclusion of others, but entails instead a commitment to cooperate for the good of the international community at large"[93]. Against the backdrop of recent events in the international affairs (Russian aggression, China's foreign policies etc.), it is certainly questionable, if one can still speak of a development in which states are growing together more closely in a political sense. However, in the legal sense, the progression towards more international cooperation concerning shared issues like depleting resources has already taken place, as it is shown in the development of concepts and principles which encompass the need to safeguard natural resources.[94] The principle of permanent sovereignty thus represents the first hint that international law is capable to intrude into national jurisdiction in the context of resource scarcity. In other words, permanent sovereignty is not equivalent with an impermeability regarding international regulation.

Furthermore, this development is reflected in the concretization of this principle in the Stockholm Declaration and later in the Rio Declaration with the already introduced Principle 21.[95] With the necessity for cooperation in the field

---

[87] UN General Assembly, Resolution on Permanent Sovereignty over Natural Resources.

[88] Human Rights Council, Report of the Special Rapporteur on the issue of human rights obligations relating to the enjoyment of a safe, clean, healthy and sustainable environment, 2017, para. 37.

[89] Rayfuse (2016), 16.

[90] Birnie, Boyle, and Redgwell (2009), 192.

[91] Birnie, Boyle, and Redgwell (2009), 191.

[92] See 2.1.3.1.

[93] Birnie, Boyle, and Redgwell (2009), 192.

[94] See 2.1.3.3.

[95] Sands et al. (2012), 191.

of environmental protection, it became apparent that there must be a corresponding limitation of state sovereignty to achieve international cooperation.[96] This balance between state sovereignty over its own resources and its responsibility for the environment including natural resources was then reflected in Principle 21.[97] From the primarily exclusive sovereignty over its resources, this principle evolved towards preserving these resources and imposes, next to the right of disposing of them, a responsibility of safeguarding natural resources for the sake of future generations.[98] With the establishment of this principle in the Stockholm and Rio Declaration, sovereignty was put into the context of environmental protection and conservation and the principle, therefore, limits the "exercise of sovereignty over natural resources by implicitly referring to international law principles such as diligence and due care, good-neighborliness, and State responsibility"[99].

Already referred to in the context of defining the content of sustainable development,[100] Principle 21 plays a vital role in international environmental law regarding the use of natural resources and its content thus needs to be analyzed to determine the interplay of sovereignty and a duty of safeguarding resources.

4.2.2.2 Significance of Principle 21 vis-à-vis State Sovereignty

A closer look at the content of Principle 21 reveals two aspects which form the key claims of this principle: Besides the sovereign right to exploit their own resources, it imposes the responsibility on states to not cause transboundary environmental harm.[101] The sovereignty over their resources is thus inherently limited by the obligation of preventing damage to the environment of other states or areas beyond national jurisdiction.[102] These inseparable elements evolved to an important rule under international environmental law.[103] Moreover, the second element regarding a responsibility of not causing transboundary harm when exercising their sovereign right of exploiting resources means that states' action concerning their resources is subdued to environmental limits.[104] Thereby the principle itself

[96] Sands et al. (2012), 192.

[97] Sands et al. (2012), 192.

[98] Beyerlin and Holzer (2018), para. 8.

[99] Schrijver (2008), para. 14.

[100] See 2.1.1.2.

[101] Sands et al. (2012), 191.

[102] Rayfuse (2016), 16.

[103] Sands et al. (2012), 191.

[104] Sands et al. (2012), 195.

balances the national interests of states regarding resource exploitation and transboundary environmental damage.[105] It can therefore be assumed that Principle 21 can already be described as a balancing parameter between state sovereignty and environmental standards in the field of resource management as it comprises both aspects which need to be reconciled. Applied to the issue of resource scarcity, it shows that national resource exploitation is subject to international environmental legal standards. Weighing criterion is the prevention of environmental damage in a transboundary context.[106] Traditionally, it is applied to cases like the Trail Smelter Case,[107] in which the action of one country causes concrete environmental damage to another state. Nonetheless, as demonstrated in Chap. 2, resource scarcity represents an international concern with huge environmental consequences. The overexploitation of resources in one country directly and indirectly affects areas beyond national jurisdiction due to the global significance of a sufficient availability of natural resources. Of course, applying this rule to a global concern involves the question of who (other states, the international community) is entitled to invoke this responsibility.[108] As already highlighted above,[109] this principle is reinforced by a framework of other principles and rules under international environmental law and there exist initial approaches of unraveling questions of competence.[110] Despite this issue concerning its enforcement, the main message of this rule does incorporate a further pillar to solve the conflict between state sovereignty and resource use: Principle 21 establishes a mutual limitation between sovereignty and environmental protection in general.[111] Like every weighing rule, it must be applied to the concrete circumstances of each situation.[112] With regard to resource scarcity, this balancing parameter of reconciling the states' sovereignty to exploit their resources and the obligation not to cause transboundary harm, entails that states can freely dispose of their resources as long as other states do not suffer from environmental consequences. Once, a resource is threatened to be depleted, this right can be restricted. As *Eshbach*

---

[105] Brunnée (2003), 44.

[106] Brunnée (2003), 44.

[107] Trail Smelter Case (United States v. Canada) Arbitration, Reports of International Arbitral Awards, vol. III, 1905–1982.

[108] Brunnée (2003), 44.

[109] See 2.1.3.3.

[110] See section about erga omnes obligations in 2.1.3.2.

[111] Brunnée (2003), 43.

[112] Sands et al. (2012), 200.

suggests, the elements restricting state sovereignty include the well-being of people outside national jurisdiction and therefore their human right to a healthy environment.[113] This right, which also depends on the sufficient availability of resources,[114] thus also finds entry in the balancing process and is capable of limiting the states' sovereignty. Moreover, the consequences of depleting resources become visible on an individual level: It is discussed whether states can violate their obligation of not causing transboundary harm also by affecting human rights of people outside their jurisdiction. This evolution is rooted in the recognition that action of state sovereignty must be challengeable in order to engage with transboundary issues.[115] As a question concerning human rights, this will be further elucidated below. Consequently, the significance of the impacts—at the individual as well as at the general level—resulting from overexploitation in most cases prevail the national interest of exploitation. That does not lead to a complete prohibition of national resource use but argues in favor of a restriction in case of a threating scarcity. Hence, Principle 21 including its development forms a strong pillar towards the limitation of state sovereignty in the field of depleting resources, giving priority to environmental and individual concerns over the right to freely dispose of their national resources.

4.2.2.3 Legal Status of Principle 21

From the theory of this principle to its practical implementation, it is now to analyze its embedment in international law as well as its reflections in the jurisprudence. In how far these results can be verified in practice can be best revealed by taking a closer look at international case law. As already noted above in the context of sustainable development, Principle 21 is accepted as a principle of customary law.[116] This is underscored by the ICJ Case of Armed Activities (Democratic Republic of the Congo v. Uganda) that confirmed the acceptance of the permanent sovereignty principle as customary law,[117] and by the ICJ Advisory Opinion on Nuclear Weapons, holding that the "existence of the general obligation of States to ensure that activities within their jurisdiction and control respect the environment of other States or of areas beyond national control is now

---

[113] Eshbach (1990), 272.

[114] As proven in 2.2.2.6.

[115] Freestone (1999), 137.

[116] See 2.1.1.3.

[117] Case Concerning Armed Activities on the Territory of the Congo (Democratic Republic of the Congo v. Uganda), ICJ Rep 2005, p. 168 para. 244 (International Court of Justice 2005).

part of the corpus of international law relating to the environment"[118], referring to both aspects of Principle 21. By acknowledging its customary law status,[119] the principle and its content can be treated as binding international law. At the same time, this status does not impede its further evolution, meaning its applicability to new issues.[120] Accordingly, its content can still evolve in light of the increasing concern of depleting resources.

Especially one aspect is missing in the classical wording of this principle: the international responsibility regarding resource depletion. At the time of the Trail Smelter Case, the urgence of safeguarding resources at the global level was not as widely acknowledged as now.[121] Consequently, this principle could not entirely encompass all aspects of depleting resources. Like every principle of international law, it evolves over the time, as it was already demonstrated in the first section and continuously obtains new elements, according to the actual state of knowledge. Therefore, the development of its content did not stop at the status of addressing the sovereign right of exploiting resources and the prohibition of causing transboundary harm. It can as well provide answers to the issue of resource scarcity, since this issue is firmly recognized by now. The no harm rule of Principle 21 represents the first evidence, that states cannot freely manage their own resources, but must act in accordance with international law,[122] which imposes "corresponding international responsibilities requiring careful management [...] taking into account international law on sustainable development including the interests of future generations"[123]. These corresponding responsibilities involve rights and duties vis-à-vis other states or—broadly speaking—vis-à-vis the international community. Resource management is not a national issue anymore but became an international concern and thus requires international action.[124] In the light of the threating scarcity of resources, this joint action is more important than before, since a global interdependence exists regarding different natural resources. Moreover, the concept of common concern of humankind, which is also applicable to the issue of resource depletion,[125] supports this evolution towards more

---

[118] Advisory Opinion on the Legality of the Threat or Use of Nuclear Weapons, ICJ Rep 1996 para. 29.

[119] Ng'ambi (2018), 8.

[120] Schrijver (2008), para. 23.

[121] Parrish (2005), 7.

[122] Parrish (2005), 6.

[123] Schrijver (2008), para. 24.

[124] Ng'ambi (2018), 3.

[125] See 2.1.3.1.

joint action.[126] *Schrijver* thus speaks of a pathway from "resource allocation to resource co-operation"[127], suggesting that states must exercise their sovereignty over natural resources for the sake of humankind.[128] *Parrish* complements this statement by ascribing a crucial role in encountering environmental issues to this principle.[129] With the actual international needs regarding the depletion of resources, it becomes clear that an international responsibility towards a sustainable management of resources in order to protect their sufficient supply is indispensable and thus must be part of the obligations under a modern principle of permanent sovereignty.

4.2.2.4 Principle 21 as a Balancing Parameter

What follows from this analysis is twofold: First, the analysis sheds light on the general legal status of the principle of permanent sovereignty. Its content is not fixed but can and did evolve over the years in light of the actual issues regarding environmental protection. Hence, the principle is capable of reconciling the tension between state sovereignty over their own resources and environmental issues. Therefore, it developed towards a parameter for balancing sovereignty in regard of resource use and environmental concerns.

Applying this parameter to the topic of resource depletion has led to the conclusion that the huge consequences of a threatening scarcity of resources build strong arguments for a priority for safeguarding resources vis-à-vis a continuous freedom over resource exploitation. In this case, the balancing process results in favor of environmental concerns and prioritizes ensuring a sufficient supply of natural resources. A duty of safeguarding resources, hence, does not question the existence of state sovereignty in this field, but limits the free disposition of natural resources due to crucial environmental and developmental concerns. After weighing the conflicting interests with this principle as the balancing parameter, it became clear that environmental concerns have developed towards a greater significance and one key aspect in solving these issues effectively is international action. Since international law permits rules for restricting the free exploitation of resources, it shows that both state sovereignty and environmental concerns regarding resource management can be reconciled rather than mutually excluding one another.

---

[126] Schrijver (2008), para. 24.

[127] Schrijver (2008), para. 25.

[128] Schrijver (2008), para. 25.

[129] Parrish (2005), 7.

4.2.3 Balancing Sovereignty and Environmental Law

Continuing with the next aspect of the balancing process, the duty of waste prevention and minimization must be placed into relationship with sovereignty. This follows from the huge interference of such a duty on economic decisions not only relating to waste management but with regard to the whole product's life cycle. As set out above, preventing and minimizing waste require a different treatment of a product and its components, which optimally starts at the beginning of the production process. Taking this thought one step further and including the issue of resource scarcity, it eventually leads to a closed cycle of resources, which stands in contrast to the actual way the states create their economies.[130] That is why the aspects of state sovereignty must be considered, when concretizing the duty of waste prevention and minimization. The question whether international law can prescribe waste prevention and minimization vis-à-vis sovereignty must therefore be answered by balancing both aspects. In the field of waste management, the foregoing Principle 21 cannot be applied as a balancing parameter, since it focusses only on resources rather than on issues surrounding waste. On these grounds, it will be started with the general relation between environmental law and sovereignty, moving over to the concrete issue of waste generation.

4.2.3.1 Environmental Protection vis-à-vis Sovereignty

This evaluation must start with the general need of environmental protection, which encompasses the negative environmental impacts of the excessive waste generation: The transboundary character of environmental consequences, such as these resulting from waste, requires international action that constitutes a limitation of sovereignty.[131] How to weigh the environmental protection necessary to impede the consequences of waste with the implications of sovereignty can be shown best by an introductory example of regional case law: In the Case of Hamer v. Belgium, acknowledging the importance of environmental protection in general, the judgment clarified that rights such as ownership should not generally prioritized over environmental matters.[132] It highlights that there must be achieved a fair balance between individual and collective interests.[133] Although

---

[130] See 3.3.3.

[131] Bifulco and Nato (2020), 13.

[132] Case of Hamer v. Belgium, Judgment, Reports of Judgments and Decisions 2007-V para. 79 (European Court of Human Rights 2007).

[133] Case of Hamer v. Belgium, Judgment, Reports of Judgments and Decisions 2007-V para. 79.

this case does not directly refer to the conflict between sovereignty and environmental protection, it has ascribed a responsibility to public authorities of taking action in case of ineffective environmental protection in the interplay between economic interests and environmental concerns.[134] *Sands* thus concludes that economic and other considerations must not have priority over environmental protection as the latter must be conducted effectively.[135] Therefore, this case builds a hierarchy upon environmental matters and reinforces their significance vis-à-vis other interests like economic or financial ones. With regard to waste management, it can be transferred that the environmental impacts of waste must not be disregarded in terms of economic considerations concerning its management. *Bifulco and Nato* put this in the context of the general relation between sovereignty and environmental protection. They hold that protection of the environment challenges sovereignty as it transcends national boundaries and demands for international action and therefore puts limits to exercising sovereign rights.[136]

4.2.3.2 Concretizing this Relation to Waste Generation

Regarding the criterion of transboundary environmental protection and to refer back to the issue of waste, the already cited preventive principle moves to the scene again. Due to the fact that this principle marks one of the basic principles under international environmental law and incorporates the issue of transboundary and even global environmental harm,[137] it becomes apparent, why this principle deserves a closer look in finding a tool for the weighing process. The reason, why the preventive principle may serve as a balancing parameter lies in its broad scope of application.[138] The fact that it applies to waste management, has already been proven.[139] However, which statements does the preventive principle provide regarding state sovereignty? In order to prevent transboundary environmental damage, states are required to control action within their jurisdiction.[140] The answer thus lies in its capability to limit state action that occurs within national boundaries for the benefit of preventing environmental damage outside

[134] Case of Hamer v. Belgium, Judgment, Reports of Judgments and Decisions 2007-V para. 79.

[135] Sands et al. (2012), 785.

[136] Bifulco and Nato (2020), 14.

[137] Reynolds (2019), 567.

[138] De Sadeleer (2002), 64.

[139] See 3.1.3.2.

[140] Advisory Opinion OC-23/17 para. 102.

its jurisdiction.[141] The shield of sovereignty is often seen as hindering the solution of international issues.[142] In contrast, the preventive principle overcomes this obstacle by demanding to prevent this action in case of transboundary damage. Applied to waste management, it thus declares the consequences of current waste treatment, which undoubtedly entail transboundary environmental harm, as an international issue. In other words, this principle limits national action for the sake of the international community. With the help of the preventive principle, international law can intrude into the state's national jurisdiction and prescribe anticipatory action.

Accordingly, this principle already incorporates the balancing process between the state's right to decide freely about their action and the transboundary consequences of not preventing environmental harm. It does not restrict national activities as long as the potential consequences do not impact on the other states' welfare in terms of environmental damage.[143] If transboundary harm is likely, it imposes due diligence obligations of preventing these consequences.[144] Thereby, it unifies the implications of both sovereignty and environmental law and implements a priority for environmental concerns in case of transboundary or even global damage.

On top of that, it has already been clarified that the entire international community depends on the same global environment. Therefore, the state's independence decreases in light of the interdependence in the field of environmental protection.[145] Together with the increasing global environmental issues, the traditional concept of sovereignty is outdated, as these problems demand for joint international action.[146] A redefinition of sovereignty, as proposed by *Bifulco and Nato*,[147] towards more flexibility, is thus necessary. With the preventive principle as a balancing parameter, these developments are taken into account in the continuous debate between sovereignty and environmental protection. As a result, this underscores that waste prevention is generally compatible with sovereignty and international law can impose such a duty in accordance with the requirements of national sovereignty. This principle, therefore, does not entail any

---

141 Advisory Opinion OC-23/17 para. 97.

142 Bifulco and Nato (2020), 12.

143 Reynolds (2019), 569.

144 See 2.1.2.2.

145 Bifulco and Nato (2020), 16.

146 Advisory Opinion on the Legality of the Threat or Use of Nuclear Weapons, Dissenting Opinion Judge Weeramantry, 1996 I.C.J. Reports at 505.

147 Bifulco and Nato (2020), 13.

concrete decision in favor or against an obligation to transform the economy. However, it involves a general argument for balancing environmental concerns with sovereignty, which can be applied to the issue of transboundary waste streams as well, since this principle is applicable to a range of environmental concerns, which do not necessarily must be named in agreements.[148] In how far this duty reaches must, nevertheless, identified by looking at the basis for such an obligation, which lies in the human rights regime.

4.2.4 Balancing Human Rights and Sovereignty

The fact that environmental protection does not only represent an objective itself, but also serves for protecting humanity from the adverse affects of environmental degradation,[149] has already been set out.[150] Since human rights build the hard law basis for a duty to safeguard resources and to prevent and minimize waste, its relation to sovereignty remains the missing piece for concretizing such an obligation. It must, hence, be examined, in how far human rights, especially in the environmental context of resources and waste, can limit state sovereignty. On these grounds, the relationship between human rights and sovereignty is to be analyzed in order to find out a parameter for balancing their different demands. Although the general relation between human rights and sovereignty must be shortly examined to understand their interdependence, the core task consists in applying these findings to the concrete topic of an obligation to transform the economy.

4.2.4.1 Development of Human Rights vis-à-vis Sovereignty

Generally, human rights restrict state action concerning the treatment of their peoples, which leads to limitations to the state's sovereignty.[151] With the emergence of the human rights regime and the related obligations, international law has developed even more towards a system, intruding into multiple areas.[152] Therefore, *Reus-Smit* assumes on one side, that sovereignty and human rights

---

[148] Advisory Opinion on the Legality of the Threat or Use of Nuclear Weapons, Dissenting Opinion Judge Weeramantry, 1996 I.C.J. Reports at 505.

[149] Bifulco and Nato (2020), 15.

[150] See 3.2.4.1.

[151] Reus-Smit (2001), 519.

[152] Fassbender (2003), 139.

are "two separate regimes, that stand in a zero-sum relationship"[153], underscoring their opposing character. On the other side, *Ruiz Fabri* refers to the idea that both can complement and oppose each other at the same time.[154] The relation between sovereignty and human rights is thus far from being uncontested. What is clear, nevertheless, is that there exist tensions between both regimes: While the protection of human rights represents an inevitable obligation of states, this duty does not justify the violation of international accepted concepts like this of sovereignty, which thus imposes limitations on the realization of human rights as well.[155] The traditional understanding, hence, focusses on their separateness and mutual restriction that cause conflicts regarding their respective fulfillment.[156] With that focus, balancing both requirements in a concrete context remains difficult. However, the development of their relation did not stop at that point.

Moving from the classical perception with a focus on state sovereignty towards its modern perception, it becomes clear that the people and their well-being are now in the center of modern sovereignty.[157] States shall act not only in favor of their own (economic) interests, but with the objective of ensuring human well-being.[158] According to this understanding, sovereignty exists for the sake of the individuals and shall serve for protecting their rights.[159] In its press release to its annual report, the former Secretary General *Kofi Annan* describes this development as the following: "State sovereignty, in its most basic sense, is being redefined by the forces of globalization and international cooperation. The State is now widely understood to be the servant of its people, and not vice versa."[160]

As already touched upon,[161] the internationalization of human rights challenges the freedom of action under state sovereignty[162] and so its internal affairs must open up to the new development as well. These limitations to state

[153] Reus-Smit (2001), 519.

[154] Ruiz Fabri (2008), 33.

[155] Advisory Opinion OC-23/17 para. 90.

[156] Reus-Smit (2001), 520.

[157] Besson (2011), para. 153.

[158] Besson (2011), para. 93.

[159] Besson (2011), para. 93.

[160] Annan (1999), 1.

[161] See 1.3.2.

[162] Ruiz Fabri (2008), 36.

sovereignty are based on the necessity of protecting human rights.[163] Nonetheless, they do not require the exclusion of either sovereignty or the protection of human rights. The Wimbledon Case describes this situation correctly by stating that international law places limits to the sovereign rights of a state, but at the same time this right entails the freedom of agreeing to treaties that impose obligations on this state.[164] According to the newer development of placing human beings in the center of sovereignty, this perspective allows reconciling both regimes. If the protection of human rights is one of the main objectives of sovereignty, both can be fulfilled rather than being played off against each other. *Besson* concretizes this by holding that "without sovereignty, many human rights-related developments [...] would not have taken place and without the role human rights played in their creation, many of today's sovereign States would not exist"[165]. *Ruiz Fabri* adds that the protection of human rights is thus "structurally dependent upon the existence of an authority capable of guaranteeing them"[166], which requires the existence of state sovereignty. In this context, the cosmopolitan approach evolved, which recognizes human beings as the central subjects of international law from an ethical perspective.[167] This approach addresses the relation between human rights and sovereignty with regard to the developments towards a human-centered perspective and argues in favor of opening the state's internal affairs to take into account the increasing significance of human rights.[168] This ethical approach—although not being a purely legal point—can serve to find a balancing parameter because this perspective is also legally embedded in the emergence of the universal human rights regime. *Pogge* already applies this idea to the issue of production and consumption and criticizes that the actual "state-centric model"[169] does not meet the demands of the people as the national regulation excludes them from this process and hinders international solutions.[170] In light of the massive impacts of global issues concerning production processes, which touch upon both resource depletion and waste generation, uncoordinated national initiatives impede the effective protection of human rights. The cosmopolitan approach, supporting a human-centered focus, hence

---

[163] Ruiz Fabri (2008), 39.

[164] Ruiz Fabri (2008), 43.

[165] Besson (2011), para. 50.

[166] Ruiz Fabri (2008), 84.

[167] Pogge (1992), 48.

[168] Pogge (1992), 58.

[169] Pogge (1992), 63.

[170] Pogge (1992), 63.

serves as a model to balance sovereignty and human rights with due regard to the newer developments including globalization and transboundary issues.

4.2.4.2 Consequences of Human Rights on Sovereignty

What does this perspective mean in terms of a practical application and regarding an obligation? Through the lens of this approach, the traditional concept of sovereignty is challenged, and its boundaries must be redefined.[171] In light of the development of the human rights regime, state sovereignty must be limited, but at the same time not entirely weakened due to its necessity of guaranteeing human rights.[172] A redefinition of sovereignty thus has to include more flexibility regarding its adaption to different historical and practical situations: In that regard, *Reus-Smit* argues in favor of a "variable, practically constituted institution [...] [that is] subject to the same constitutive processes as all other norms, rules and principles"[173]. Instead of a fixed and static concept, it must rather be adaptable to a new context and needs to be detached from its untouchable role. With a variable content, it can evolve over time and adapt to actual needs and issues, serving the people more by providing new solutions than a stuck concept that hinders them. This evolving character is not only desirable but mandatory in light of its objective of protecting the people's well-being including their human rights. Their effective protection requires an adapted perception of sovereignty that is capable of constituting a solid basis for realizing human rights. Such as the rules under the human rights regime and environmental principles, the concept of sovereignty must react to new threats and demands and can therefore be considered as an evolving concept as well.

First, this leads to a general conclusion concerning the existence of human rights obligations: The development of a human rights regime, which still evolves and offers a range of obligations, involve a "cumulative effect"[174] of them, resulting in an extended legal framework. Accordingly, there is a set of human rights obligations limiting the free decision-making of states. Together with the already analyzed environmental law principles, this framework is even more enhanced. In terms of a concrete application of this result, it is to be detected, how far such an obligation can reach without completely undermining the state's right to determine its economy. Regarding the economic leeway vis-à-vis human rights and the environment, a regional case law example is again to be outlined because

[171] Ruiz Fabri (2008), 34.

[172] Ruiz Fabri (2008), 41.

[173] Reus-Smit (2001), 526.

[174] Ruiz Fabri (2008), 46.

it ostensively shows how these aspects are balanced, although in another context than resources and waste: In its Case of Hatton and Others v. United Kingdom, the European Court of Human Rights first demands for a "fair balance that had to be struck between the competing interests of the individual and the community as a whole"[175], including a margin of appreciation for the state in deciding about the steps in order to comply with the rights. In finding this fair balance, the state is thus not entirely bound regarding the way, how to fulfill its duty. Apart from that, the judgment decided that concerning the protection of the environment, economic well-being cannot outbalance the rights of individuals and that states must find the best alternative—also regarding a regulation of private entities—in order to minimize the impact on human rights.[176] This case highlights the importance of human rights related to environmental protection and demonstrates that economic concerns cannot outweigh these rights. Although a state is not forced to set its scope for decision-making to zero, it is required to implement the measure which has the least impact on individual rights. It is self-evident that this regional case cannot determine in how far unwritten international obligations are concretized. However, this case builds a guidance of how to balance human rights in an environmental context vis-à-vis economic considerations.

Moreover, the ICJ in its Advisory Opinion of the Crime of Genocide recognizes the existence of principles that are binding, although lacking a codification,[177] seconded by the acknowledgement of fundamental rules without ratification in the Nuclear Weapons Advisory Opinion.[178] Additionally, the Barcelona Traction Case speaks of obligations that derive from principles and basic human rights.[179] These case law examples, although not directly applicable to this topic, build a strong argument for the existence of unwritten obligations, resulting from human rights together with (environmental law) principles, that have a binding character. Against the backdrop of the findings concerning the development of sovereignty, the existence of unwritten obligations derived from human rights and environmental law principles does not collide with the modern

[175] Case of Hatton and Others v. The United Kingdom, Judgment, Reports of Judgments and Decisions 2003-VIII para. 86 (European Court of Human Rights 2003).

[176] Case of Hatton and Others v. The United Kingdom, Judgment, Reports of Judgments and Decisions 2003-VIII para. 86.

[177] Reservations to the Convention on the Prevention and Punishment of the Crime of Genocide, Advisory Opinion, 1951 I.C.J. Reports 15, 23 (International Court of Justice 1951).

[178] Advisory Opinion on the Legality of the Threat or Use of Nuclear Weapons, ICJ Rep 1996 para. 79.

[179] Case Concerning the Barcelona Traction, Light and Power Company, Limited (Belgium v Spain), Second Phase, Judgment, ICJ Rep 1970, 3 para. 34.

perception of sovereignty anymore. Before reaching a final conclusion, the missing aspect of the states' differentiated situations regarding their capacity for an economic transformation is to be illuminated.

4.3 Special Status of Less Developed Countries

One last issue remains to be solved in order to clarify the content and scope of the discussed obligation. With the huge discrepancies between states not only regarding their economic situation and relating financial capacities but also in terms of their waste management systems,[180] it is questionable if the same obligation applies for every state. Therefore, it appears to be necessary to take a look at the differences between states concerning waste management and other conditions which are important for an economic transformation in order to complete the picture surrounding the sort of obligation.

Before considering the differences between states, it is first to briefly clarify the terminology and classification of states, especially regarding the term "developing countries". Second their general differences will be considered in order to frame their different situations. In a next step, these differences will be embedded in a legal context, taking a closer look at the environmental law principle of common but differentiated responsibilities in this context. Ultimately, this will be evaluated from a human rights perspective, touching upon the notion of socioeconomic rights and their significance for transnational cooperation.

4.3.1 Terminology

First of all, it is difficult to name an appropriate term to summarize those states which face major difficulties regarding their waste management or lack other financial or organizational resources to start a shift towards a circular economy. The often-cited categories of "developing countries", "Third World", or "global South" to describe states which do not achieve certain standards such as the degree of prosperity, industrialization, or political power,[181] are rightly said to be

[180] See already 1.3.4.

[181] Natarajan (2012), 179.

outdated. They are criticized due to the significant discrepancies and the increasing diversity between every state, formerly classified as the "Third World"[182], so that it would no longer be accurate to lump them altogether.

Although the question about the best classification cannot be answered here, since the topic touches upon multiple aspects and requires more background information to be properly discussed, a categorization of the different situations serves to keep these discrepancies in mind. There does exist a group of states and people that share distinct issues like lacking financial power or underdeveloped waste treatment systems. Despite the critique about each term, it is clear that without a joint category, these shared concerns remain less visible.[183] Without neglecting their disparate challenges, but in order to display their current obstacles, the need for a classification is evident. Hence, these discrepancies will be highlighted by speaking of less developed countries, referring to their weaker capabilities of investing into an economic transformation or insufficient waste management. What these differences consist in, will be set out in the following.

4.3.2 Current Obstacles of an Economic Transformation

As already referred to in Chap. 1, less developed countries share a range of obstacles and difficulties regarding their waste management systems,[184] e.g. insufficient waste infrastructure that is necessary for introducing a circular economy[185] or lacking financial capacities for investment.[186] Besides the insufficient financial resources, the establishment of waste services is in a competition with other issues of development and requires institutional structures as well as organizational knowledge and management.[187] Moreover, the access to necessary technology for creating the basis for a circular economy such as institutional capacities for guiding this process are often limited in these countries.[188] Without getting lost in the details of the varied issues, less developed countries face a range of difficulties regarding the establishment of a system that allows safeguarding resources and preventing and minimizing waste. However, it is to be

[182] Natarajan (2012), 180.

[183] Natarajan (2012), 181, 182.

[184] See 1.4.4.

[185] Halog and Anieke (2021), 224, 224; Schulze (2020), 181, 195.

[186] Kaza and et al. (2018), 88.

[187] Kaza and et al. (2018), 88.

[188] Preston et al. (2019), 13.

noted that these obstacles are often neglected in the discussion about how an economy can be designed more sustainable.[189] The concept of circular economy as a possible solution to fulfill these duties thus plays a minor role in less developed countries.[190]

At the same time, the common narrative concerning less developed countries reduces their developmental aim to a narrow focus on poverty reduction, ascribing a negligence of environmental protection to them.[191] *Halog and Anieke*, therefore, criticize that the debate surrounding circular economy does not involve the progress of many less developed countries regarding sustainability.[192] In fact, there exist promising case studies of the positive contribution of circular economic business models in less developed countries like India, Brazil or Kenya.[193] With its capability to increase productivity, leading to economic growth and reducing environmental impacts, which contributes to environmental conservation and human health, the advantages of a circular economic system in those countries are evident.[194] What is more: With their less developed waste management systems, these countries have the possibility to avoid mistakes, more developed countries have made, and pursue the pathway to a green economy at an earlier stage.[195] A transformation towards a circular economy thus could mean a great opportunity for these countries,[196] again depending on investment and support to make use of this chance.[197]

These examples of the disparate challenges and possible approaches render a one-fits-all solution inappropriate. It is thus to be put in a legal context, whether a potential duty of safeguarding resources and preventing and minimizing waste through taking steps towards a circular economy can equally address all states to the same extent and what is necessary to fulfill these duties. This will be illuminated under the environmental law principle of common but differentiated responsibilities and by considering the implications of socioeconomic rights under the human rights regime.

---

[189] Preston et al. (2019), 2.

[190] Halog and Anieke (2021), 225.

[191] Halog and Anieke (2021), 225.

[192] Halog and Anieke (2021), 225.

[193] Halog and Anieke (2021), 225.

[194] Halog and Anieke (2021), 225.

[195] Schulze (2020), 196.

[196] Preston et al. (2019), 2.

[197] Preston et al. (2019), 3.

4.3.3 Common but Differentiated Responsibilities

In the first place, it must be detected whether the principle of common but differentiated responsibilities is suitable to solve this conflict, resulting from the different contributions to the issues of resource depletion and waste generation as well as the divergent capacities of more and less developed countries. Thereby, the general content of this principle including its legal status will be set out in order to apply it to the issue at stake. Together with its connections to other environmental law concepts like sustainable development and the common concern of humankind, its legal consequences are to be analyzed to answer the question from an environmental law perspective.

4.3.3.1 The Principle's General Content

From the perspective of a formal equality of states, "de iure all states are assumed to be equal and subject to the same rights and duties"[198], neglecting the de facto inequalities. *Kelsen*, however, does not speak of an equality of duties and rights, but rather of an equality of capacity for duties and rights.[199] Generally, the principle of common but differentiated responsibilities addresses this issue of different capacities between more and less developed countries and builds the bridge to a joint protection of the global environment.[200] Although embedded in a range of multilateral treaties and declarations by now, its reflection in Principle 6 and 7 Rio Declaration entails its most accepted formulation: Applying a special priority for the needs and (environmental) vulnerability of less developed countries,[201] Principle 7 highlights the different contributions to global environmental degradation and demands for global cooperation for environmental conservation.[202] *Hey* summarizes this by stating that this concept incorporates "that while pursuing a common goal, States take on different obligations, depending on their socio-economic situation and their historical contribution to the environmental problem at stake"[203]

On the side of the prerequisites, it includes two elements: Firstly, it constitutes a common responsibility for global environmental issues. Secondly, the states' differing situations are recognized, both regarding their contributions to

[198] Hey (2011), para. 12.

[199] Kelsen (1944), 209.

[200] Brunnée (2003), 46.

[201] Principle 6 Rio Declaration.

[202] Principle 7 Rio Declaration.

[203] Hey (2011), para. 1.

these issues and to their capability to handle them.[204] This involves the existence of a global environmental issue, which is not specified further. As already set out within the discussion of the concept of common concern of humankind,[205] resource depletion can be considered as a common environmental concern and with its multiple environmental impacts at the global level, it can surely be acknowledged as a global environmental issue under this principle. Furthermore, the consequences of the massive waste generation and its treatment equally impact on the environment[206] and can therefore be subsumed under this requirement as well. Hence, this principle prescribes a common responsibility for the issue of depleting resources and waste. As clarified in the above part, especially less developed states face difficulties regarding the establishment of an adequate waste treatment and lack financial and institutional measures to achieve this responsibility. Concerning the divergent contributions, industrialized countries are responsible for the major part of waste generation per capita, while less developed countries generate more than half of the total amount of waste.[207] The responsibility for overexploitation evidently depends on the supply of natural resources within each state and, therefore, varies between the states. Accordingly, there are differences between their contributions to these issues and between their capabilities as well.

4.3.3.2 Concrete Legal Consequences

It remains questionable, what this principle then entails as a legal consequence. Although it still cannot be qualified as a binding rule, it is accepted as a soft law principle with normative implications not only in the field of environmental law but also in general international law.[208] It is supported by state practice at different levels[209] and provides a basis for less developed countries in the debate about different capacities in fulfilling international law obligations.[210]

---

[204] Sands et al. (2012), 233.

[205] See 2.1.3.1.

[206] See 3.1.1.

[207] See https://www.imf.org/en/Blogs/Articles/2020/01/31/waste-woes-in-the-world#:~:text=While%20high%2Dincome%20countries%20generate,tourism%20plays%20a%20large%20role accessed 28 March 2024.

[208] Hey (2011), para. 18.

[209] Sands et al. (2012), 233.

[210] Hey (2011), para. 19.

Its exact implications in the respective field are, nevertheless, more difficult to concretize.[211]

First of all, the part of "common responsibility" leads to a shared obligation of the states towards handling this environmental issue.[212] Applied to resource depletion and waste generation, it thus constitutes a joint obligation of all states to fulfill the duties of safeguarding resources and preventing and minimizing waste. The second part, however, reflects the differences and thus imposes different legal obligations on the states, dependent on their degree of contribution and their capabilities.[213] Therefore, differing obligations may include less strict commitments or more leeway regarding the way of how such a duty is implemented.[214] However, the concrete legal consequences did not remain undisputed, as the United States at Rio did not accept any interpretation of Principle 7 that would mean a diminution of the responsibility of less developed states under international law.[215] This position is reinforced in the context of a duty of prevention by the Inter-American Court which holds in its Advisory Opinion OC 23/17 that the "existence of this obligation does not depend on the level of development; in other words, the obligation of prevention applies equally to both developed and developing States"[216]. Instead of a lower normative responsibility of less developed countries or those with a lower degree of contribution, this suggests only diverging approaches to fulfill these duties. Their capabilities do not challenge the existence of these duties but influence their way of implementation.

What is necessary to still render the common responsibility effective is the key obligation under this principle: The duty of cooperation. The global responsibility incorporates a duty to cooperate according to their different contributions as well as their access to the necessary technology and financial resources.[217] Less developed states can only achieve their part of the common responsibility if they receive financial and organizational support. The duty of cooperation has already been thematized within the section about the concept of common concern of humankind.[218] The important connection between the concept of common concern of humankind and the principle of common but differentiated responsibilities

[211] Handl (2012), 5, 6.

[212] Sands et al. (2012), 234.

[213] Sands et al. (2012), 233.

[214] Sands et al. (2012), 235.

[215] Handl (2012), 5, 6.

[216] Advisory Opinion OC-23/17 para. 142.

[217] Hey (2011), para. 5.

[218] See 2.1.3.2.

has thereby been touched upon. Since both are connected by their demand for a common responsibility for environmental issues like resource depletion and the impacts of waste[219] and by their relation to a duty of cooperation, they are complementing and reinforcing each other. Whereas the concept of common concern constitutes a framework for a common responsibility, the principle of common but differentiated responsibilities shapes this framework in terms of distributing the obligations between more and less developed countries. Financial support through investments and funds as well as the transfer of knowledge and technology for establishing a circular economy are thus crucial to achieve this common responsibility. Cooperation also involves the development of common rules and standards for achieving circular resource flows on a global level.[220] More developed countries, which entail the financial and organizational capabilities,[221] and which are front runner states in terms of a circular economy, are obliged under this principle to share their measures and knowledge to contribute to the common goal. This can even be described as a component of international solidarity.[222] On that account, the duty to cooperate leads to the concrete obligations of financial aid and transfer of knowledge and technology for establishing better waste management systems and starting a shift away from resource-intensive business models.

Similarly, the principle of common but differentiated responsibilities is connected to the concept of sustainable development and translates the issue of intragenerational equity towards achieving sustainable development to the interstate level.[223] Applying the idea of equity to the interpretation of international law rules means to take into account the needs of less developed countries.[224] It thereby connects the obstacles of less developed countries with the concept of sustainable development. Intragenerational equity as one component of sustainable development,[225] transferred to the divide between more and less developed countries leads to a "shared but heavier responsibility in working towards sustainable development"[226] for more developed states. Since it has been clarified that sustainable development builds one pillar for a binding duty to safeguard

---

[219] See Rayfuse (2016), 12.

[220] Preston et al. (2019), 3.

[221] Preston et al. (2019), 4.

[222] Beyerlin (2013), para. 20.

[223] Hey (2011), para. 5.

[224] Sands et al. (2012), 233.

[225] See 2.1.1.5.

[226] Barral (2012), 381.

resources and prevent and minimize waste, it thus reinforces the argument that the connected principle of common but differentiated responsibilities is also applicable to this obligation. As this principle entails that more developed countries must support the sustainable development efforts of less developed states,[227] this support is also owed in terms of the concrete duties of safeguarding resources and preventing and minimizing waste. Both the concept of sustainable development and the principle of common but differentiated responsibilities deal with different facets of the same issue and are, hence, intertwined regarding the concrete design of these duties.

The necessity of international cooperation in light of the global character of the issue of resource depletion and waste is thus reinforced by the principle of common but differentiated responsibilities. It influences on the duties to safeguard resources and prevent and minimize waste by applying a common responsibility for all states and, at the same time, obliges more developed states to transfer knowledge, technology, and financial resources to less developed countries in order to meet their joint responsibility.

4.3.3.3 Implications of Socioeconomic Rights

Regarding questions of equity and the disparate situations between states, the human rights regime offers provisions dealing with these inequalities as well: Further insights on how human rights handle the different capabilities of states can be found in the ICESCR. Within the analysis of human rights, it has already been set out that socioeconomic rights merely demand for a progressive realization of these rights and that the states' efforts depend on their maximum available resources.[228] Furthermore, Art. 2 (1) ICESCR offers more insights on the significance of the states' capabilities regarding the fulfillment of their duties and—on top of that—on international cooperation.[229] Art. 2 (1) ICESCR explicitly requires "international assistance and cooperation, especially economic and technical" and thereby highlights the relevance of international cooperation in fulfilling human rights. Moreover, the need for cooperation is repeated in the specific rights, e.g. Art. 11 (1) or (2) ICESCR, and demanded by the Special Rapporteur concerning the right to a healthy environment.[230]

---

[227] Barral (2012), 381.

[228] See 2.2.1.2.

[229] Sajo (2002), 225.

[230] UN General Assembly, Report of the Special Rapporteur on the issue of human rights obligations relating to the enjoyment of a safe, clean, healthy and sustainable environment, para. 19.

Socioeconomic rights thus recognize the different economic and developmental situations of states through limiting their duties by their maximum available resources on the one hand. On the other hand, the Covenant acknowledges the need for cooperation to jointly fulfill its rights. Support for other states as a legal obligation is, hence, embedded in the system of socioeconomic rights.[231] Therefore, socioeconomic rights are described as the "foundation of a more equitable order"[232]. In terms of a concrete obligation to safeguard resources and prevent and minimize waste generation, these implications have a huge effect on these duties, since the latter are largely based on socioeconomic rights. They reinforce the approach, that different countries with different capabilities do not have exactly the same obligation and that more developed countries are obliged to cooperate with less developed states to support their economic shift. Parallel to the findings from the principle of common but differentiated responsibilities, including the differentiated design of their obligations, dependent on their capabilities, as well as the duty to cooperate with each other, involving i.a. transfer of knowledge and financial support, the character of socioeconomic leads to similar consequences.

In the interplay between national sovereignty and cooperation, there is one aspect about socioeconomic rights that moves the discussion beyond a duty to cooperation: The existence of transnational human rights obligations. Although the topic of transnational human rights obligations is too broad to be entirely discussed in this framework, the idea of a transboundary facet of socioeconomic rights needs to be touched upon when thinking about a global economic transformation. With due regard to the transboundary impacts of waste, this idea has already been touched upon.[233] Concerning the potential of socioeconomic rights of contributing to a more equitable economic order, *Sajo* poses the question if states may also have human rights obligations to people outside their jurisdiction.[234] When thinking about a duty of cooperation, which involves an obligation of financial support or other assistance, this alone entails a transboundary facet. The idea of helping each other in achieving the fulfillment of human rights is said to be based on the assumption that states "must respect the human rights of all humans"[235] and that they must support those countries which are not able to fulfill these duties alone. This is rooted in the understanding that one state alone

[231] Besson (2011), para. 125.

[232] Sajo (2002), 221.

[233] See 3.2.2.7.

[234] Sajo (2002), 235.

[235] Sajo (2002), 235.

may not have the capacity of solving global obstacles which inhibit the fulfillment of human rights, e.g. the sufficient provision of adequate food hindered by a changing climate which impacts on the local agriculture.[236] Hence, *Sajo* derives transnational obligations for other states to equally address these issues from socioeconomic rights.[237] He argues that socioeconomic rights demand for a fair and equitable system that allows less developed countries to fulfill their human rights obligations.[238] Since the foundation of many issues surrounding socioeconomic rights lies in the economic order, he ascribes to these rights the capability of challenging the current economic system.[239]

Nonetheless, the existence of transnational human rights obligations which affect the whole economic order again raises a conflict with state sovereignty.[240] Although it has already been discussed how human rights and sovereignty can be reconciled in this context, the implications of sovereignty determine the concrete design of a duty of cooperation. Regarding this issue, *Attaran* offers a plausible approach of both acknowledging the need for international cooperation and taking the limits by state sovereignty into account: The demand for international assistance and cooperation in Art. 2 (1) ICESCR represents the recognition that no state is left alone with its duties under this Covenant and that this assistance involves obligations towards humans outside the own jurisdiction.[241] In fact, such cooperation entails i.a. the funding of foreign projects, which does transcend the national boundary.[242] However, the development has shown that state sovereignty has opened up for such transboundary action for fulfilling human rights. As already discussed above, the effective fulfillment of human rights necessitates international action and thus cooperation. As long as the principle of non-intervention is observed, such transboundary action is in accordance with a modern perception of sovereignty.[243] Therefore, *Attaran* seconds *Sajo* in acknowledging transnational duties towards humans outside national jurisdiction derived from the duty of cooperation under socioeconomic rights.[244]

---

[236] Sajo (2002), 235.
[237] Sajo (2002), 235.
[238] Sajo (2002), 251.
[239] Sajo (2002), 250.
[240] Attaran (1999), 33.
[241] Attaran (1999), 33.
[242] Attaran (1999), 34.
[243] Attaran (1999), 35.
[244] Attaran (1999), 33.

In the context of a joint responsibility under the principle of common but differentiated responsibilities and the concept of common concern of humankind, this consequence might have seemed clear. The interpretation of socioeconomic rights, moreover, reinforces this approach in the legally binding context of human rights obligations and it is thus based on another solid pillar. It must, nevertheless, be kept in mind that the existence of such transnational duties is not entirely accepted and subject to a range of consequential problems, so that this issue cannot be solved in its entirety. The assumption of such duties of course leads to follow-up questions, in how far the states owe support in light of their own capacities and issues of fulfilling this duty. However, such questions of distribution are far beyond the scope of the actual research question and thus cannot be discussed within this framework.[245] Notwithstanding that the extent of those transnational duties entails elements of uncertainty, this development forms a strong argument in favor of a high degree of international cooperation, involving transboundary measures and support. Cooperation based on the environmental law principle of common but differentiated responsibilities and the concept of common concern of humankind, as well as on the character of socioeconomic rights is thus a crucial element of bridging the divide between more and less developed countries.

4.4 Conclusion on the Concretization of the Obligation

Taking the results from the balancing process as well as the divergent situations of states into account, a final answer for the overall research question can be found by building five categories to concretize the conclusive obligation.

4.4.1 Priority for Human Rights and Environmental Concerns

After weighing the requirements of human rights combined with international environmental law with the implications of sovereignty regarding implicit obligations, the high importance of human rights in the environmental context has been set out. According to the different balancing parameters, the issue of resource depletion and the consequences of waste can be prioritized vis-à-vis the sovereign right to decide upon a state's economic system. Although economic decisions fall

[245] See for more insights on that topic Attaran (1999), 39.

under the *domaine réservé*, the concerns under human rights law together with environmental law outweigh the state's interest to continue with overexploiting resources or unlimitedly generating waste. It follows that human rights, especially regarding a healthy environment or which are otherwise related to environmental issues, have gained importance and, therefore, a higher priority. In the context of resource and waste management, this approach gives these obligations a higher significance and requires finding solutions for these issues. Therefore, international law may intrude into these internal affairs and prescribe rules, even those rules have not been explicitly consented to. Implicit obligations in the context of resource and waste management, which are derived from the human rights regime and environmental law principles and concepts, can thus be reconciled with the demands of state sovereignty. Sovereign rights including economic decisions can, hence, be degraded and restricted by the needs of humanity in this context. On these grounds, the first criterion of concretizing this duty lies in the higher significance of human rights and environmental concerns vis-à-vis sovereignty regarding this specific context, which generally permits the deduction of an implicit duty to both safeguard resources and prevent and minimize waste generation.

4.4.2 Margin of Appreciation

However, the second criterion considers the still important role of sovereignty and the remaining margin of appreciation: Since sovereignty including its inherent rights is not outdated, but only adapted, there is still leeway for state action that cannot be excluded entirely. The actual state of the relation between sovereignty and international law does not provide a foundation of fully prescribing necessary rules and specific measures, which on top of that directly challenge the whole economic system. In order to take the status of sovereignty and its requirements into account, an obligation to apply a concrete product design or certain production processes cannot follow from this implicit obligation. Similar to the consequences of economic, social and cultural rights, this obligation leads towards a process of legislating rules in order to implement cyclical material flows rather than a fixed result of a distinct production pattern. Applied to the duty of safeguarding resources and preventing and minimizing waste, the margin of appreciation does not permit a certain target, but rather involves a duty of conduct that implements these objectives step by step. Although the high importance of these duties can restrict sovereignty, it cannot undermine the state's right to decide upon their economy entirely. The way of how to achieve safeguarding resources and preventing and minimizing waste underlies a margin of appreciation and cannot be concretized to one specific measure.

4.4.3 Principle of Effectiveness

This leads over to the third criterion, which is the effective realization of human rights. It has been clarified that the protection of human rights, particularly in the environmental context, requires the limitation of sovereignty on the one side, but still leaves room for national leeway on the other. In this conflicting area, the principle of effectiveness sharpens the concretization of the obligation. Human rights must be realized effectively, which means that vague general goals do not meet the requirements of human rights protection. Although the margin of appreciation only prescribes a process, this does not allow inaction. On the contrary, it involves positive action initiating this process. Most effective are thus positive obligations.[246] In the case of depleting resources and threats of waste, the most effective way to fulfill these rights consists in concrete rules of an adapted economy, including rules for product design that allow a cyclical use. Leaving the economy as it is cannot meet the requirement of an effective realization—independent from the degree of leeway. Therefore, this criterion requires steps towards an economic transformation that include an adapted product design in order to effectively implement the duty of safeguarding resources and minimizing waste altogether.

4.4.4 Due Diligence

The fourth criterion reinforces the latter point by concretizing the steps demanded by the effective realization of these obligations. The duty of due diligence, derived from the preventive principle, entails the obligation to use the best available technology. It, hence, influences on the compromise between the economic leeway and the needs from human rights and environmental law principles by specifying the required measure. Due diligence involves finding the best solution that has the least impacts. A cyclical resource use with a regulation for product design entails the maximum benefit for the aim of minimizing waste and safeguarding resources and is, therefore, the most suitable solution for human well-being.

[246] Ruiz Fabri (2008), 55.

At the same time, a duty of due diligence does not aim for a specific result and thereby considers the state's margin of appreciation. As the current linear economy cannot meet the standards in terms of environmental protection and human rights, it certainly does not represent the best available technology. However, a circular economy is not well established and, therefore, demands for huge economic changes including financial and institutional efforts. A completely regulated transformation would entirely diminish the significance of sovereignty. The duty of due diligence thus only requires initiating this process and starting a transformation towards a cyclical resource use. It considers the remaining economic leeway by not demanding for a concrete framework of how to achieve this including timetables and special measures, but rather provides a flexible approach with a certain objective.

This approach is underscored by the character of socioeconomic rights, on which the obligation is largely based. The positive duty, derived from the analyzed human rights, does not involve a specific result, but rather entails to undertake steps to achieve it. With the requirement of a minimum core, it is clear that inaction does not suffice to fulfill the human rights obligations. On the contrary, socioeconomic rights demand for taking at least first steps towards fulfilling the underlying obligations. In terms of an economic transformation, socioeconomic rights thus oblige states to start the process towards the establishment of a system that effectively stops resource depletion and waste generation. Both environmental law and human rights thus prescribe a duty of conduct including steps towards a circular economy.

4.4.5 Cooperation

Lastly, the consideration of the aforementioned socioeconomic rights as well as the application of the principle of common but differentiated responsibilities lead to recognizing the states' different economic and developmental situations in deriving a duty of cooperation. With due regard to their differentiated situations, the overall obligation applies for every state the same, but the way how to achieve its fulfillment varies between states according to their capabilities. Both fields of international law acknowledge the need for cooperation and entail the obligation of international support through the transfer of knowledge and technology as well as financial support as the necessary measure. With due regard to the concrete duties of safeguarding resources and waste prevention and minimization, this leads to additional duties of more developed states of supporting an economic shift in less developed countries. With a transfer of knowledge and technology and together with financial support, the process towards establishing a circular economy can be started in every country, so that the global responsibility of solving the issues of resource depletion and waste generation is thereby met. As the missing puzzle piece, this duty to cooperate enhances the concretized obligation of starting the process towards a circular economy in order to meet the objectives in the field of resource and waste management. By considering the aspect of international cooperation, the concretization of this duty has been conducted comprehensively including all relevant perspectives.

In the end, it is to be concluded that a binding duty of safeguarding resources for future generations and for preventing and minimizing waste generation through a transformation towards a circular economy including adapted product design can be derived from the human rights regime together with the environmental law principles. This duty entails to initiate the transformative process towards a cyclical resource use, leaving leeway concerning a concrete implementation and elaboration of this process. In contrast to restrictions on resource-extraction or the dumping of waste, a positive duty of supporting the transformation of the economy into a circular one provides a proactive solution for fulfilling the duty of safeguarding resources and preventing and minimizing waste in a sustainable way.

Conclusion

After analyzing the fields of international environmental law and human rights law with the focus on resource and waste management as well as considering the concept of sovereignty, the overall research question on an obligation of an economic transformation has been answered. Although the concept of a circular economy does not form the economic foundation of most states yet, the interpretation of the analyzed principles and concepts under international environmental law such as of the written and unwritten rights under the human rights regime leads to an implicit obligation of due diligence to undertake steps towards a cyclical resource flow with an adapted product design. With the underlying duties of safeguarding natural resources for future generations and preventing and minimizing the generation of waste, it builds the basis of a transformation towards a circular economy.

This thesis has proven that the roots of such a future-oriented obligation lie within the interlinked body of human rights law together with international environmental law. After clarifying the scope of circular economy including the development of a working definition, this project approached this concept from an international law perspective using doctrinal analysis. Without specific hard law agreements on this topic and only fragmented literature in legal research, it developed a conception of how this relatively new concept can be linked to international law. Surrounding the product's life cycle, its findings regarding the field of resource management such as its conclusions on waste management, both from an environmental law and a human rights perspective, paved the way for embedding circular economy into a legal framework.

Within the field of international environmental law, this project found a way to interpret the respective concepts and principles in order to reveal their legal

V. Wefringhaus, *Circular Economy and International Law*, Juridicum—Bochumer Schriften zur Friedenssicherung und zum Humanitären Völkerrecht I Bochum Studies on the International Law of Peace and Armed Conflict 70,
https://doi.org/10.1007/978-3-658-49936-5

significance as well as their interrelation to circular economy. The concept of sustainable development, the common concern of humankind, and the principles of precaution and prevention have thereby been illuminated in depth and applied to the issue of resource depletion, which is only fragmentarily researched upon in a legal context. What is new, is not only their combined consideration but also their application to resource exploitation in this degree of profundity. By revealing the modifying character of sustainable development and the implications of preventive action regarding resource management under the preventive and precautionary principle, a strong argument for an alternative resource management has been developed. Whereas the topic of waste is already embedded in international treaties, this thesis carved out its implications on waste prevention and minimization and reinforced the argumentation on a principle of waste prevention and minimization by an extensive analysis of the preventive and precautionary principle in the context of waste management. Carrying the actual state of literature on the issue of waste forward, this project involved international law documents such as international and regional case law. By comparing regional developments on that issue to the international level, the development of this broad field is extensively portrayed.

Regarding the involvement of human rights, the classic interpretation methods under the VCLT have been enhanced by the principle of effectiveness and the evolutive interpretation, which underscored the special development of the human rights regime and allowed to derive more concrete results. With the help of an extensive evaluation of judgements in the field of resource and waste management, the close connection between human rights and these issues has been revealed. In addition to their detailed separate analysis, their combined consideration has illuminated their linkages to each other and has provided answers for the status of human rights regarding resource depletion and waste management, linking up with the current state of research.

The most important step, however, consists in the joint interpretation of human rights and international environmental law, which did not build a focal point of international legal research yet. After clarifying the legitimacy of interpreting both regimes together from a methodological point of view, the findings of international environmental law and human rights in the context of resource and waste management have been combined. The thesis thus builds on common interpretation methods and applies them to the rarely touched upon topics of resources and waste and, moreover, involves a new methodological approach of considering different fields of law together. This consideration has led to the first insightful conclusion that states are obliged to safeguard resources for future generations and to prevent and minimize waste generation.

As a logical next step regarding the overall topic of circular economy, it has been justified why both stages (resource and waste management) have to be regarded together in a practical and legal context and whether they constitute inseparable parts of a product's life cycle. By carving out their interdependence and the need for considering the whole production process, the product design moved into focus. Therefore, this project started to illuminate its legal embedment by setting out the current EU legislation, which serves as a first mover in this field, and compared it to the international level. It thereby incorporated the concept of sustainable development with its integrative function again, arguing in favor of a system that entails sustainable production and consumption through implementing resource efficiency and minimizing pollution. With this approach, the need for a joint fulfillment of both duties in the production phase through an adapted product design has been set out.

This conclusion under Part 1 builds a strong argument in favor of a mandatory economic transformation under international law. Nonetheless, the question of such an implicit obligation could not be answered without having taken the concept of sovereignty into account. Since sovereignty is discussed extensively in legal literature, this thesis focused on its implications on implicit obligations and referred to its theoretical foundation only in terms of defining its limitations. It thereby ties up with the existing research framework and developed it further on the question of an implicit obligation for an economic transformation. An adapted understanding of sovereignty has resulted, as it has evolved towards a limited concept that permits the limitation through international law also in terms of economic decisions. Core task of Part 2 is the balancing process, which describes in how far the free determination of the state's economic decisions can be restricted and regulated by international law. First, due to the lack of established structure for balancing these findings, the parameters of the weighing process have been defined for each field of law. Second, the boundaries between sovereignty on the one side, and the provisions under both international environmental law and human rights law on the other side have been clarified in this balancing process. By including sovereignty, this project illuminates the obligation from all necessary perspectives and anticipates potential hurdles of its implementation. Together with examining the differentiated situation of less developed countries with the help of the principle of common but differentiated responsibilities and the implications of socioeconomic rights, the final conclusion has been derived. In describing five categories, the duty of states is concretized to a duty of due diligence which takes the state's margin of appreciation into account and prescribes to undertake steps to start a shift to an economic system, which is based on a cyclical use of resources including an adapted product design and thereby entails to safeguard resources for future generations and prevent and minimize waste generation.

With this implicit obligation under international law, although not being a defined duty of result regarding the establishment of a circular economy, the transformative character of especially the human rights regime and international environmental law has been highlighted. Their potential to provide solutions for new problems is generally underestimated and has been demonstrated by this examination. Whereas the topic of circular economy has already found entry into the literature surrounding its technical perception, this thesis builds an important cornerstone regarding its implications in the legal context. This duty paves the way for further legal research concerning its implementation and measures of how to achieve a global economic shift towards more resource efficiency. Especially the role of businesses and other relevant stakeholders deserves an in-depth consideration since they represent the actual addressees of such an obligation. Future research on the general relation between international law and private entities like companies as well as on the special case of concrete regulation concerning a cyclical resource use for the industry, hence, becomes necessary.

Regarding its influence in a political context, national governments and, particularly, international and regional organizations are called upon to find a way to translate this duty into concrete legislation and measures. The states' awareness of this issue is already visible; however, the actual state of implementation still leaves much to be desired. This thesis' result may help to support the already identifiable developments in this direction by explicitly naming that such an obligation under international law exists. Besides this duty, it shows how the concept does not only entail additional efforts but also offer economic chances for every state, which will pay off in the future—for the economy, the environment and the people. Within the framework of legal research, this thesis, therefore, marks the first step towards the global establishment of a circular economy.

Bibliography

Table of Cases

Advisory Opinion OC-23/17, No. OC-23/17 (Inter-American Court of Human Rights November 15, 2017).

Case Concerning Military and Paramilitary Activities in and Against Nicaragua (Nicaragua v. United States of America), I.C.J. Reports 14 (International Court of Justice 1986).

Case of Di Sarno and others v. Italy, No. Application no. 30765/08 (European Court of Human Rights January 10, 2012).

Case of Giacomelli v. Italy, No. Application no. 59909/00 (European Court of Human Rights November 2, 2006).

Case of Guerra and Others v. Italy, No. 116/1996/735/932 (European Court of Human Rights February 19, 1998).

Case of López Ostra v. Spain, No. Application no. 16798/90 (European Court of Human Rights December 9, 1994).

Case of Öneryildiz v. Turkey, Judgment, No. Application no. 48939/99 (European Court of Human Rights November 30, 2004).

Case of the Indigenous Communities of the Lhaka Honhat (Our Land) Association v. Argentina, Jugment (Inter-American Court of Human Rights February 6, 2020).

Case of Zander v. Sweden, No. Application no. 14282/88 (European Court of Human Rights November 25, 1993).

European Court of Human Rights. Guide on Article 8 of the European Convention on Human Rights (2022).

Inter-American Commission on Human Rights. "Community of San Mateo de Huanchor and Its Members v. Peru," October 15, 2004.

Tătar v. Romania, No. No. 67021/01 (European Court of Human Rights January 27, 2009).

V. Wefringhaus, *Circular Economy and International Law*, Juridicum—Bochumer Schriften zur Friedenssicherung und zum Humanitären Völkerrecht I Bochum Studies on the International Law of Peace and Armed Conflict 70,
https://doi.org/10.1007/978-3-658-49936-5

International Jurisdiction

Advisory Opinion on the Legality of the Threat or Use of Nuclear Weapons, ICJ Rep 1996 226 (International Court of Justice (ICJ) 1996).
Advisory Opinion on the Legality of the Threat or Use of Nuclear Weapons, Dissenting Opinion Judge Weeramantry, 1996 I.C.J. Reports 226 (International Court of Justice 1996).
Advisory Opinion on the Responsibilities and Obligations of States Sponsoring Persons and Entities with Respect to Activities in the Area, ITLOS Reports 2011, 10 (International Tribunal of the Law of the Sea (ITLOS) 2011).
Arbitration regarding the Iron Rhine Railway (Belgium v Netherlands), Award, ICGJ 373 (Permanent Court of Arbitration (PCA) 2005).
Case Concerning Armed Activities on the Territory of the Congo (Democratic Republic of the Congo v. Uganda), I.C.J. Reports 2005, p. 168 (International Court of Justice 2005).
Case Concerning the Barcelona Traction, Light and Power Company, Limited (Belgium v Spain), Second Phase, Judgment, ICJ Rep 1970, 3 (International Court of Justice (ICJ) 1970).
Case of the S.S. Wimbledon, ICGJ 235 (Permanent Court of Justice 1923).
Customs Régime Between Germany and Austria Advisory Opinion, Individual Opinion Judge Anzilotti, No. 41 (Permanent court of International Justice September 5, 1931).
Gabčikovo-Nagymaros Project (Hungary v Slovakia), Judgement (Separate Opinion of Vice-President Weeramantry), ICJ Rep 7 (International Court of Justice (ICJ) 1997).
Gabčikovo-Nagymaros Project (Hungary v Slovakia), Judgement, Merits, ICJ Rep 7 (International Court of Justice (ICJ) 1997).
Nationality Decrees Issued in Tunis and Morocco, Advisory Opinion, No. 4 (Permanent Court of International Justice February 7, 1923).
Nuclear Tests (New Zealand v France), Request for an Examination of the Situation in Accordance with Paragraph 63 of the Court's Judgment of 20 December 1974, Dissenting Opinion of Judge Weeramantry, ICJ Reports 1995, 288 (International Court of Justice (ICJ) 1995).
Pulp Mills on the River Uruguay (Argentina v Uruguay), Judgement, ICJ Rep 113 (2006) (International Court of Justice (ICJ) 2006).
Reservations to the Convention on the Prevention and Punishment of the Crime of Genocide, Advisory Opinion, 1951 I.C.J. Reports 15 (International Court of Justice 1951).
The Case of the S.S. "Lotus," Publications of the Permanent Court of International Justice (Permanent Court of International Justice 1927).

Regional Jurisdiction

Case of Demir and Baykara v. Turkey, Judgment, No. Application no. 34503/97 (European Court of Human Rights November 12, 2008).
Case of Golder v. The United Kingdom, Judgment, No. Application no. 4451/70 (European Court of Human Rights February 21, 1975).
Case of Hamer v. Belgium, Judgment, Reports of Judgments and Decisions 2007-V (European Court of Human Rights 2007).

Case of Hatton and Others v. The United Kingdom, Judgment, Reports of Judgments and Decisions 2003-VIII (European Court of Human Rights 2003).
Case of Tyrer v. The United Kingdom, Jugment, No. 5856/72 (European Court of Human Rights April 25, 1978).
European Court of Human Rights, Press Unit. "Factsheet—Environment and the European Convention on Human Rights," October 2022.
United Kingdom of Great Britain and Northern Ireland v. Commission of the European Communities, Judgment, 1998/-02265 European Court Reports (European Court of Justice 1998).

National Jurisdiction

German Federal Constitutional Court, Order of 24 March 2021, 1 BvR 2656/18, 1 BvR 288/20, 1 BvR 96/20, 1 BvR 78/20, headnote 4, available at https://www.bundesverfassungsgericht.de/SharedDocs/Entscheidungen/DE/2021/03/rs20210324_1bvr265618.html (also available in English) accessed 12 January 2022.
Minors Oposa v Secretary of the Department of Environmental and Natural Resources, 33 ILM 173 (1994) (Supreme Court of the Philippines 1993).
Urgenda Foundation v. State of the Netherlands, Hoge Raad, December 20 2019, 19/00135, available at https://www.urgenda.nl/wp-content/uploads/ENG-Dutch-Supreme-Court-Urgenda-v-Netherlands-20-12-2019.pdf (English translation) https://uitspraken.rechtspraak.nl/inziendocument?id=ECLI:NL:HR:2019:2006 (original Dutch version) accessed 12 January 2022.

Table of Legislation

Basel Convention on the Transboundary Movements of Hazardous Waste and their Disposal (adopted on 22 March 1989, entered into force on 5 May 1992) UN Treaty Series vol. 1673, 57.
Brundtland, Gro Harlem. Report of the World Commission on Environment and Development: Our Common Future, UN Doc. A/42/427 § (1987). available on https://www.netzwerk-n.org/wp-content/uploads/2017/04/0_Brundtland_Report-1987-Our_Common_Future.pdf.
Statute of the International Court of Justice (adopted on 26 June 1945, entered into force on 24 October 1945) UN Treaty Series vol. 993, 33.
Vienna Convention on the Law of Treaties (adopted on 23 May 1969, entered into force on 27 January 1980) UN Treaty Series vol. 1155, 331.

Treaties

African Charter on Human and Peoples' Rights (adopted on 27 June 1981, entered into force on 21 October 1986) UN Treaty Series 1520, 217.

African Convention on the Conservation of Nature and Natural Resources (adopted on 11 July 2003, entered into force on 23 July 2016) available at https://au.int/sites/default/files/treaties/41550-treaty-Charter_ConservationNature_NaturalResources.pdf
Arab Charter on Human Rights (adopted on 22 May 2004, entered into force on 15 March 2008) reprinted in 12 Int'l Hum. Rts. Rep. 893 (2005).
Bamako Convention on the Ban of the Import into Africa and the Control of Transboundary Movement and Management of Hazardous Wastes within Africa (adopted on 30 January 1991, entered into force on 22 April 1998) UN Treaty Series vol. 2101, 177.
Convention on the Prevention of Marine Pollution by Dumping of Wastes and Other Matter 1972 (adopted on 13 November 1972, entered into force on 30 August 1975) UN Treaty Series vol. 1046, 120.
Convention to Ban the Importation of Hazardous and Radioactive Wastes into Forum Island Countries and to Control the Transboundary Movement and Management of Hazardous Waste within the South Pacific Region (Waigani Convention) (adopted on 16 September 1995, entered into force on 21 October 2001) UN Treaty Series vol. 2161, 91.
European Convention for the Protection of Human Rights and Fundamental Freedoms (adopted on 4 November 1950, entered into force on 3 September 1953) UN Treaty Series vol. 213, 221.
German Waste Management Act (KrWG), https://www.umweltbundesamt.de/en/topics/waste-resources/waste-management/waste-regulations accessed 25 March 2024.
International Convention for the Conservation of Atlantic Tunas (adopted on 14 May 1966, entered into force on 20 May 1969) UN Treaty Series No. 9587, 64.
International Convention for the Prevention of Pollution from Ships (adopted on 2 November 1973, entered into force on 2 October 1983) UN Treaty Series vol. 1340, 184.
International Covenant on Civil and Political Rights (adopted on 16 December 1966, entered into force on 23 March 1976) UN Treaty Series vol. 999, 171.
International Covenant on Economic, Social and Cultural Rights (adopted on 16 December 1966, entered into force on 3 January 1976) UN Treaty Series vol. 993, 3.
Marrakesh Agreement Establishing the World Trade Organization (adopted on 15 April 1994, entered into force on 1 January 1996) UN Treaty Series vol. 154, 33, preamble.
Montreal Protocol on Substances that Deplete the Ozone Layer (adopted on 16 September 1987, entered into force on 1 January 1989), UN Treaty Series, vol. 1522, 3.
Paris Agreement (adopted on 12 December 2015, entered into force on 4 November 2016) UN Treaty Series vol. 3156.
Rotterdam Convention on the Prior Informed Consent Procedure for Certain Hazardous Chemicals in International Trade (adopted on 10 September 1998, entered into force on 24 February 2004) UN Treaty Series vol. 2244, 337.
Stockholm Convention on Persistent Organic Pollutants (adopted on 22 May 2001, entered into force on 17 May 2004) UN Treaty Series vol. 2256, 119.
The Convention on Biological Diversity (adopted on 5 June 1992, entered into force 29 December 1993) UN Treaty Series vol. 1760, 79.
The UN Agreement for the Implementation of the Provisions of the UN Convention on the Law of the Sea of 10 December 1982 relating to the Conservation and Management of Straddling Fish Stocks and Highly Migratory Fish Stocks (adopted on 4 August 1995, entered into force on 11 December 2001) UN Treaty Series vol. 2167, 3.

UN Educational, Scientific and Cultural Organization (UNESCO), Convention Concerning the Protection of the World Cultural and Natural Heritage, adopted by the General Conference at its seventeenth session, Paris, 16 November 1972.
United Nations Framework Convention on Climate Change (adopted on 9 May 1992, entered into force on 21 March 1994) UN Treaty Series vol 1771, 107.

Legal Documents

African Commission on Human and Peoples' Rights. Communication 155/96: Social and Economic Rights Action Center (SERAC) and Center for Economic and Social Rights (CESR)/Nigeria, Ogoni Case, No. 155/96 (2001).
Commission on Sustainable Development. International Legal Instruments and Mechanisms (Chapter 39 of Agenda 21), Report of the Secretary-General Addendum, E/CN.17/1996/17/Add.1 § (1996). available at https://www.un.org/esa/documents/ecosoc/cn17/1996/ecn171996-17a1.htm accessed 18 July 2022.
Committee on Economic, Social and Cultural Rights. General Comment No. 4: The Right to Adequate Housing, E/1992/23 § (1991).
Committee on Economic, Social and Cultural Rights. General Comment No. 12: The Right to Adequate Food, E/C.12/1999/5 § (1999).
Committee on Economic, Social and Cultural Rights. General Comment No. 14: The Right to the Highest Attainable Standard of Health, E/C.12/2000/4 § (2000).
Committee on Economic, Social and Cultural Rights. General Comment No. 15: The Right to Water (Arts. 11 and 12 of the Covenant), E/C.12/2002/11 § (2003).
Committee on Economic, Social and Cultural Rights. General Comment No. 23: The Right To Just and Favourable Conditions of Work, E/C.12/GC/23 § (2016).
Conference of the Parties to the Basel Convention. Cartagena Declaration on the Prevention, Minimization and Recovery of Hazardous Wastes and Other Wastes (2011).
Council Directive 1999/31/EC of 26 April 1999 on the Landfill of Waste (OJL 182, 16.7.1999, 1–19).
Council of Europe, Parliamentary Assembly. Recommendation 1614 (2003), Environment and human rights, 1614 § (2003).
Council of Europe. Resolution 2396 (2021), Anchoring the right to a healthy environment: need for enhanced action by the Council of Europe, 2396 § (2021).
European Council. Integrated Pollution Prevention and Control (IPPC) Directive, 96/61/EC § (1996).
European Council. Recomendation 1885 (2009), Drafting an additional protocol to the European Convention on Human Rights concerning the right to a healthy environment, 1885 § (2009).
European Parliament, and European Council. Waste Framework Directive, 2008/98/EC § (2008).
European Parliament. Directive (EU) 2018/851 of the European Parliament and of the Coucil amending Directive 2008/98/EC on Waste, 2018/851 § (2018).
European Parliament. Directive 2012/19/EU of the European Parliament and of the Council on Waste Electrical and Electronic Equipment, 2012/19/EU § (2012).
Human Rights Committee, *Portillo Cáceres et al. v. Paraguay* (CCPR/C/126/D/2751/2016).

Human Rights Committee, *Teitiota v. New Zealand* (CCPR/C/127/D/2728/2016).
Human Rights Committee, *Toussaint v. Canada* (CCPR/C/123/D/2348/2014).
Human Rights Committee. General Comment No. 36: Article 6 of the International Covenant on Civil and Political Rights, the Right to Life, CCPR/C/GC/36 § (2018).
Human Rights Committee. General Comment No. 6: The Right to Life (1982).
Human Rights Committee. Views adopted by the Committee under article 5 (4) of the Optional Protocol, concerning communication No. 3624/2019, No. CCPR/C/135/D/3624/2019 (September 22, 2022).
Human Rights Council. Guidelines for the Implementation of the Right to Adequate Housing, A/HRC/43/43 § (2019).
Human Rights Council. Human Rights and the Global Water Crisis: Water Pollution, Water Scarcity and Water-Related Disasters—Report of the Special Rapporteur on the Issue of Human Rights Obligations Relating the Enjoyment of a Safe, Healthy and Sustainable Environment, A/HRC/46/28 § (2021).
Human Rights Council. Issue of human rights obligations relating to the enjoyment of a safe, clean, healthy and sustainable environment, A/HRC/40/55 § (2019).
Human Rights Council. Principles on human rights and the protection of workers from exposure to toxic substances, A/HRC/42/41 § (2019).
Human Rights Council. Report of the Special Rapporteur on the implications for human rights of the environmentally sound management and disposal of hazardous substances and wastes, A/HRC/36/41 § (2017).
Human Rights Council. Report of the Special Rapporteur on the implications for human rights of the environmentally sound management and disposal of hazardous substances and wastes, A/HRC/39/48 § (2018).
Human Rights Council. Report of the Special Rapporteur on the issue of human rights obligations relating to the enjoyment of a safe, clean, healthy and sustainable environment, A/HRC/34/49 § (2017).
Human Rights Council. Report of the Special Rapporteur on the issue of human rights obligations relating to the enjoyment of a safe, clean, healthy and sustainable environment, A/HRC/37/58 § (2018).
Human Rights Council. Resolution adopted by the Human Rights Council—The human right to a clean, healthy and sustainable environment, A/HRC/RES/48/13 § (2021).
Human Rights Council. Right to Science in the Context of Toxic Substances, A/HRC/48/61 § (2021).
Human Rights Council. The right to a clean, healthy and sustainable environmnet: non-toxic environment, A/HRC/49/53 § (2022).
International Law Association. Sofia Guiding Statements on the Judicial Elaboration of the 2002 New Delhi Declaration of Principles of International Law Relating to Sustainable Development, Resolution No. 7/2012 § (2012).
International Law Commission. Report of the International Law Commission on the work of its fifty-third session, A/56/10 § (2001).
Office of the High Commissioner of Human Rights, and UN Environment Programme. "Human Rights and the Environment—Rio+20: Joint Report OCHR and UNEP." Rio de Janeiro, June 19, 2012.

The Office of the High Commissioner for Human Rights. "Human Rights, Poverty Reduction and Sustainable Development: Health, Food and Water—A Background Paper." Johannesburg: World Summiot on Sustainable Development, September 26, 2002.

UN Environment Assembly of the UNEP. Report on the work of the ad hoc open-ended expert group on marine litter and microplastics at its fourth meeting, UNEP/AHEG/4/7 § (2020).

UN Environment Programme. "Governing Council Approval of the Report of the Intergovernmental Working Group of Experts on Natural Resources Shared by Two or More States." *International Legal Materials*, no. vol. 17 No. 5 (September 1978): 1091–99.

UN Environment Programme. Cairo Guidelines and Principles for the Environmentally Sound Management of Hazardous Wastes, Decision 14/30 § (1987).

UN Environment Programme. Conference of the Parties to the Basel Convention on the Control of Transboundary Movements of Hazardous Wastes and their Disposal, UNEP/CHW.5/29 § (1999).

UN Environment Programme. Draft guidance to assist Parties in developing efficient strategies for achieving the prevention and minimization of the generation of hazardous and other wastes and their disposal, UNEP/CHW.13/INF/11 § (2017).

UN Environment Programme. Report of the Ad Hoc Working Group of Legal and Technical Experts on Biological Diversity on the Work of its Second Session, UNEP/Bio.Div/WG.2/2/5 § (1991).

UN Environment Programme. *UNEP Training Manual on International Environmental Law*, 2006. available on https://wedocs.unep.org/20.500.11822/20599 last accessed 6 September 2022.

UN General Assembly. Adequate housing as a component of the right to an adequate standard of living, and the right to non-discrimination in this context, A/74/183 § (2019).

UN General Assembly. Human rights obligations relating to the enjoyment of a safe, clean, healthy and sustainable environment, A/76/179 § (2021).

UN General Assembly. Human rights obligations relating to the enjoyment of a safe, clean, healthy and sustainable environment, A/77/284 § (2022).

UN General Assembly. Implications for human rights of the environmentally sound management and disposal of hazardous substances and wastes, A/75/290 § (2020).

UN General Assembly. Implications for human rights on the environmentally sound management and disposal of hazardous substances and wastes, A/74/480 § (2019).

UN General Assembly. International Development Strategy for the Third United Nations Development Decade, UN Doc. A/RES/35/56/Add. 1 § (1980). https://documents-dds-ny.un.org/doc/RESOLUTION/GEN/NR0/390/75/IMG/NR039075.pdf?OpenElement.

UN General Assembly. Programme for the Further Implementation of Agenda 21, UN Doc. A/RES/S-19/2 § (1997). available on https://documents-dds-ny.un.org/doc/UNDOC/GEN/N97/774/73/PDF/N9777473.pdf?OpenElement.

UN General Assembly. Protection of global climate for present and future generations of mankind, A/RES/43/53 § (1988).

UN General Assembly. Report of the Economic Commission for Europe on the Bergen Conference, A/CONF.151/PC/10 § (1990).

UN General Assembly. Report of the Special Rapporteur on the implications for human rights of the environmentally sound management and disposal of hazardous substances and wastes, Marcos Orellana, A/76/207 § (2021).

UN General Assembly. Report of the Special Rapporteur on the issue of human rights obligations relating to the enjoyment of a safe, clean, healthy and sustainable environment, A/73/188 § (2018).

UN General Assembly. Report of the United Nations Conference on Environment and Development, UN Doc. A/CONF.151/26 § (1992). available on https://www.un.org/en/development/desa/population/migration/generalassembly/docs/globalcompact/A_CONF.151_26_Vol.I_Declaration.pdf.

UN General Assembly. Report of the United Nations Conference on the Human Environment, UN Doc. A/CONF.48/14/Rev. 1 § (1972). available on https://documents-dds-ny.un.org/doc/UNDOC/GEN/NL7/300/05/IMG/NL730005.pdf?OpenElement.

UN General Assembly. Report of the World Commission on Environment and Development, UN Doc. A/RES/42/187 § (1987). http://www.un-documents.net/a42r187.htm.

UN General Assembly. Resolution adopted by the General Assembly on 28 July 2010, 64/292. The human right to water and sanitation, A/RES/64/292 § (2010).

UN General Assembly. Resolution on Permanent Sovereignty over Natural Resources, A/RES/1803(XVII) § (1962).

UN General Assembly. The human right to a clean, healthy, and sustainable environment, A/76/L.75 § (2022).

UN General Assembly. World Charter for Nature, A/RES/37/7 § (1982).

UN Interagency Framework Team for Preventive Action, "Toolkit and Guidance for Preventing and Managing Land and Natural Resources Conflict", available at https://www.un.org/en/land-natural-resources-conflict/pdfs/EU-UN%20Introduction%20and%20overview.pdf accessed 4 April 2024.

United Nations Human Settlements Programme, and United Nations, eds. *Housing Rights Legislation: Review of International and National Legal Instruments*. Series of Publications in Support of the Global Campaign for Secure Tenure, no. 05. Nairobi: United Nations Human Settlements Programme : Office of the High Commissioner for Human Rights, 2002.

List of References

Abbott, Kenneth W., and Duncan Snidal. "Hard and Soft Law in International Governance." *International Organization* 54, no. 3 (2000): 421–56. https://doi.org/10.1162/002081800551280.

Ahmad, Zaker. *WTO Law and Trade Policy Reform for Low-Carbon Technology Diffusion: Common Concern of Humankind, Carbon Pricing, and Export Credit Support*. Brill | Nijhoff, 2021. https://doi.org/10.1163/9789004446090.

Andrews, Deborah. "The Circular Economy, Design Thinking and Education for Sustainability." *Local Economy: The Journal of the Local Economy Policy Unit* 30, no. 3 (May 2015): 305–15. https://doi.org/10.1177/0269094215578226.

Annan, Kofi. "Two Concepts of Sovereignty." *The Economist*, September 18, 1999. http://www.kentlaw.edu/faculty/bbrown/classes/HumanrsemFall2008/CourseDocs/12Twoconceptsofsovereignty-Kofi%20Annan.pdf last accessed 3 November 2023.

Atapattu, Sumudu A. “The Paris Agreement and Human Rights: Is Sustainable Development the New Human Right.” *Journal of Human Rights and the Environment*, no. 9 (March 2018): 68–88.

Atapattu, Sumudu A. “The Right to a Healthy Life or the Right to Die Polluted: The Emergence of a Human Right to a Healthy Environment under International Law.” *Tulane Environmental Law Journal*, no. 16 1 (2002): 65–126.

Attaran, Amir. “Human Rights and Biomedical Research Funding for the Developing World: Discovering State Obligations under the Right to Health.” *Health and Human Rights* 4, no. 1 (1999): 26. https://doi.org/10.2307/4065167.

Awan, Usama, Narmeen Kanwal, and Mohammed Khurrum S. Bhutta. “A Literature Analysis of Definitions for a Circular Economy.” In *Logistics Operations and Management for Recycling and Reuse*, edited by Paulina Golinska-Dawson, 19–34. EcoProduction. Berlin, Heidelberg: Springer Berlin Heidelberg, 2020. https://doi.org/10.1007/978-3-642-33857-1_2.

Backes, Chris. *Law for a Circular Economy*. ’s-Gravenhage: Eleven international publishing, 2017.

Ballardini, Rosa Maria, Janne Kaisto, and Jukka Similä. “Developing Novel Property Concepts in Private Law to Foster the Circular Economy.” *Journal of Cleaner Production* 279 (January 2021): 123747. https://doi.org/10.1016/j.jclepro.2020.123747.

Barral, V. “Sustainable Development in International Law: Nature * and Operation of an Evolutive Legal Norm.” *European Journal of International Law* 23, no. 2 (May 1, 2012): 377–400. https://doi.org/10.1093/ejil/chs016.

Barsalou, Olivier, and Michael Hennessy Picard. “International Environmental Law in an Era of Globalized Waste.” *Chinese Journal of International Law* 17, no. 3 (September 1, 2018): 887–906. https://doi.org/10.1093/chinesejil/jmy016.

Barstow Magraw, Daniel, and Lisa D. Hawke. “Legal Status and Function.” In *The Oxford Handbook of International Environmental Law*, edited by Daniel Bodansky. Oxford: Oxford Univ. Press, 2008.

Bartenstein, Kristin, Wolfgang Durner, and Astrid Epiney. “Internationales Umweltrecht.” In *Internationales Umweltrecht*, edited by Alexander Proelß. Berlin: De Gruyter, 2022. https://doi.org/10.1515/9783110248296.

Bartl, Andreas. “Moving from Recycling to Waste Prevention: A Review of Barriers and Enables.” *Waste Management & Research: The Journal for a Sustainable Circular Economy* 32, no. 9_suppl (September 2014): 3–18. https://doi.org/10.1177/0734242X14541986.

Bassiouni, M. Cherif. “A Functional Approach to General Principles of International Law,” no. 11 (1990): 768–818.

Besson, Samantha. “Sovereignty.” In *Max Planck Encyclopedia of Public International Law*, edited by Rüdiger Wolfrum, April 2011.

Beyerlin, Ulrich, and Vanessa Holzer. “Conservation of Natural Resources.” In *Max Planck Encyclopedia of Public International Law*, edited by Rüdiger Wolfrum, October 2018.

Beyerlin, Ulrich. “Policies, Principles, and Rules.” In *The Oxford Handbook of International Environmental Law*, edited by Daniel Bodansky. Oxford: Oxford Univ. Press, 2010.

Beyerlin, Ulrich. “Sustainable Development.” In *Max Planck Encyclopedia of Public International Law*, edited by Rüdiger Wolfrum. Oxford Public International Law, October 2013.

Beyerlin, Ulrich. "Umweltschutz Und Menschenrechte." *Zeitschrift Für Ausländisches Öffentliches Recht Und Völkerrecht*, no. 65 (2005).

Biermann, Frank, Norichika Kanie, and Rakhyun E Kim. "Global Governance by Goal-Setting: The Novel Approach of the UN Sustainable Development Goals." *Current Opinion in Environmental Sustainability* 26–27 (June 2017): 26–31. https://doi.org/10.1016/j.cosust.2017.01.010.

Biermann, Frank. "Common Concern of Humankind: The Emergence of a New Concept of International Environmental Law." *Archiv Des Völkerrechts* 34, no. 4 (December 1996): 426–81.

Bifulco, Raffaele, and Alessandro Nato. "The Concept of Sovereignty in the EU—Past, Present and the Future," April 30, 2020. https://ec.europa.eu/research/participants/documents/downloadPublic?documentIds=080166e5ceba74f0&appId=PPGMS accessed 22 August 2023.

Birnie, Patricia W., Alan E. Boyle, and Catherine Redgwell. *International Law and the Environment*. 3rd ed. Oxford ; New York: Oxford University Press, 2009.

Bogale, Zelalem. "E-Responsibility: E-Waste, International Law and Africa's Growing Digital Wasteland." *U.C. Davis Journal of International Law and Policy* 18 (January 2011): 225–59.

Bowling, Chelsea and Pierson, Elizabeth; Ratté, Stephanie. "The Common Concern of Humankind: A Potential Framework for a New International Legally Binding Instrument on the Conservation and Sustainable Use of Marine Biological Diversity in the High Seas," 2021 https://www.un.org/depts/los/biodiversity/prepcom_files/BowlingPiersonandRatte_Common_Concern.pdf.

Boyd, David R. "Catalyst for Change: Evaluating Forty Years of Experience in Implementing the Right to a Healthy Environment." In *The Human Right to a Healthy Environment*, edited by John H. Knox and Ramin Pejan, 1st ed., 17–41. Cambridge University Press, 2018. https://doi.org/10.1017/9781108367530.002.

Boyd, David R. "The Right to a Healthy and Sustainable Environment." In *A Global Pact for the Environment—Legal Foundations*, edited by Yann Aguila and Jorge E. Viñuales. C-EENRG, 2019.

Boyle, A. "Human Rights and the Environment: Where Next?" *European Journal of International Law* 23, no. 3 (August 1, 2012): 613–42. https://doi.org/10.1093/ejil/chs054.

Boyle, A.E. "The Gabčíkovo-Nagymaros Case: New Law in Old Bottles." *Yearbook of International Environmental Law* 8, no. 1 (December 1, 1997): 13–20. https://doi.org/10.1093/yiel/8.1.13.

Bringezu, Stefan. "Assessing Global Resource Use, A Systems Approach to Resource Efficiency and Pollution Reduction." *UNEP*, 2017. available at https://www.unep.org/news-and-stories/press-release/resource-use-expected-double-2050-better-natural-resource-use accessed 11 October 2021.

Brown Weiss, Edith. "Agora: Trade and Environment." *The American Journal of International Law* 86, no. 4 (October 1992): 700–735.

Brunnée, Jutta, and André Nollkaemper. "Between the Forests and the Trees—an Emerging International Forest Law." *Environmental Conservation* 23, no. 4 (December 1996): 307–14. https://doi.org/10.1017/S0376892900039163.

Brunnée, Jutta. "Common Areas, Common Heritage, and Common Concern." In *The Oxford Handbook of International Environmental Law*, edited by Daniel Bodansky, Reprinted. Oxford: Oxford Univ. Press, 2010.

Brunnée, Jutta. "The Stockholm Declaration and the Structure and Process of International Environmental Law." In *The Stockholm Declaration and Law of the Marine Environment*, edited by Myron H. Nordquist, John N. Moore, and Said Mahmoudi, 41–62. COLP 7. The Hague: Nijhoff, 2003.

Chenwi, Lilian. "The Right to a Satisfactory, Healthy, and Sustainable Environment in the African Regional Human Rights System." In *The Human Right to a Healthy Environment*, edited by John H. Knox and Ramin Pejan, 1st ed., 59–85. Cambridge University Press, 2018. https://doi.org/10.1017/9781108367530.004.

Chimni, B.S. "Critical Theory and International Economic Law: A Third World Approach to International Law (TWAIL) Perspective." In *Research Handbook on Global Justice and International Economic Law*, edited by John Linarelli. Research Handbooks on Globalisation and the Law. Cheltenham, UK Northampton, MA, USA: Edward Elgar, 2013.

Chioatto, Elisa, and Paolo Sospiro. "Transition from Waste Management to Circular Economy: The European Union Roadmap." *Environment, Development and Sustainability* 25, no. 1 (January 2023): 249–76. https://doi.org/10.1007/s10668-021-02050-3.

Cohen, Jean L. *Globalization and Sovereignty: Rethinking Legality, Legitimacy, and Constitutionalism.* 1st ed. Cambridge University Press, 2012. https://doi.org/10.1017/CBO9780511659041.

Cooney, Rosie. *The Precautionary Principle in Biodiversity Conservation and Natural Resource Management: An Issues Paper for Policy-Makers, Researchers and Practitioners.* IUCN Policy and Global Change Series, no. 2. Gland, Switzerland ; Cambridge: IUCN-the World Conservation Union, 2004.

Cortat Simonetti Goncalves, Luisa, and Michael G. Faure. "International Law Instruments To Address The Plastic Soup." *SSRN Electronic Journal*, 2019. https://doi.org/10.2139/ssrn.3405968.

Da Rosa, Alexandre Morais, and Ana Luisa Schmidt Ramos. "CIRCULAR ECONOMY, HUMAN BEHAVIOR AND LAW," 35–44. Alicante, Spain, 2018. https://doi.org/10.2495/UG180041.

De Sadeleer, Nicolas. "*The Principle of Prevention.*" In *Environmental Principles*, by Nicolas de Sadeleer, 61–90, 1st ed. Oxford University PressOxford, 2002. https://doi.org/10.1093/acprof:oso/9780199254743.003.02.

Duvic-Paoli, Leslie-Anne. *The Prevention Principle in International Environmental Law.* 1st ed. Cambridge University Press, 2018. https://doi.org/10.1017/9781108553728.

Ekardt, Felix. *Sustainability: Transformation, Governance, Ethics, Law.* Environmental Humanities: Transformation, Governance, Ethics, Law 1. Cham, Switzerland: Springer, 2020.

Ekins, Paul, Nick Hughes, Stefan Bringezu, Charles Arden Clarke, Marina Fischer-Kowalski, Thomas Graedel, Maarten Hajer, et al. "Resource Efficiency: Potential and Economic Implications Summary for Policymakers," 2016. https://doi.org/10.13140/RG.2.2.18978.43204.

Elia, Valerio, Maria Grazia Gnoni, and Fabiana Tornese. "Measuring Circular Economy Strategies through Index Methods: A Critical Analysis." *Journal of Cleaner Production* 142 (January 2017): 2741–51. https://doi.org/10.1016/j.jclepro.2016.10.196.

Ellis, Jaye. "Sustainable Development as a Legal Principle: A Rhetorical Analysis." *SSRN Electronic Journal*, 2008. https://doi.org/10.2139/ssrn.1319360.

Eshbach, Roseann. "A Global Approach to the Protection of the Environment: Balancing State Sovereignty and Global Interests." *Temple International and Comparative Law Journal* 4, no. 2 (1990): 271–305.

Fassbender, Bardo. "Sovereignty and Constitutionalism in International Law." In *Sovereignty in Transition*, edited by Neil Walker, 115–43. Oxford ; Portland, Or: Hart, 2003.

Feichtner, Isabel. "Der Kampf Um Rohstoffe Im Völkerrecht." *Verfassung und Recht in Übersee* 49, no. 1 (2016): 3–15. https://doi.org/10.5771/0506-7286-2016-1-3.

Fitzmaurice, Malgosia. "Interpretation of Human Rights Treaties." In *The Oxford Handbook of International Human Rights Law*, edited by Dinah Shelton, 1st ed. Oxford University Press, 2013. https://doi.org/10.1093/law/9780199640133.001.0001.

Francioni, F. "International Human Rights in an Environmental Horizon." *European Journal of International Law* 21, no. 1 (February 1, 2010): 41–55. https://doi.org/10.1093/ejil/chq019.

Freestone, David. "International Fisheries Law Since Rio: The Continued Rise of the Precautionary Principle." In *International Law and Sustainable DevelopmentPast Achievements and Future Challenges*, edited by Alan Boyle and David Freestone. Oxford University Press, 1999. https://doi.org/10.1093/acprof:oso/9780198298076.001.0001.

Geng, Yong, Joseph Sarkis, and Raimund Bleischwitz. "How to Globalize the Circular Economy." *Nature* 565, no. 7738 (January 2019): 153–55. https://doi.org/10.1038/d41586-019-00017-z.

Ghisellini, Patrizia, Catia Cialani, and Sergio Ulgiati. "A Review on Circular Economy: The Expected Transition to a Balanced Interplay of Environmental and Economic Systems." *Journal of Cleaner Production* 114 (February 2016): 11–32. https://doi.org/10.1016/j.jclepro.2015.09.007.

Ghisolfi, Verônica, Gisele de Lorena Diniz Chaves, Renato Ribeiro Siman, and Lúcia Helena Xavier. "System Dynamics Applied to Closed Loop Supply Chains of Desktops and Laptops in Brazil: A Perspective for Social Inclusion of Waste Pickers." *Waste Management* 60 (February 2017): 14–31. https://doi.org/10.1016/j.wasman.2016.12.018.

Gilbert, Jérémie. *Natural Resources and Human Rights: An Appraisal*. First edition. Oxford, United Kingdom: Oxford University Press, 2018.

Gottberg, Annika, Joe Morris, Simon Pollard, Cecilia Mark-Herbert, and Matthew Cook. "Producer Responsibility, Waste Minimisation and the WEEE Directive: Case Studies in Eco-Design from the European Lighting Sector." *Science of The Total Environment* 359, no. 1–3 (April 2006): 38–56. https://doi.org/10.1016/j.scitotenv.2005.07.001.

Grant, Evadne. "International Human Rights Courts and Environmental Human Rights: Re-Imagining Adjudicative Paradigms." *Journal of Human Rights and the Environment*, no. 6 (September 2015): 156–76.

Gwam, Cyril Uchenna. "Toxic Wastes and Human Rights." *The Brown Journal of World Affairs* 7, no. 2 (Summer/Fall 2000).

Halog, Anthony, and Sandra Anieke. "A Review of Circular Economy Studies in Developed Countries and Its Potential Adoption in Developing Countries." *Circular Economy and Sustainability* 1, no. 1 (June 2021): 209–30. https://doi.org/10.1007/s43615-021-00017-0.

Handl, Günther. "Declaration of the United Nations Conference on the Human Environment (Stockholm Declaration), 1972 and the Rio Declaration on Environment and Development, 1992," n.d. available on https://legal.un.org/avl/pdf/ha/dunche/dunche_e.pdf accessed 1 July 2022.

Hannum, Hurst. "The UDHR in National and International Law." *Health and Human Rights* 3, no. 2 (1998): 144. https://doi.org/10.2307/4065305.

Hertogen, An. "Letting *Lotus* Bloom." *European Journal of International Law* 26, no. 4 (November 2015): 901–26. https://doi.org/10.1093/ejil/chv072.

Hey, Ellen. "Common but Differentiated Responsibilities." In *Max Planck Encyclopedia of Public International Law*. Oxford Public International Law, February 2011.

Hutchinson, Terry, and Nigel Duncan. "Defining and Describing What We Do: Doctrinal Legal Research." *Deakin Law Review* 17, no. 1 (October 1, 2012): 83. https://doi.org/10.21153/dlr2012vol17no1art70.

Jolly, Stellina. "The Vedanta (Niyamgiri) Case: Promoting Environmental Justice and Sustainable Development." In *The Cambridge Handbook of Environmental Justice and Sustainable Development*, edited by Sumudu A. Atapattu, Carmen G. Gonzalez, and Sara L. Seck, 1st ed., 289–302. Cambridge University Press, 2021. https://doi.org/10.1017/9781108555791.022.

Jonas, Hans. *Das Prinzip Verantwortung: Versuch einer Ethik für die technologische Zivilisation*. 6. Auflage. Suhrkamp Taschenbuch 3492. Frankfurt am Main: Suhrkamp, 2017.

Kaza, Silpa, and et al. *What a Waste 2.0—A Global Snaphsot of Solid Waste Management to 2050*. World Bank Group, 2018. available at https://openknowledge.worldbank.org/handle/10986/30317 accessed 9 November 2023.

Kelsen, Hans. "The Principle of Sovereign Equality of States as a Basis for International Organization." *The Yale Law Journal* 53, no. 2 (March 1944): 207. https://doi.org/10.2307/792798.

Khan, Sabaa A. "Chemical Pollution and the Role of International Law in a Future Detoxified." In *The Cambridge Handbook of Environmental Justice and Sustainable Development*, edited by Sumudu A. Atapattu, Carmen G. Gonzalez, and Sara L. Seck, 1st ed., 243–56. Cambridge University Press, 2021. https://doi.org/10.1017/9781108555791.019.

Kirchherr, Julian, Denise Reike, and Marko Hekkert. "Conceptualizing the Circular Economy: An Analysis of 114 Definitions." *Resources, Conservation and Recycling* 127 (December 2017): 221–32. https://doi.org/10.1016/j.resconrec.2017.09.005.

Kohen, Marcelo, and Bérénice Schramm. "General Principles of Law." In *International Law*, by Marcelo Kohen and Bérénice Schramm. Oxford University Press, 2013. https://doi.org/10.1093/obo/9780199796953-0063.

Korhonen, Jouni, Antero Honkasalo, and Jyri Seppälä. "Circular Economy: The Concept and Its Limitations." *Ecological Economics* 143 (January 2018): 37–46. https://doi.org/10.1016/j.ecolecon.2017.06.041.

Korhonen, Jouni, Cali Nuur, Andreas Feldmann, and Seyoum Eshetu Birkie. "Circular Economy as an Essentially Contested Concept." *Journal of Cleaner Production* 175 (February 2018): 544–52. https://doi.org/10.1016/j.jclepro.2017.12.111.

Kotzé, Louis J. "Human Rights and Socioecological Justice through a Vulnerability Lens." In *The Cambridge Handbook of Environmental Justice and Sustainable Development*, edited by Sumudu A. Atapattu, Carmen G. Gonzalez, and Sara L. Seck, 1st ed., 86–100. Cambridge University Press, 2021. https://doi.org/10.1017/9781108555791.008.

Lazarevic, David, and Helena Valve. "Narrating Expectations for the Circular Economy: Towards a Common and Contested European Transition." *Energy Research & Social Science* 31 (September 2017): 60–69. https://doi.org/10.1016/j.erss.2017.05.006.

Leib, Linda Hajjar. *Human Rights and the Environment: Philosophical, Theoretical, and Legal Perspectives*. Queen Mary Studies in International Law, v. 3. Leiden ; Boston: Martinus Nijhoff Publishers, 2011.

Lowe, Vaughan. "Sustainable Development and Unsustainable Arguments." In *International Law and Sustainable DevelopmentPast Achievements and Future Challenges*, edited by Alan Boyle and David Freestone. Oxford University Press, 1999. https://doi.org/10.1093/acprof:oso/9780198298076.001.0001.

Maitre-Ekern, Eléonore. "Re-Thinking Producer Responsibility for a Sustainable Circular Economy from Extended Producer Responsibility to Pre-Market Producer Responsibility." *Journal of Cleaner Production* 286 (March 2021): 125454. https://doi.org/10.1016/j.jclepro.2020.125454.

Mies, Annika, and Stefan Gold. "Mapping the Social Dimension of the Circular Economy." *Journal of Cleaner Production* 321 (October 2021): 128960. https://doi.org/10.1016/j.jclepro.2021.128960.

Muigua, Kariuki. "Fostering the Principles of Natural Resource Management in Kenya." *Journal of Conflict Management & Sustainable Development*, no. 8 (2022): 1–47.

Murray, Alan, Keith Skene, and Kathryn Haynes. "The Circular Economy: An Interdisciplinary Exploration of the Concept and Application in a Global Context." *Journal of Business Ethics* 140, no. 3 (February 2017): 369–80.

Natarajan, Usha. "TWAIL and the Environment: The Statem of Nature, the Nature of the State, and the Arab Spring." *Oregon Review of International Law*, no. vol. 14 (2012): 177–202.

Ng'ambi, Sangwani Patrick. "Reconciling Permanent Sovereignty Over Natural Resources and Pacta Sunt Servanda." *SSRN Electronic Journal*, 2018. https://doi.org/10.2139/ssrn.3246211.

Nolte, Georg. "Sovereignty as Responsibility?" *Proceedings of the Annual Meeting (American Society of International Law)*, no. 99 (April 30, 2005): 389–92.

Orrego Vicuña, Francisco. *International Dispute Settlement in an Evolving Global Society: Constitutionalization, Accessibility, Privatization.* 1st ed. Cambridge University Press, 2004. https://doi.org/10.1017/CBO9780511735257.

Parrish, Austen. "Sovereignty's Continuing Importance? Traces of Trail Smelter in the International Law Governing Hazardous Waste Transport." In *Transboundary Harms in International Law: Lessons from the Trail Smelter Arbitration*, edited by Rebecca Bratspies and Russell Miller. 2005/06. available at https://papers.ssrn.com/sol3/papers.cfm?abstract_id=765404 last accessed 23 February 2023, n.d.

Peters, Anne. "Global Constitutionalism." In *The Encyclopedia of Political Thought*, edited by Michael T Gibbons, 1st ed. Wiley, 2014. https://doi.org/10.1002/9781118474396.

Peters, Birgit. "Clean and Healthy Environment, Right to, International Protection." In *Max Planck Encyclopedia of Public International Law*, edited by Rüdiger Wolfrum, January 2021.

Pogge, Thomas. "Cosmopolitanism and Sovereignty." *Ethics, The University of Chicago Press* 103, no. 1 (October 1992): 48–75.

Pouikli, Kleoniki. "Concretising the Role of Extended Producer Responsibility in European Union Waste Law and Policy through the Lens of the Circular Economy." *ERA Forum* 20, no. 4 (March 2020): 491–508. https://doi.org/10.1007/s12027-020-00596-9.

Precautionary Principle Project. "Guidelines for Applying the Precautionary Principle to Biodiversity Conservation and Natural Resource Management," n.d. available on http://www.onlyoneplanet.com/marinePPguidelines2005.pdf accessed 16 August 2022.

Preston, Felix, Johanna Lehne, Laura Wellesley, and Royal Institute of International Affairs. *An Inclusive Circular Economy Priorities for Developing Countries*, 2019. https://www.chathamhouse.org/sites/default/files/publications/research/2019-05-22-Circular%20Economy.pdf.

Proelß, Alexander. "Prinzipien Des Internationalen Umweltrechts." In *Internationales Umweltrecht*, edited by Alexander Proelß, 2. De Gruyter, 2022.

Raffensperger, Carolyn, and Joel Tickner. "Wingspread Statement on the Precautionary Principle," n.d. available on https://www.gdrc.org/u-gov/precaution-3.html accessed on 23 August 2022.

Rayfuse, Rosemary. "Principles of International Environmental Law Applicable to Waste Management." In *Waste Management and the Green Economy*, by Katharina Kummer Peiry, Andreas Ziegler, and Jorun Baumgartner, 11–32. Edward Elgar Publishing, 2016. https://doi.org/10.4337/9781783473816.00010.

Reus-Smit, Christian. "Human Rights and the Social Construction of Sovereignty." *Review of International Studies* 27, no. 4 (October 2001): 519–38.

Reynolds, Jesse L. "An Economic Analysis of International Environmental Rights." *International Environmental Agreements: Politics, Law and Economics* 19, no. 6 (December 2019): 557–75. https://doi.org/10.1007/s10784-019-09454-7.

Ritchie, Hannah, and Max Roser. "Emissions by Sector," n.d. available at https://ourworldindata.org/emissions-by-sector accessed 13 January 2022.

Rublack, Susanne. "Fighting Transboundary Waste Streams: Will the Basel Convention Help?" *Verfassung und Recht in Übersee* 22, no. 4 (1989): 364–91. https://doi.org/10.5771/0506-7286-1989-4-364.

Ruiz Fabri, Hélène. "Human Rights and State Sovereignty: Have the Boundaries Been Significantly Redrawn?" In *Human Rights, Intervention, and the Use of Force*, edited by Philip Alston and Euan Macdonald, 33–86. Oxford University Press, 2008. https://doi.org/10.1093/acprof:oso/9780199552719.003.0002.

Rylander, Håkan. "Solid Waste Management International Perspectives." *Linnaeus Eco-Tech*, April 2, 2019, 81–89. https://doi.org/10.15626/Eco-Tech.1997.009.

Sajo, Andras. "Socioeconomic Rights and the International Economic Order." *New York University Journal of International Law and Politics* 35, no. 1 (Fall 2002): 221–62.

Sands, P. "International Law in the Field of Sustainable Development." *British Yearbook of International Law* 65, no. 1 (January 1, 1995): 303–81. https://doi.org/10.1093/bybil/65.1.303.

Sands, Philippe, Jacqueline Peel, Adriana Fabra Aguilar, and Ruth MacKenzie. *Principles of International Environmental Law*. 3rd ed. Cambridge; New York: Cambridge University Press, 2012.

Saul, Ben, David Kinley, and Jacqueline Mowbray. *The International Covenant on Economic, Social and Cultural Rights: Commentary, Cases, and Materials*. First edition. Oxford, United Kingdom: Oxford University Press, 2014.

Schabas, William, and Manfred Nowak. *U.N. International Covenant on Civil and Political Rights: Nowak's CCPR Commentary*. 3rd revised edition. Kehl: N.P. Engel, Publisher, 2019.

Schrijver, Nico. "ILA New Delhi Declaration of Principles of International Law Relating to Sustainable Development." *Netherlands International Law Review* 49, no. 02 (August 2002): 299. https://doi.org/10.1017/S0165070X00000528.

Schrijver, Nico. "Permanent Sovereignty over Natural Resources." In *Max Planck Encyclopedia of Public International Law*, edited by Rüdiger Wolfrum, June 2008.

Schröder, Meinhard. "Precautionary Approach/Principle." In *Max Planck Encyclopedia of Public International Law*. Oxford Public International Law, March 2014.

Schröder, Patrick, Alexandre Lemille, and Peter Desmond. "Making the Circular Economy Work for Human Development." *Resources, Conservation and Recycling* 156 (May 2020): 104686. https://doi.org/10.1016/j.resconrec.2020.104686.

Schröder, Patrick, Kartika Anggraeni, and Uwe Weber. "The Relevance of Circular Economy Practices to the Sustainable Development Goals." *Journal of Industrial Ecology* 23, no. 1 (February 2019): 77–95. https://doi.org/10.1111/jiec.12732.

Schulze, Sven. "Abfall- und Kreislaufwirtschaft im Kontext der Agenda 2030." In *Die Agenda 2030 als Magisches Vieleck der Nachhaltigkeit*, edited by Estelle Herlyn and Magdalène Lévy-Tödter, 179–97. FOM-Edition. Wiesbaden: Springer Fachmedien Wiesbaden, 2020. https://doi.org/10.1007/978-3-658-25706-4_10.

Shelton, Dinah. "Common Concern of Humanity," *Environmental Policy and Law*, No. 39/2 (2009).

Shelton, Dinah. "Complexities and Uncertainties in Matters of Human Rights and the Environment: Identifying the Judicial Role." In *The Human Right to a Healthy Environment*, edited by John H. Knox and Ramin Pejan, 1st ed., 97–121. Cambridge University Press, 2018. https://doi.org/10.1017/9781108367530.006.

Shelton, Dinah. "Human Rights and the Environment: Substantive Rights." In *Research Handbook on International Environmental Law*, edited by Malgosia Fitzmaurice, David M. Ong, and Panos Merkouris. Cheltenham, UK ; Northampton, MA: Edward Elgar, 2011.

Shelton, Dinah. "Human Rights and the Environment: What Specific Environmental Rights Have Been Recognized," Denv. J. Int'l L. & Pol'y, No. 35 (2006): 129.

Shresta, Zubin. "The Integration of Circular Economy into Municipal Solid Waste Managemnt of Kathmandu Metropolitan City in Nepal", 54 https://essay.utwente.nl/77393/1/2012685_Zubin_Shrestha_17-18.pdf accessed 25 March 2024.

Streeten, Paul. "Basic Needs and Human Rights." *World Development* 8, no. 2 (February 1980): 107–11. https://doi.org/10.1016/0305-750X(80)90019-4.

Velenturf, Anne P.M., and Phil Purnell. "Principles for a Sustainable Circular Economy." *Sustainable Production and Consumption* 27 (July 2021): 1437–57. https://doi.org/10.1016/j.spc.2021.02.018.

Viñuales, Jorge E. "Sustainable Development." In *The Oxford Handbook of International Environmental Law*, by Jorge E. Viñuales, 284–301. edited by Lavanya Rajamani and Jacqueline Peel. Oxford University Press, 2021. https://doi.org/10.1093/law/9780198849155.003.0017.

Voigt, Christina. *Sustainable Development as a Principle of International Law: Resolving Conflicts between Climate Measures and WTO Law*. Legal Aspects of Sustainable Development, vol. 2. Leiden: M. Nijhoff, 2009.

Wilson, David C, United Nations Environment Programme, and International Solid Waste Association. *Global Waste Management Outlook*, 2015.

Wiprächtiger, Maja, Melanie Haupt, Martina Rapp, and Stefanie Hellweg. "Waste Not, Want Not—Ambiguities around Waste and Waste Prevention." *Resources, Conservation and Recycling* 173 (October 2021): 105742. https://doi.org/10.1016/j.resconrec.2021.105742.

Wolfrum, Rüdiger. "Common Heritage of Mankind." In *Max Planck Encyclopedia of Public International Law*. Oxford Public International Law, November 2009.

Woods, Kerri. *Human Rights and Environmental Sustainability*. Cheltenham, UK ; Northampton, MA: Edward Elgar, 2010.

Zhang, Chunbo, Mingming Hu, Francesco Di Maio, Benjamin Sprecher, Xining Yang, and Arnold Tukker. "An Overview of the Waste Hierarchy Framework for Analyzing the Circularity in Construction and Demolition Waste Management in Europe." *Science of The Total Environment* 803 (January 2022): 149892. https://doi.org/10.1016/j.scitotenv.2021.149892.

MIX
Papier aus verantwortungsvollen Quellen
Paper from responsible sources
FSC® C105338

If you have any concerns about our products, you can contact us on
ProductSafety@springernature.com

In case Publisher is established outside the EU, the EU authorized representative is:
Springer Nature Customer Service Center GmbH
Europaplatz 3, 69115 Heidelberg, Germany

Printed by Libri Plureos GmbH
in Hamburg, Germany